July 2019

Valley Cottage Library

110 Route 303
Valley Cottage, NY
10989

www.vclib.org

Liars, Leakers, and Liberals

The Case Against the Anti-Trump Conspiracy

Judge Jeanine Pirro

CENTER STREET

LARGE 🔲 **PRINT**

Center Street
Hachette Book Group
1290 Avenue of the Americas, New York, NY 10104
centerstreet.com
twitter.com/centerstreet

First published in July 2018
First Large Print Edition: August 2018

Center Street is a division of Hachette Book Group, Inc.
The Center Street name and logo are trademarks of Hachette Book Group, Inc.

The publisher is not responsible for websites (or their content)
that are not owned by the publisher.

The Hachette Speakers Bureau provides a wide range of authors for speaking events.
To find out more, go to www.HachetteSpeakersBureau.com or call (866) 376-6591.

Print book interior design by Timothy Shaner, NightandDaydesign.biz

Library of Congress Cataloging-in-Publication Data has been applied for.

ISBN: 978-1-5460-8295-8

Printed in the United States of America

LSC-C

10 9 8 7 6 5 4 3

To all the men and women who've made it their life's mission to enforce our laws without fear or favor, leaving their politics at the door to ensure equal justice under the law for everyone. We salute them for their service to us and their unrelenting determination to protect this great nation.

Contents

Liars,
Leakers,
and
Liberals

CHAPTER ONE

Here's My Open

As we approach the publication date for this book, I continue to be amazed at how quickly the news moves, especially in the age of Trump. And, as if Donald J. Trump's election itself weren't enough of a shock to our nation's political core, the subsequent months have proved to be an even greater jolt.

The left-wing liberal media have savaged not only President Trump, but everyone around him. Anyone connected to the president is fair game: Melania, Ivanka, Jared, Don Jr., Eric, Lara, Tiffany, and even twelve-year-old Barron! The media have criticized everything about them, from their hair, accents, mannerisms, and styles, to their intelligence and patriotism. They've even been attacked for their choice of footwear. No one and nothing has been spared. If the first family had a dog, they would probably call it a Russian bot.

It was worse on social media. Lara told me when her pregnancy was announced there were posts from people saying they hoped she fell down the stairs and had a miscarriage. Just when you thought the Left couldn't sink any lower, they did. Horrifying.

Those working in the White House haven't been spared, either, from the highest-ranking marine general in the nation, now Chief of Staff John Kelly, to counselor to the president Kellyanne Conway, to White House Press Secretary Sarah Huckabee Sanders, to former director of communications Hope Hicks.

The haters march, protest, riot, resist, obstruct, and jump into their ninja Antifa getups, suffering from "Trump derangement syndrome." One woman, in particular, is still suffering as she wanders around the woods in Chappaqua, New York, searching for the reasons she lost.

Not even the people who voted for Trump have been spared. A chief White House correspondent for CNN recently said, "They don't have all their faculties and in some cases their elevator might not hit all floors." Jim Acosta has since said he wasn't talking about Trump supporters, but we know what the liberal media think of Trump voters: They're deplorables, idiots, rednecks, and people who cling to God, guns, and religion.

To those charges, I plead guilty—guilty and proud!

How We Got Here

Donald Trump came to us at a time when we needed his tough talk and unvarnished perspective. We had just suffered under an administration riddled with corruption, double talk, a feckless foreign policy, and a disastrous economy. This was an administration that approved the sale of 20 percent of America's uranium to Russia with a $145 million payback to the Clinton Foundation, and a quick $500,000 to Bill for a speech in Moscow. Obama's Department of Justice was so corrupt, so unlawful, so immoral that they tried to drag a corrupt woman across the 2016 presidential election finish line after she put our classified secrets at risk. They watched as she deleted thirty thousand emails and destroyed evidence. Those running a more than one-year-long so-called criminal investigation with no grand jury, no search warrants, no subpoenas, and prophylactic immunities for everyone involved—without requiring their testimony—allowed her to get away with it.

Our economy was in shambles. The workforce participation rate was lower than at any time in our nation's history. Millions weren't employed because they simply gave up looking for work. Hundreds of thousands were working three part-time jobs to make ends meet. While the Obama team said it was a healthy economy, there was barely a pulse. One percent annual GDP growth was the new normal for these bozos.

Meanwhile, there were some in the workforce who should not have been in the country in the first place. Record numbers of illegal aliens had crossed our borders. Along with jobs, they and their families helped themselves to tax-funded education, medication, and housing. And when the illegals committed crimes, they were given the best lawyers and translators the criminal justice system could buy. The same people who burned and trashed the American flag, driving around with the foreign flags of their home countries waving atop their vehicles, would kick, scream, and demand their constitutional rights, calling Americans racist if, God forbid, we tried to send them back to the countries their flags represented.

Speaking of God, people of faith across the country were faced with the dilemma of upholding the secular Obamacare law to provide abortifacients to pregnant women or violating God's law. It seemed the government was not there to defend our First Amendment religious freedoms, but to gut them. Christians were horrified as the Obama administration dragged the Little Sisters of the Poor all the way to the US Supreme Court to force them to violate their religious beliefs.

Gun owners across the country were being blamed

for every lunatic who took a weapon and killed others, while at the same time being lectured about not blaming all Muslims for the actions of a violent few. We were told how many guns we should own, how big our clips should be, how many bullets we could keep in our magazines, or that we really should not have guns at all.

Globally, we had a president who couldn't comprehend terrorism, calling ISIS a "JV team." He couldn't figure out whether to "contain them," "dismantle them," or "destroy them," none of which he did. As this JV team unleashed brutal, inhumane genocide on innocent Christians across the Middle East and Africa, Obama spouted off at the National Prayer Breakfast that "people committed terrible deeds in the name of Christ."

Yes, Donald Trump arrived just in time, when our nation needed him most, when we needed to be protected and inspired.

To be sure, Trump was not your typical, politically correct candidate. Unlike the two-faced parasites in Washington, he really wanted to make America great again. They tagged him with every negative characterization they could. They called him a fascist, a racist, and twisted everything he said. Why? Because he was a threat to the greedy, corrupt Washington insiders who had captured our government. And he did what other candidates wouldn't dream of. In addition to the Establishment, he took on the media. They said it was suicide. They were wrong.

Donald Trump was speaking to the rest of America in a way they understood. He prioritized law and order and the safety of American citizens over criminal illegal immigrants and terrorists. As a Christian, he took on those who made believers uncomfortable for stating their Judeo-Christian beliefs. He stood for the hardworking, forgotten men and women who didn't get a fair shot at a better life, but were instead made to pay for those who violate the rules. He criticized the $1.7 billion cash transfer of funds to a nation committed to our destruction, as well as the destruction of Israel.

That is why Donald Trump stepped into the spotlight, a patriot who believed in putting America's interests first, who believed the decline of a great nation was a choice we could reject. He reignited the flame of liberty by swearing to rebuild our bare-bones military. Americans bought into the promise of a man whose views were most like the moral vision of the framers of the Constitution—a man whose philosophy was based not on politics, but reason. Donald Trump understands we are born with certain natural rights that come not from government, but from God, and that government wields power only with the consent of the governed.

The Anti-Trump Conspiracy

When Donald Trump reawakened the American spirit, the establishment was far more corrupt and deeply rooted than we imagined. We knew most politicians enter office with modest means and leave with enormous wealth for themselves or close family members. We knew that one hand washed the other, accepting horse trading across the aisle as the way democracy was supposed to work.

What we didn't know was how little it mattered which party was in power. It didn't matter because the Establishment was the power. Once Donald Trump entered the political landscape, a rogues' gallery of LIARS, LEAKERS, and LIBERALS joined forces to ensure the Establishment stayed in power, regardless of what all those "deplorable" voters wanted.

The anti-Trump movement is a conspiracy by the powerful and connected to overturn the will of the American people. Among the co-conspirators are FBI officials illegally exonerating their favorite candidate of violating well-defined federal criminal statutes, first to help her get elected and then to frame Donald J. Trump for "Russia collusion" that never happened.

It all began when members of the Obama administration, seeking a Hillary Clinton presidency and continuation of Obama's platform, used the intelligence community to spy on the campaign of the Republican candidate for president. But once the unelected Deep State got on board, the anti-Trump conspiracy grew from mere dirty politics to an assault on our republic itself.

Continuing beyond Election Day and throughout President Trump's term to date, the LYING, LEAK-ING, LIBERAL Establishment has sought to nul-lify the decision of the American people and continue the globalist, open-border oligarchy that the people voted to dismantle in 2016. The perpetrators of this anti-American plot include, but are not limited to, the leadership at the FBI, the CIA, NSA, and other intel-ligence agencies, the Democrat Party, and perhaps even the FISA (Foreign Intelligence Surveillance Act) courts. And let's not forget the media and entertain-ment industries that are waging a nonstop propaganda campaign that would render envious their counter-parts in the worst totalitarian states of history.

Yes, this is a conspiracy, and you and anyone who loves the America described in our founding doc-uments, are among its victims. The rule of law has become irrelevant and politically motivated fiction has become truth.

The Fake News Media are trying their hardest to deny this conspiracy. One of their arguments is that key players at the FBI and elsewhere are Republicans, meaning they supposedly would not help Democrat Hillary Clinton get elected or Donald Trump be defeated. They're either missing the point or deliberately ignoring it. Donald Trump was more than a Republican candidate, running against more than the Democrat Party. He was the outsider candidate, the populist candidate, virtually his own party. As far as his voters were concerned, the Establishment's major parties are meaningless.

Plenty of Republicans lined up against Trump in 2016, even during the general election. *National Review* did an entire issue during the primaries called "Against Trump" in an attempt to prevent him from winning the nomination. Plenty of Democrats and Independents who voted for Barack Obama in 2012 voted for Trump in 2016. There were two completely new parties in that election: the Swamp Party and the American People's Party.

The former is comprised of longtime incumbents, entrenched government employees in the intelligence community and Pentagon, popularly known as the "Deep State," the rest of the DC bureaucracy, the Fake News Media and the connected corporations, with their army of lobbyists. They all had a vested interest in maintaining the status quo. The latter is made up of the forgotten men and women who comprise the real America, on whose backs these globalist elites ride to unprecedented power and wealth, along with those few politicians who remain true to the oaths they took to the Constitution. The American People's Party is led by the man who gave up the fairy-tale life of a successful billionaire to be their champion: Donald J. Trump.

Yet, despite a media focused on "whack-a-mole" Trump-Russian collusion nonsense, and the haters continuing to hate, the outsider president has thundered forward with his America First agenda. With a Kryptonite-proof aura of invincibility, the forty-fifth president, often working without the support of his own party, has accomplished more during his first year and a half than most presidents in two full terms.

That's why, in addition to exposing the vast conspiracy against it, I'm going to tell you about the *real* Trump presidency, which has accomplished so much despite the dark forces arrayed against it. That includes tax reform, a booming economy, record-low unemployment, and a renewed manufacturing base. ISIS is vanquished, there are historic peace talks on the Korean peninsula, and we are moving toward a more mutually respectful relationship with China. I'm talking about fairer trade with partners who have run roughshod over previous administrations, cared little for what happened to most Americans as long as their Wall Street and corporate donors kept the contributions flowing.

You haven't heard much about the real Trump presidency, because the media we rely on for news are part of the dishonest "Resistance." They're too busy pushing distorted or flatly untrue narratives against Donald Trump to simply report on the great things happening in their own country under his leadership.

In this book you'll hear all about the accomplishments of this historic presidency, but first let's shine a light on the rogues' gallery of LIARS, LEAKERS, and LIBERALS who will stop at nothing to bring down a duly elected president and keep you, the American people, from taking your country back.

CHAPTER TWO

Lying, Liberal Fake News and Fiction

When it comes to politics, I've been around. I've won four elections and lost one. While doing so, I've had my share of good press, bad press, and blatantly untrue and unfair press. But in my four decades in law enforcement, politics, and television, I've never seen anything like the way the media treats President Trump.

It's one thing to publish slanted, misleading, or demonstrably false stories during a presidential campaign. It's another to publish lies. The media outdid themselves in that respect during the 2016 election. And, it didn't end with the election. Can you remember the last time the media continued vilifying the winner of a presidential election after an inauguration with as much negative coverage as Donald Trump has endured?

No, of course you can't, because the media's treatment of President Trump is unprecedented. The LIBERAL press didn't like George W. Bush. It despised Richard Nixon. But nothing the media wrote or said about either of them compares to the unabashed hatred they've displayed toward Donald Trump. Forget the customary honeymoon the media usually give presidents during their first hundred days; Donald Trump wasn't given even a hundred hours. As Kellyanne Conway put it, "We are well beyond describing the bent as 'liberal' or 'biased.' They are chasing stories that don't matter to most of America."

A year and a half later, they haven't relented, not even a little. At the 2018 White House Correspondents' Dinner (a tradition going back almost a hundred years), President Trump, and anyone associated with him, was assaulted with hateful remarks by whiny-voiced Michelle Wolf. Now, don't get me wrong, I have attended several of these dinners and understand part of the tradition is some good-natured ribbing of the president and his administration. No one likes a well-delivered jab better than I do.

Let's be honest. There was a marked difference between the "jokes" made by Michelle Wolf about the president, Kellyanne Conway and, especially, Sarah Sanders, and the ribbing directed at President Obama or any of his predecessors. Wolf's comments were way over the line of even edgy comedy. Can you imagine if a conservative guest speaker insulted Susan Rice's or Michelle Obama's appearance, even as part of a supposed comedy routine? Apparently, liberals have no problem with such treatment of a woman, as long as she is in some way connected to Donald Trump.

Worst of all, Wolf wasn't remotely funny. Her hatred of the president completely short-circuited her talent as a comedian. Instead of witty barbs, she produced nothing but shrill invective. Even if her target had been a president I didn't support, it would have been equally cringe-worthy for me.

One of the most hypocritical moments in Wolf's embarrassing diatribe was her lame joke lead-in, "And I know as much as some of you might want me to, it's 2018 and I am a woman, so you cannot shut me up." She should have said, "I'm a liberal woman, so you cannot shut me up," because, like mocking their physical appearance, the Left sees nothing wrong with "shutting up" conservative women. And they're perfectly willing to use violence to do so.

Street Injustice

I have a segment on my Fox News show, *Justice with Judge Jeanine*, called "Street Justice." I go out onto the street with a cameraman, a producer, and, of course, security, to try to get people to answer some questions. It's all in good fun; we try to have a few laughs.

Usually, I stick close to Fox News headquarters, but sometimes we travel around. Recently, I went down toward lower Manhattan, to a park very close to New York University. We got a few people to stop and got great, funny footage, until some nut jobs in the park realized who I was. Every time I started talking to someone on camera, those guys would scream as loud as they could. "FOX NEWS! FAKE NEWS! EFF TRUMP! GRAB HER BLEEP [a reference to the female anatomy]!"

The eyes in the back of my head were on full alert. They were so aggressive and angry I thought one of them was going to hit me with a bottle he was carrying.

But there was one kid, a student, who was also following me that day. "I'm a conservative, but I don't dare say anything, because it will affect my friendships and my grades," he said. I tried to talk to him, but then he screamed, yelled, and jumped in front of the camera to fit in with the others. He was too scared, I guess, to let anyone know how he truly felt.

The Trump campaign experienced the same as this kid and I did, but much worse. "Well, it's the 'free speech for me but not for thee' mentality that's always on the left," Don Jr. told me. "It's the do as I say, not as I do thing. Listen, I think what we learned from this election is that they are the greatest hypocrites in the history of hypocrisy. All the things that they said, 'This is what the evil Trump supporters are going to do,' they're doing it in droves."

My crew ended up packing and leaving. As we rode back to Fox, I was stunned. Those clowns had no respect for the First Amendment. It was a public park. I had every right to be there. They treated me like I'm a fascist, yet they were the ones trying to deny me my free speech.

That's the Left today. And don't tell me for one minute that Antifa and the women's marches are not supported by George Soros—a socialist with an agenda to destroy this country and the capitalist system.

For too long, people on the Right have allowed this to happen. Rather than get our hands dirty fighting such fights, conservatives have ignored the Left's violent rhetoric. I don't know anyone on the Right today who would try to do what those people outside NYU did to me. Not a single one.

The Fake News Awards

Not only does this all-consuming hatred for Donald Trump render comedians not funny, it has rendered the news media virtually incapable of reporting basic facts. The lies were so outrageous during Trump's first year in office that he created the Fake News Awards. It was a somewhat tongue-in-cheek move that injected some much-needed humor into the poisonous political atmosphere, but each award was richly deserved.

First prize went to Paul Krugman, who predicted, in the opinion pages of the *New York Times,* that the stock market would plummet and then "never recover" from the election of Donald Trump;[1] this from a Nobel prize–winning economist! I've often wondered how people like him can become so blinded by their hatred of Donald Trump that they forget decades of training in their chosen fields. Krugman, a renowned economist, is not a moron.

Second prize went to ABC's Brian Ross, whose "investigative" unit at ABC did some Inspector Clouseau–level investigating when it ran a story[2] that Michael Flynn was prepared to testify against the president, alleging he had personally directed Flynn to contact Russia *before* the election. That was a lie. The request by the president occurred *after* the election and was completely proper.

The story was false. It was poorly sourced and involved about as much investigative journalism as a tabloid gossip column. Like everyone else in the media, Ross, a previously well-respected, award-winning reporter, allowed his hatred of Donald Trump to cloud his judgment. ABC News retracted the story the next day[3] and eventually demoted Ross.[4] It was a demotion well deserved.

The bronze medalist was my personal favorite. The team over at CNN published a story alleging members of Trump's campaign had intimate ties with people at WikiLeaks.[5]

Those knuckleheads managed to convince their editors the Trump campaign had plotted to coordinate the release of stolen emails to damage Hillary Clinton. Specifically, it erroneously reported the Trump campaign received an email from WikiLeaks giving the campaign access to the Clinton emails on September 4, 2016, before the emails were made public. The Trump campaign did not have any advance access nor, more importantly, a relationship with WikiLeaks.

The email from WikiLeaks to the Trump campaign was actually sent on September 14th, the day *after* WikiLeaks had published the Clinton emails, which CNN's online version of the story now acknowledges. To add insult to injury, the Clinton News Network suffered the indignity of being corrected by fellow Fake News outlet the *Washington Post*.[6]

It's not as if Donald Trump had needed any help from WikiLeaks in the first place. WikiLeaks only confirmed what everyone ostensibly knew. In addition to being crooked, Hillary was a hypocritical oligarch who largely had contempt for her deluded supporters. All the emails did was confirm that.

Fake news is profitable to CNN. I get it. Without Trump, CNN would be suffering a deficit rather than a Trump-fueled cash infusion.

The Fake News Awards list goes all the way to eleven, but you get the idea. The press in America has become the public relations arm of the Democrat Party, which is so blinded by rage for its loss of the White House and Congress that it will stop at nothing to cook up a negative story about Donald Trump, with no regard for truth.

One of the chief differences between President Trump and other presidents is his transparency. He doesn't hide behind political correctness. He doesn't spout two-faced doubletalk. He's just a hard-nosed, what-you-see-is-what-you-get successful businessman and negotiator. Rather than applaud him, the so-called Resistance, including its Fake News mouthpiece, would rather take him down, sacrificing our economic success and international strength for the sake of their agenda. *They would rather see America fail than see Donald Trump succeed.*

It is shocking, for example, that in the week that North Korea announced, as a precondition to meeting with the president, it would shut down its nuclear testing, the press coverage of Michael Cohen and Stormy

Daniels was wall-to-wall. They get a search warrant for Trump's lawyer's office, but HRC (Her Royal Clinton) doesn't even get a subpoena. Instead, she gets a heads-up that "it's time to destroy" the evidence of her crimes. And rather than applaud the president for what no other president had accomplished, the media relegated the story to secondary reporting. It didn't matter that so many Americans were able to breathe a sigh of relief, or that a war seemed to have been averted.

On Friday, April 13, 2018, McClatchy reported that Special Counsel Robert Mueller had evidence the president's personal attorney, Michael Cohen, had in fact traveled to Prague in 2016, as the Steele dossier alleged, for a meeting with Putin agents. The Mueller team had to put out a statement that said in part: "Be very cautious about any source that claims to have knowledge about our investigation and dig deep into what they claim before reporting on it. If another outlet reports something, don't run with it unless you have your own sourcing to back it up."

This hatred is all consuming and puts the security of our country in danger. Regardless of the damage they do to our country, its institutions, and its traditions of freedom, these LIARS, LEAKERS, and LIBERALS are determined to sabotage the Trump presidency.

The very same publications that used to call President Trump when he was a real estate mogul now stop at nothing to make him look bad. Gone are the days when they would cover both sides of an issue or call anyone—let alone their old pal Donald Trump—for a fair, on-the-record quote. They twist words and play with facts until the American people can't tell what's true anymore. Fake News reporters don't need to interview people on the record anymore, because their sources can all be anonymous. There's no longer any accountability for what they say, because names will never be attached to anything.

As of this writing, the lies haven't stopped. There was a time when the press would self-reproach for publishing inaccurate information. Today, the media's strategy is if you repeat something often enough, people will believe it is true. That includes telling you LYING, LEAKING James Comey is some kind of hero, instead of the politically-motivated weasel he appears to be to anyone with any grip on reality. More on "Cardinal" Comey later.

Doubling Down on Dishonesty

A favorite narrative of the Left says the White House is in chaos. I have been in the White House on several occasions. Based on these crazy reports, I expected to see people hanging from chandeliers and vomiting or hiding under their desks.

In March, with this anticipated scene in mind, I sat down with Chief of Staff John Kelly, who completely refuted the media's representation of the White House as "chaotic."[7] Suffice it to say both the general's remarks and my firsthand observations in the West Wing confirm the reports are demonstrably false.

Even more egregious is the media's characterization of the Robert Mueller investigation. The president rightly calls this fiasco a "witch hunt," while the media would have you believe that any day it will conclusively prove the outlandish Russiagate conspiracy theory to be true. Headline after headline uses the words "closing in" to describe the special counsel's progress.

The Russia collusion investigation is over. Deputy Attorney General Rod Rosenstein announced that himself, for all intents and purposes, when he indicted thirteen Russians for interfering in the election and said explicitly that no Americans had been knowingly involved.[8] That means neither Donald Trump nor any of his campaign team was involved, as they are all Americans.

"Think about the campaign in the early days, when they say this Russia stuff happened," Don Jr. said to me. "We couldn't have colluded to order a cheeseburger."

So, any suggestion, explicit or implicit, that Mueller is getting close to proving the Democrats' unhinged conspiracy theory is just plain wishful thinking. As the president has said, there was no collusion by the Trump campaign. The investigators have yet to admit that the actual effect the Russians had on election results did not change the numbers or the outcome of the election. That's why Mueller has all but given up on the original theory, and is now supposedly focusing on trying to prove the president obstructed justice when he fired LIAR and LEAKER James Comey.[9]

Lots of luck with that. The president has a constitutional right to fire the head of the FBI. He is expressly given this power in Article II of the Constitution. How are you going to prove impropriety if the president fires one of his own subordinates? Even Comey himself admitted, almost immediately after his dismissal, that the president had unqualified authority to fire him for any reason or no reason. The whole idea that unelected members of executive agencies are supposed to act "independently" of the elected executive they report to is preposterous to begin with. But the idea that Trump fired Comey to obstruct a legitimate investigation into his own actions is absurd.

After more than a year, there is no evidence of collusion or coordination with Russia by the Trump campaign to influence the election, nor any evidence of obstruction of justice. The special counsel is now simply looking for anything and everything with which they can make a case against the president, no matter how unrelated to the election or his duties. "This is the nature of special counsels," Kellyanne Conway astutely observed. "Don't forget that Monica Lewinsky didn't exist until fifteen months into the Whitewater special counsel. She was somewhere across the country in college when that all started."

There would be no special counsel, and Robert Mueller wouldn't be a household name, but for spineless Attorney General Jeff Sessions unnecessarily recusing himself from all things Russia, and Jim Comey illegally leaking federal records to his Columbia professor pal Dan Richman to give to the *New York Times*. When this cockamamie narrative finally implodes and backfires on the real criminals, the media will come up with a new fake story with which to slander the president. Their hatred has no limits and knows no shame, but it wasn't always like this.

The Donald and The Press

Believe it or not, there was a time when the media adored Donald Trump. Throughout the 1980s and '90s, you could hardly pass a newsstand without seeing Donald's face on the covers of glossy tabloids and fifty-cent newspapers. There were stories about him gallivanting around New York and attending charity galas, photographs of him standing in front of new buildings, and long stories about business in which he'd give tips to aspiring entrepreneurs. Whether it was about renovating a dilapidated hotel into a showpiece, erecting soaring towers that drew the envy of his peers or, mostly out of his own pocket, building a skating rink in Central Park, the media reported positive news about Donald Trump on a very regular basis.

Before Donald Trump even thought about running for president, he ran his real estate business out of an office on the twenty-sixth floor of Trump Tower in New York City. You've probably seen pictures of it. His office had floor-to-ceiling windows with a jaw-dropping view of Central Park, regalia and awards from his life, and a big wooden desk in the middle. Walking in, you'd often find him leaning back in his chair with the phone to his ear.

The man was always on the phone.

As he said in *The Art of the Deal*, "There's rarely a day with fewer than fifty calls, and often it runs to over a hundred. In between, I have at least a dozen meetings. The majority occur on the spur of the moment, and few of them last longer than fifteen minutes. I rarely stop for lunch. I leave my office by six-thirty, but I frequently make calls from home until midnight, and all weekend long."

I can confirm this.

No matter who was calling him—business affiliates, the press, or the Westchester County district attorney—Donald would take the call. By the way, never in my life have I met someone who'd drop everything to help another person faster than Donald Trump. Aside from his friends and business partners, the people who called most often were newspaper and magazine reporters. He always took their calls, too. Reporters couldn't get enough of Donald Trump. He was funny and engaging, and his quotes always sold newspapers, magazines, and ad space on news shows.

If you were in Manhattan in the mid-1980s, you knew all about the saga of Wollman Rink—it was all over the newspapers.[10] At the time, before Mayor Rudy Giuliani took the reins, New York City was the epitome of failed liberal policies and government dysfunction. Falling into disrepair, the rink was a symbol of urban decay. You had a better chance of buying a bag of dope there than renting a pair of skates.

The city had spent nearly six years and $13 million trying to rebuild the rink but had made very little progress. The press was having a field day, eating liberal mayor Ed Koch alive. Enter Donald Trump. He made a public offer to Koch: give me six months, and I'll build a new rink for the cost of the materials.

Koch wanted no part of the deal—he didn't want to look any more foolish than he already did. But pressure from the press, nearly all of it backing Donald Trump, forced the mayor's hand. Koch and his crooked Limousine Liberal pals secretly hoped Donald would fail. Instead, he built the rink in four months, not six, and brought the project in 25 percent below budget. Wollman Rink is a Central Park attraction today. If you visit New York City in the winter and go for a skate, you can thank our current president for it.

Even when the press was taking shots at Donald's lavish lifestyle, there was respect for him.

Occasionally, the press would even publish the acts of charity that Trump preferred to keep secret. Donald tipped waiters, doormen, workers, and everyone in between. And I mean tipped! Like hundreds of dollars. He rarely leaves one of his restaurants or building sites without slipping someone a wad of bills that could choke a horse, with instructions to distribute it among the people staffing the place.

He's also quick to help in bigger ways. When a terminally ill three-year-old boy needed treatment he could only get in New York, Donald Trump flew him across the country on his private jet. When ex–Buffalo

Bills quarterback Jim Kelly battled cancer at Memorial Sloan Kettering Cancer Center, Donald gave the Kelly family use of his townhouse.

Even the New York *Daily News* ran a story about a botched mugging on Fifth Avenue, with a picture of Donald Trump. The headline read "Mugger's Trumped."[11] According to the reporter, Trump had been riding by in his limo and had seen one man hitting another with a baseball bat. Before anyone could intervene, Donald opened the door and ran out onto the sidewalk, screaming:

"Stop that! Put that bat down!"

The assailant took one look at Donald, dropped the bat, and took off.

That's the way American journalism used to be. Stories weren't driven by some reporter's agenda, and they weren't printed to further a cause or bring a person down. Not in the best cases, anyway.

Coverage of Donald Trump wasn't all positive, even back then. The *Daily News* took its share of shots at him over the years. Along with usual suspects such as the *New York Times* and the *New York Post*, the *News* didn't hold back when he had some trouble in his casino ventures or when his net worth began falling in the 1990s. They mostly ran stories that were deeply sourced and included both sides of the argument when it was necessary. When the stories concerned him,

Donald was always happy to be interviewed. Between 1980 and 2015, Trump graced the covers of thousands of newsmagazines and sold countless tabloids and broadsheets. There's no telling how much money he made for the media back then—and the money he made for them back then doesn't hold a candle to the money he's made for them since he decided to run for president.

When CNN Worldwide president Jeff Zucker, who put Donald Trump on TV in the first place with *The Apprentice* on NBC, decided to air Trump campaign rallies from beginning to end, the cable network's viewership skyrocketed. It was a sign of things to come. A few months into the election, online readership of the *New York Times* climbed above 1 million for the first time in history. In the first month of his presidency, the *Times* sold 132,000 new subscriptions.[12] Two months after the election, the *Washington Post* added sixty new newsroom jobs and set records for digital traffic and advertising. *Vanity Fair*, *The New Yorker*, *The Atlantic*, and other magazines also set subscription records.[13]

Those news organizations called it "the Trump bump," and without it many of them would be heading to the big recycling bin in the sky. But as soon as the Trump campaign began picking up steam in 2016, positive stories about the real Donald Trump became harder to find than one of Hillary Clinton's emails. The news organizations no longer had any interest in telling the truth. Instead, they sold their collective soul to the conspiracy to take Donald Trump down. They knew that phony, negative stories would sell.

The Media's 2016 About-Face

During the primary, Donald Trump provided the media with never-before-seen viewership. He drove home his policies while punching and counterpunching his opponents. With a blend of humor and name-calling, the ratings went through the roof. Then the unexpected happened. Trump won!

Suddenly the media shifted gears—it damned Donald Trump and crowned Hillary Clinton.

Coverage of the 2016 election became the most negative in the history of US politics, and coverage only got worse during President Trump's first months in office. Every day, establishment hacks who'd weaseled their way into the White House would collect information, store it, then leak it to reporters to make themselves look and feel powerful. Those LEAKERS teamed up with LIARS and LIBERALS at newspapers and television stations on both coasts, all of whom were starving for negative information about the president.

In 2013, the *New York Times* reported that their readers' number one concern was anonymous sources.[14] Did the newspaper listen? Of course not. Pull out a copy of the *Times* tomorrow morning—swipe it from your dentist's office if you can—and count the number of identified sources in stories about Donald Trump. I bet you'll be able to count them on one hand.

In 1974, when Deep Throat brought down President Richard Nixon, no one doubted the veracity of the claims being made because the press was held in such high regard. Bob Woodward, Carl Bernstein, and their peers took thorough steps to verify claims made by the anonymous source. They would not move a story forward without looking into it more closely. Watching Carl Bernstein today, as he predicts Trump's imminent impeachment, you have to wonder if he's forgotten everything that made him the quintessential investigative journalist.

What Donald Trump says about the media is true. If news organizations continue to make up sources, improperly fact-check, and knowingly lie, they should face major consequences, even if that means the person wronged has to threaten to take them to court, as Anthony Scaramucci did with CNN. Until then, news sites will continue to rely on anonymous sources to propagate their agenda.

Unfortunately, today, since there are no real consequences for journalists who lie, the press lies with impunity. That's the business model—one lies, another swears to it, and then the rest pile on. If the lies are exposed, the Fake News Media just moves on to the next lie. They never cop to their falsehoods; they just spin the next false narrative, and on it goes.

The genius of Donald Trump was recognizing that Americans instinctively felt that the press was lying. He was the one who put the laser focus on the press and their lack of accountability, and America came along with him.

With just one phrase, "Fake News," the president has deflected and defeated billions of negative words written about him. With the Fake News Awards, he raised exposure of dishonest media to an art form. When the president tweeted the link to the awards at GOP.com, the website was so inundated it crashed!

The awards were humorous. But they served to send a much larger, more important message to the American public: that the relationship between Donald Trump and the press—which had been long and healthy for years and beneficial to both parties—was over.

What changed?

Donald J. Trump certainly didn't. Go back and look at video of his appearances on programs such as *The Oprah Winfrey Show* in the late 1980s, or read some of his comments on trade and foreign policy in the newspapers. Nothing's different. He's been advocating for fairness in international trade, promoting his America First agenda, and denouncing political correctness for decades. You won't find him switching positions like other politicians. That's because Donald Trump has guiding principles, and one of his core principles is fairness.

"Fairness is equality of opportunity, not equality of outcome. Candidate Trump elevated fairness as a core governing value in this country," said Kellyanne Conway. "And he took fairness and used it as a thread. Fairness undergirds his policy on trade. He doesn't say I'm going to rip up all the trade deals and walk away. He says 'I want free trade. I want trade but I want it to be fair to America.' Reciprocal and fair! It's never fair to American interests, workers. It needs to be.

"For years, people, including Republicans, ran around and said, 'What's fair to the illegal immigrants? What more can we give them? Here's a driver's license, here's housing, here are benefits.' Donald Trump finally stood up and asked, 'Hey, what's fair to the American worker who's competing with the illegal immigrant for that job? What's fair to our local law enforcement who can't keep up? What's fair to the brave men and women border patrol agents? What's fair to moms in the suburbs who are struggling with the drugs that are coming over the border and into their communities?"

Fairness is about school choice and charters, it's about taxation. It's not fair that some are able to hire a coterie of accountants and lawyers over the years to favor the wealthy and well-connected—while others pay high taxes. It's not fair that in the US we pay a 35 percent corporate tax rate, and all these countries that used to have a higher rate, too, saw how foolish we were being and lowered theirs. It's not fair you've got trillions of unpatriated dollars that are legally overseas. So fairness is very important to him. And if you listen to many female voters long enough, they're talking about fairness."

As the president's son Don Jr. told me, the only thing that's changed about Donald Trump is his tolerance for the nonsense going on around him. "Just watch him," Don Jr. said. "You can see him on those shows, even then. You can tell he's getting a little more fed up, a little more fed up, a little more fed up. And he's not a man who won't take action. He stepped up when it was time."

That was the beginning of the end. Donald Trump, a longtime fixture of the tabloids and political newspapers, saw how the system worked and got sick of it. By the time he'd watched Barack Obama float from nowhere to the top of the American political class, carried along by fawning news coverage from virtually every media outlet in the country, he had finally had enough. So, while Obama was running America down on the world stage and caving in to deals with our enemies in Iran, he decided to act. When it was time, he launched the most successful campaign in the history of US politics, not by going to war with the press or trying to play its game, but by going completely around it.

On Twitter, Donald Trump can reach more people than CNN, the *New York Times*, the *Daily News*, and the rest of the media combined. He reaches people those media outlets ignore. It seems the only time the "flyover states" show up in the pages of the *New York Times* is when factory workers lose their jobs. We see the victims of crooked trade deals staring out the dirty window of a diner. After the reporters get a few quotes and file their stories, they leave town and the newspaper quickly forgets all about the people in those diners. But Donald Trump sent a message: I'm listening to you, and I'm going to help.

For caring about those people and what happened to the country he loves, Donald Trump became a media target. Stirring up hate and conflict has always been an integral part of the Fake News business model.

According to the Pew Research Center, this is not unique to Donald Trump or to political coverage in general. Newspapers have been falling down this slippery slope for years, getting more and more negative with time. Ever heard the saying "If it bleeds, it leads"? It's a common joke around newsrooms. It means that if you've got a story about a factory that's been saved from shutting down by a shrewd policy move and another story about a bomb that went off and killed three people in a country no one's ever heard of, you lead with the second one. The more negative, the better. The more sex, violence, and palace intrigue, the better.

Trust me, I know.

As an assistant district attorney, I prosecuted domestic violence cases for years before they ever got coverage in the media. So, when did the media start covering me? During the O. J. Simpson case. A professional football player is accused of murdering his ex-wife and her friend in cold blood. That was what it took for people to start paying attention to domestic violence.

Suddenly I was all over *Larry King Live*, even hosting the show, breaking down details of the case for Larry's viewers. I was again under the glare of TV lights when I reopened the investigation against accused murderer Robert Durst. Fake News survives on the sensational with no regard for substance. According to a study by the *International Journal of Press/Politics*, negative news has been increasing steadily since the early twentieth century. When a newspaper runs a headline bashing someone its readers don't like, it has a 33 percent chance of selling more newspapers that day. Bad news happens quickly, and it's easy to report on. The media just have to find a body or a victim, interview some people who saw the crime occur, and print the story. Progress, on the other hand, takes time. Stories about accomplishments in foreign policy or immigration are made up of slow events and small decisions, which the press has no interest in covering.

That's not even mentioning the negative coverage of Trump himself. If the trend toward negative news was bad, it got much worse when he took office. A study by the Pew Research Center found that of all newspaper and network stories about Trump, 62 percent were negative.[15] That's compared to just 20 percent for Barack Obama and 28 percent for George W. Bush. Our current president is a man who used to appear frequently in the pages of those same news outlets and enjoyed a symbiotic relationship with them for years.

The minute Donald Trump announced his presidential run, on a platform that didn't politely acquiesce to their progressive, globalist agenda, they turned on him like a pack of feral dogs. As expected, they're alienating a large percentage of their audience by doing so. As Eric Trump put it, "I learned that these people do not understand the sentiment of this country. You have certain individuals from the mainstream media, who sit in their ivory towers, their fancy offices and multi-million-dollar apartments. They have never spent 18 months in America's heartland, they never saw shuttered factories, hardworking farmers, struggling families, ill-cared for veterans and tens of millions of people who feel that they have been forgotten by their own government. Candidly, despite what you saw on TV, when I was in those states, I saw significantly more 'Hillary for Prison' signs than I did signs with her first logo "I'm with Her." (After intense criticism, her logo changed to "I'm with you.") There is a major disconnect between the elitist media and the patriots in this country and that is missed every single day."

Today, funded by deep pocket LIBERALS such as Amazon and *Washington Post* owner Jeff Bezos, and supplied by LEAKERS from the Deep State, the Fake News LIARS have the means and the motive to help perpetuate what amounts to a coup d'état: the attempt to remove a sitting president based on a completely fabricated story.

Sloppy Steve's Ghostwriter and His Work of Fiction

A yet unidentified LEAKER told the *New York Times* this book would largely be a refutation of that dime novel, *Fire and Fury*. Leave it to the Gray,

Failing Lady to get the story wrong even when they cheat. By the time you read this, you may have trouble even remembering who Michael Wolff is. But I would be remiss if I didn't commit a few lines to his work of fiction.

Not since the days when I was the district attorney—when it was my job to prosecute and convict society's worst dirtbags—have I seen a story this separated from reality. It would have been thrown out of any court had he tried to read it into the record. Yet, somehow, he got a major publishing house to print it.

For a few weeks, self-admitted LIAR Michael Wolff, the counterfeit king of fabrication, floated on a sea of cash and liberal adulation. There was a time in journalism when hacks like him were publicly shamed rather than applauded and rewarded with millions of dollars. But last January, liberals waited in line to get their hands on his work of "bargain basement fiction," as a spokesperson for First Lady Melania Trump so aptly described it.

It's hard to understand why anyone would believe what this guy has to say when he boldly admits his dishonesty. He told Savannah Guthrie he had "certainly said whatever was necessary to get the story." He sure did. He misled the president and his staff about the book to get into the West Wing, then used his minimal access as cover to write a hit piece on the administration that has been largely refuted by the people he wrote about.

He also created scenes out of whole cloth, and not artfully, either, often portraying events he orchestrated as if he were only an observer.

For example, he begins his book with a dinner arranged by "mutual friends in a Greenwich Village town house." It reads as though he had no hand in setting up the intimate gathering, and that the late Roger Ailes, a former CEO of Fox News, and LEAKER Steve Bannon just happened to wander in. But the dinner occurred in Wolff's own town house! Wolff set the whole thing up and made the attendees believe that they were all pals and everything they said was off the record. Not publishing comments made off the record is a time-honored code among journalists. But Wolff abides by no journalistic principles or moral code.

So, just how did he remember so many intimate details of what was said that night? He says he has audiotapes. Did he have the room bugged? I doubt he had a tape recorder sitting on the dinner table for everyone to see. Was he relying on his flawless memory? The same memory that couldn't distinguish between lobbyist Mike Berman and *Washington Post* reporter Mark Berman?

Or, maybe his memory has nothing to do with anything he writes. Maybe he just makes it up as he goes along.

Case in point: In chapter one, he writes that Kellyanne Conway, Donald Trump's campaign manager, sat in Trump Tower on Election Day in a "remarkably buoyant mood" because she was convinced Trump would lose a close election, which would put her into an ideal spot to get her dream job on television.

What crap. Kellyanne is too smart to have believed any such thing. Not only is she admitted to practice law in four jurisdictions (Maryland, New Jersey, Pennsylvania, and the District of Columbia), she studied at Oxford. Her forte is polling. A pollster for twenty-two years, she's worked with just about everyone who's anyone in the business, including Richard Wirthlin, Ronald Reagan's pollster and strategist, and Frank Luntz, Newt Gingrich's pollster during the Contract with America. No one knows how to read the political winds better.

Kellyanne was on the road with candidate Trump and saw firsthand the energy he created. She was by his side from the moment she joined the campaign, except when she was needed to help coordinate headquarters. She knew lightning was about to strike, probably better than anyone but Donald Trump himself.

Before the sun came up on Election Day morning,

just two hours after being with the candidate in Grand Rapids, Michigan—while most of the men who worked on the campaign were asleep on their couches—she was on the morning shows in New York touting the president's path to victory. Does that seem like someone who thought Trump would lose?

"He always wins!" his son, Don Jr., told me. "Doesn't matter if it's real estate. He did it with entertainment. Politics was just the next step. He understands people. He's an amazing guy. He sees things that other people don't see. And people don't give him any credit for that. Against all odds."

Anyone who's read any of Wolff's previous books knows his dishonesty is nothing new. He's been inventing stories out of thin air for years, stringing together bits of rumor and gossip into narratives and passing the results off as "reporting." Thanks to the public's appetite for cheap gossip, he's made a living on the fringes of journalism.

Michael Wolff's whole career reads like a joke, in very bad taste. Here's a loser who couldn't keep an online blog up and running during the Internet bubble writing a hit piece on Donald Trump, who built a real estate empire, had a multi-Emmy-winning, top-rated show on television for eleven seasons, and got himself elected President of the United States. Meanwhile, Wolff was begging his rich buddies, including accused serial sexual abuser Harvey Weinstein, for startup cash. And we're supposed to take his pronouncements on President Trump's competence or morality seriously?

I don't.

Wolff claims to have conducted more than two hundred interviews for his fictional opus, but it's obvious he relied mostly on one dubious source. *Fire and Fury* reads as though it was ghostwritten by none other than Sloppy Steve Bannon.

Like many of those close to the president during the last few months of the campaign, I thought Bannon had his head on straight and his priorities in order. But after the election all that changed. Proximity to power can do that to people.

"In business you form relationships over a decade or more," said Eric Trump. "Employees become family members. You would do anything for them, and they would do anything for you. You are there for one common objective. Call that capitalism. You are there to run a successful business, to create a great widget, to run a great hotel or build a successful enterprise. And if you're successful in that, it rises all boats for everyone involved. You have a very different class in politics. Politicians, other than the corrupt ones, are not motivated by money. They're motivated by power and that power can often lead to vicious and unethical behavior."

Trash such as Joshua Green's *Devil's Bargain* would

have you believe Bannon was a mighty intellect with a grand, master plan, surrounded by fools. As Kelly-anne Conway put it, "I guess Steve thought it would be bankable if the whole world—especially on a foreign stage—thought he was the brains behind the whole operation." In truth, Bannon was just trying to cover his incompetence by calling everyone else incompetent. I'm told he would sit with his P.R. team in one room trying to figure out how to take credit for policies being made in another—policies he had nothing to do with making. Bannon rose to the position he did by being lucky, nothing more. He hitched his wagon to the brightest star the political universe has ever seen—Donald J. Trump—and then tried to convince everyone he was the light in the sky.

Bannon, the "brain," was just an opportunist, and not a very smart one at that. He'd ride a wave for as long as it benefited him and got him attention. Along the way, he leaked information, turned people against each other, and fancied himself a political genius. But all he really had was five or six canned lines in his head. His "mighty intellect" amounted to a couple of cheap tricks—and leaks. As Don Jr. put it, "You think that there's anyone on earth that could change DJT? Ask yourself, was there any change in DJT or his demeanor during that time? None whatsoever. It was all Donald J. Trump. He was his own messenger."

Sloppy Steve wasn't always nice about trying to elevate himself at the expense of the president's mission. My sources in the White House tell me there was a dark side to Bannon's self-aggrandizing agenda, including threatening anyone who got in his way. "I'll cut you up in the press. That's what I do for a living," he told one such person. He'd say things like, "I'll break you," and "I'm crazier than you." This was clearly a man whose ambition overcame his reason.

Bannon might still be getting away with his threatening, leaking, and lying if he hadn't told Michael Wolff the biggest whopper of them all. Bannon's attack on Don Jr. was malicious, personal, and false. As I've said, I've known Don Jr. since he was a little kid. To call him treasonous and unpatriotic is ridiculous.

Give the Devil his due. LIAR Wolff played Bannon like a radio. Wolffie must have been licking his chops as LEAKER Steve spewed his inane bile. Wolff knew the damage Bannon's statements would do. He used them like knives stuck in the backs of those to whom he'd ingratiated himself, using that sleazy, false smile we saw plastered across every network and website last January.

They deserve each other, LEAKER Steve and LIAR Wolff. Like Abbott and Costello, they're the perfect comedy team. One has no sense of style and the other no integrity.

For a while, everywhere I looked, I saw this hack blathering about what a brilliant job he'd done reporting on the Trump administration. But he and his book are as phony as a hundred-dollar Chanel bag. Like a failed novelist who teaches a writing class filled with lonely hearts, Wolff tries to impress with French terms such as *bête noir*, *outré*, and *joie de guerre* and words nobody else ever uses such as myrmidons, but he doesn't impress me. I've seen his type countless times in the courtroom—all smoke and mirrors, double-talk and nothing of substance.

Lest I waste too many words on this loser, I'll leave it there. Suffice it to say his attempt to seriously damage the Trump administration was about as successful as his internet blog.

CHAPTER THREE

Lying, Liberal Hollywood Hypocrites

What gets my goat is LIBERAL righteous indignation, especially when columnists and pundits on the left act intellectually superior. These liberals think they are smarter and better than us, know what's good for us, how we should live and even how we should think. Don't you love when those so-called social justice warriors, the ones who claim moral and ethical superiority over the rest of us, the ones who chastise us "deplorables" because of our core American values, are hoisted by their own petard?

Even worse than the smug Fake Press is Hypocritical Hollywood. It's so bad at this point that we probably need a new awards show for them, too. Maybe we can follow President Trump's lead and create the Hollywood Hypocrites Awards.

If you watched the Oscars this past year, you would think the only person who did anything wrong in Hollywood was Harvey Weinstein. Don't get me wrong; I'm not saying Horrible Harvey doesn't deserve to get the book thrown at him. He does. In fact, I'd like to throw a lot more than the book at him.

I already missed my chance to dump a bowl of soup on him. In 2001, when I was district attorney in Westchester County, my office investigated and prosecuted a crew that stole luxury cars. Those guys were pros. They stole only the best: Audis, BMWs, Lexuses, and Mercedes-Benzes straight out of garages in the tony parts of Westchester. They used burner phones, switched warehouses regularly, and spoke to one another only in Mandarin.

They were part of an international operation. The gang would drive the cars to New Jersey and put them into shipping containers and then onto trains to the West Coast. There they drove the cars onto freighters bound for China. Back then there was a huge market for high-end cars in China, so those guys were making a killing.

How good were they? Well, after my investigators arrested one of them, they impounded his stolen car. A few hours later, a judge allowed him out on bail. He stole the same car straight out of the police impound lot!

That was a guy I wanted to meet!

At the time, Tina Brown was the editor in chief of *Talk* magazine. She invited a group of movers and shakers out to Santa Barbara, California, for what she called the "Innovators and Navigators" conference. It was a very fancy and beautiful event, held in a resort on a bluff overlooking the ocean. A cross section of media types, politicos, movie industry honchos, and others attended. Rudy Giuliani was one of the speakers, so I didn't feel totally out of place.

At the get-to-know-one-another dinner, Tina assigned me a seat right next to, of all people, Harvey Weinstein. I'm sure you've seen photos of Harvey. In person he's not exactly Paul Newman.

Tina introduced us and brought up my car theft case. At some point during the conversation, she mentioned that it might make a good movie. It was the same year the first of the *Fast and the Furious* movies had come out. Not that I cared much one way or the other, but I began to tell Weinstein a little about the case, mostly what was already in the public domain—the criminal syndicate, the walkie-talkies and the freighters, stuff like that.

"Are you into politics?" he asked me out of nowhere.

I said politics was the mechanism that allowed me to attain jobs I loved—as an elected County Judge and elected District Attorney.

"What do you think of the Clintons?"

I paused for a second, knowing I could not make small talk with him. Nope, no political correctness here.

"I think they're both crooks," I said with a smile, staring at him. That was the end of our dinner conversation.

I have a particular animus for Harvey Weinstein and people of his ilk. More than thirty years ago, as a young prosecutor, I'd started one of the first domestic violence units in the nation. Throughout my career, I litigated mostly murders, rapes, child abuse, and domestic violence cases. I know what makes a guy like him tick, and it disgusts me.

For years women had complained about Harvey Weinstein, but were ignored by LIBERAL Manhattan DA Cyrus Vance. Finally, after huge public outcry, Weinstein was indicted for rape. Another LIBERAL in New York law enforcement, Attorney General Eric Schneiderman had to resign in shame after four women accused him of assault.

Horrible Harvey and Hillary

The Harvey Weinstein sexual abuse and harassment scandal is a perfect example of Hollywood hypocrisy. During the Kennedy and Clinton presidencies, their womanizing was well known. When women came forward with accusations of sexual abuse, harassment, and even rape against Bill Clinton, reporters were silent. Hillary, showing her true cold, calculating colors, attacked and threatened victims. Not one liberal woman in Congress attacked President Clinton. Mum was the word. The Hollywood elite was not only silent on the subject, they continued to support both Clintons, raising funds and placing them on LIBERAL pedestals.

Weinstein, once a famous, now infamous, moviemaker was accused of at least three rapes and continuing sexual assault, and harassment of dozens of young women on two continents. He silenced those around him with his ability to intimidate victims, pressure business associates, buy powerful Democrats, and leverage hungry Hollywood actors.

It was an intersection of crime, money, power, and the Democrat Party. Reports are that Weinstein has given $1.5 million since 2000 to peddle influence: hundreds of thousands of dollars to the Democrat Party, nonstop donations to Hillary Clinton, hundreds of thousands of dollars to the Clinton Foundation.

After Weinstein's façade finally came tumbling down, hypocrite Hillary, the woman who created her own war room to destroy the women who credibly accused hubby Bill of rape and sexual assault, hid for five days. The woman who said women should be believed in the #MeToo movement—waited five days before saying she's shocked. Shocked. Think of it, Hillary, were you elected president, you could have done for your friend Harvey what your husband Bill did for his friend Jeffrey Epstein, the Palm Beach billionaire and convicted serial pedophile predator. Bill got the Department of Justice and the feds to intercede in a local prosecution to take child rape cases from the DA's office in Florida where Epstein was facing hard state time, to federal easy street where he quickly got home monitoring.

Hillary, could it be you said nothing because you have experience with pedophiles. As a practicing attorney you represented a child rapist, one of two men who destroyed a twelve-year-old girl by raping her so severely that she was in a coma for days, leaving her unable to have children for the rest of her life. There are recordings of you discussing the case in which you are heard laughing and giggling.

You know, Hillary, both you and Harvey are a lot alike. Both of you are addicted to power, money, and domination. Weinstein wanted to dominate Hollywood and you wanted to dominate politics. You still do.

Weinstein spread his wealth among Democrats, delivering $700,000 to another condescending liberal,

Barack Obama, who also took days to condemn Hollywood's open secret. It seems strange that not one of them knew. Obama had the FBI and IRS at his fingertips. I guess they were a little too busy going after conservatives, covering up Hillary's email scandal, and setting up Donald Trump for a Russian collusion investigation to find a predator in their midst.

Michelle Obama also was a fan of Hollywood's hypocrisy. After Hillary lost, Michelle said "Any woman who voted against Hillary Clinton voted against their own voice."[1] Michelle, does that mean you listened to your voice and voted for Hillary and against your husband when Hillary ran against him in the primary? Where was your voice on the day your daughter got a job with Harvey?

Meryl Streep—another paragon of virtue says she didn't know a thing about Harvey, while she preached to us at the Golden Globes condemning our president.

Meryl, you say you didn't know anything about Harvey's predatory behavior. Really? How much has your best bud Harvey added to your bank account while you stood oblivious to the victimization of young women who want to be you? How many of those young women came to you for advice? You arrogantly condescend to lecture the rest of us about our politics. It's no surprise. Your morals are not in line with ours. You openly rise to applaud Roman Polanski, a child rapist as Hollywood awards him when everyone knew he was a fugitive from justice.

Even comedian John Oliver gets the hypocrisy. On a recent show he had this to say about the Academy of Motion Picture Arts and Sciences' treatment of Harvey Weinstein. "Yes, finally! The group that counts among its current members Roman Polanski, Bill Cosby, and Mel Gibson has found the one guy who treated women badly and kicked him out. So, congratulations, Hollywood!

Phony Tough Guys

Now, as if Hollywood's hypocrisy and preaching aren't bad enough, since Donald Trump was elected their lectures and condescending speeches have turned into threats. Actor Robert De Niro, the movie wise guy, tells an audience from behind a lectern that he's going to punch the president in the face and curses him out. So Bobby doesn't like Donald Trump and his politics. He calls the president every name in the book while this Hollywood hypocrite is steeped knee deep in the dirty money of Harvey Weinstein. How many of Weinstein's productions have swelled DeNiro's bank account as he calls our president a punk, a pig, a thug.

Bobby, I think you're taking your roles too seriously and your punching days are behind you. Instead of throwing punches, you might want to work on your public speaking skills. When you struggle to deliver political speeches, the only time you look up from the script is to curse. You're like the street thug in a remedial reading class who got held back when the rest of the thugs graduated. Yeah, I'm talking to you. In fact—you never graduated from high school.

Folks, Hollywood's been steeped in hypocrisy for decades. As the curtain goes up on the casting couch, the town that glorifies violence, murder, and rape is the same town where the centuries-old practice of pressuring women to trade sex for a job is kept quiet.

Actors who simply repeat other people's words for a living, convince themselves they have the moral turpitude to pontificate to the rest of us on how we should act.

By the way, it's not over yet. There's more coming. It's not just adult women. It's human trafficking. It's child sex trafficking. It's real pedophilia in a town where there are no rules; where the truth is stranger than fiction and where fiction is based on reality.

Why doesn't the Department of Justice get its act together and start a federal criminal investigation into Harvey Weinstein, and his ongoing criminal activity that, no doubt, crossed state lines? I guess the DOJ is too busy redacting and hiding documents from Congress.

DeNiro isn't the only actor playing the political tough guy act. There's also Sean Penn. Remember him? Barely, right? Not too long ago he called President Trump an enemy of the state and an enemy of mankind. Just how hypocritical was that statement? Since it came out of the mouth of the guy who also said he was "blessed" to have been friends with Hugo Chávez, the Venezuelan dictator, accused of so many human rights violations, I'd say it was pretty hypocritical.

Hey, Sean, I have a question for you, too: When did you stop beating your wife?

That's a purely rhetorical question, of course.

Then there is Chelsea Handler, who led the women's march after the inauguration. Handler actually had the balls to try to embarrass Melania Trump, claiming Melania can barely speak! Right! Melania speaks five languages and the only language you speak is anti-American! And you really advocated that the military overthrow the president? Maybe you and Madonna, who pondered blowing up the White House, might ask a lawyer about 18 US Code Section 2385. It criminalizes sedition.

Kathy Griffin posed with a bloody, severed head of our president for a TMZ photographer. A Shakespeare in the Park production featured a modern-day *Julius*

Caesar modeled on Donald Trump getting stabbed to death onstage. Johnny Depp opined that "maybe it is time" to assassinate a president. Mickey "when-was-the-last-time-he-had-a-job" Rourke said he wanted to beat then-candidate Trump with a baseball bat.

Believe me, we're in a fight for our lives.

Back in June 2017, the liberal director Rob Reiner called for "all-out war" against the Right. His tweet was particularly insensitive considering that it came just a few weeks after a gunman's attack on Republicans playing baseball on a Virginia field that left Representative Steve Scalise (R-LA) in critical condition, and injured four others including a US Capitol police officer who was shot. Though heartless, his words capture the true sentiment of the Left: it is at war with America, and violence is by no means off the table.

Just a few months after President Trump took office, Chelsea Handler tweeted that she'd be giving up showbiz for a while to focus "full-time on activism." Soon afterward, Sarah Silverman said she'd be doing pretty much the same thing.

Full of righteous indignation and selfishness, these celebrities hate Donald Trump so badly they would rather our nation fail than see him succeed as president. I don't know about you, but I've had it with all of them.

Where was Hollywood's outrage when Barack

Obama was sending millions of dollars in cash to Iran on unmarked pallets in unmarked planes for the release of terrorists, some of whom returned to the battlefield? Where were the speeches and pussy hats when on his way out of 1600 Pennsylvania Avenue he gave $221 million to the PLO, which looks the other way as women are murdered in "honor killings" and sexually assaulted with relative impunity? Nowhere.

I like activism. In fact, I applaud it. But, the same celebrities who spent the first years of the new millennium screaming from the rooftops of their luxury high-rises and Hollywood Hills mansions about the injustice of the Iraq and Afghanistan wars— before the rubble from 9/11 was even cleared, in some cases—suddenly changed their tune when Obama took office. They wouldn't be seen within a few hundred feet of President George W. Bush, but a couple of years later they were just fine spending their Friday nights rubbing shoulders with and writing checks for a president who had likely ordered up a few dozen killer drone strikes that very week. In one he killed an American citizen in Yemen, Anwar al-Awlaki, an Islamic militant, without any due process. Two weeks later al-Awlaki's sixteen-year-old son was killed while eating dinner in an outdoor restaurant in a separate drone strike targeting someone else. Just kill 'em and to hell with the collateral damage.

Where was the outrage when his administration put a stop to a US international drug operation called Project Cassandra, an operation that targeted the terrorist group Hezbollah for trafficking drugs to the United States and killing Americans? Obama threw a wrench into the operation, so he could dance with the Devil in Iran to the tune of over $100 billion in funds released from sanctions.

Instead, Hollywood targets a man who has improved our economy, reduced unemployment—including African-American unemployment—to unprecedented levels, helped push the stock market to historic highs, passed tax reform, eliminated the individual health insurance mandate, and made good or is making good every one of his campaign promises.

And we're supposed to grin and bear it?

Not on my watch.

Self-Righteous Script Readers

What makes movie stars' opinions so important, anyway? These are people with a bloated sense of self-worth, little accountability, and practically no original thought. Without a Hollywood scriptwriter, most of them couldn't talk their way out of a telemarketing call. When they shoot a scene for a movie, they get twenty-one takes to get it right. How many takes do you get in your life? Real people get one shot. If we make a mistake, we must live with it. Not so for the stars. They get pass after pass and then send their assistants to fetch grande lattes for them.

My own daughter Kiki took acting lessons for almost a decade—singing, dancing, theater. When she was sixteen, she told me she didn't want to act anymore. Stunned, I asked her why. "I want the words that come out of my mouth to be mine," she said. That from a sixteen-year-old!

So, to all the actors and fellow haters out there: get a life. Real people—not actors, not ideologues—elected Donald Trump president. Real people. The forgotten men and women who live normal, hardworking lives and who, by the way, buy the movie tickets that pay for your pampered, cushy lives.

All of this would be bad enough if the product they were putting out was any good, but it's not. Hollywood is dead. If it's not dead, it's on a respirator. Look at the numbers.

Along with the Oscars' puny ratings, movie theater attendance is down to a nineteen-year low and about to drop right through the floor. Studio profits are down 40 percent. Paramount is worth the same amount as it was twenty years ago, in twenty-years-ago dollars, so it has significantly decreased in real, inflation-adjusted value.

Why? Well, people will tell you it's due to competition from Netflix and streaming videos. And maybe that's partly true. But what is also true is that the quality of movies has been steadily declining for decades. Where are movies like *Gone with the Wind*, *On the Waterfront*, or *To Kill A Mockingbird*? Hollywood once served us filet mignon; now it slings hash.

Subversive Scriptwriters

Though movie attendance is far below what it once was, Hollywood has managed to morph itself into a formidable brainwashing machine. Scriptwriters weave far-left messages into the storylines of popular TV shows that are watched by millions including millions of impressionable young people.

Writing in *The Hill*, Christian Toto, a rare conservative voice covering Hollywood and movies, called out just a sampling of television shows with overt anti-conservative and anti-Trump storylines. Included in his piece were ABC's *Designated Survivor*, which touts gun control, the CW's *Supergirl*, which equated the "Make America Great Again" slogan with slavery, and ABC's *Scandal*, in which a supporter of a vile, supposedly Trump-like character sets off a bomb in a church, killing eight people. That's what Hollywood thinks of Trump supporters.

Just as bad as those who write *for* television and movies is the liberal bias of those who write *about* television and movies. Consider the kudos given the filmmaker Michael Moore. If your film or television show doesn't fall into line with their liberal bias, they'll drum you right off the screen. It's what happened to Tim Allen, a funny guy who dared write and star in a sitcom that said something a little different than what the establishment wanted him to say.

In its fifth season, Allen's *Last Man Standing* was pulling in an average of 6.4 million viewers, making it ABC's third-most-watched show. Out of nowhere, and all while ABC was renewing left-leaning shows such as *Scandal* and *Modern Family,* it cancelled *Last Man Standing.* Make fun of political correctness and liberals for too long, and the critics and writers will come at you like wolves.

CHAPTER FOUR

Lying Liberal RINOs

At least Hollywood doesn't try to hide its Liberal bias. You can't say the same about some Republicans on the Hill. Even though Democrats lost the House, the Senate and the Oval Office, you wouldn't know it.

"RINOs" refers to elected Republicans acting like Dem-ocrats. RINOs are Republicans In Name Only—elected Republicans.

As President Trump seeks to protect us and our border because border patrol agents are overwhelmed, LIBERALS chant in unison that he's a racist and a fascist and RINOs sit on their hands. Legislators dither as to whether they even want their border protected. In the case of Oregon's governor, Kate Brown, she refused to assist other states in their efforts to control borders three days after she accepted a large donation from George Soros. The Democrats seem to be controlling the agenda. Why? Because they have learned how to wield power. As they did with their FBI and the Department of Justice when they decided one of their own would not be prosecuted. As they did when they prioritized illegal criminals over American citizens, proudly declaring themselves to be sanctuary cities. They have learned what to do when they are in power—such as covering for their own and condoning the corrupt Clinton Foundation, which in reality is a pay to play international racketeering syndicate.

They were smart enough to look to the future. They instituted a Deep State shadow government to continue their agenda even when they are not in power. Unlike Republicans, they have learned to circle their wagons.

They are in lockstep with each other on the phony Trump Russia collusion narrative, ignoring the obvious: the flow of hundreds of millions in cash that went into Bill and Hillary's corrupt foundation as Russians found fertile ground for their corruption in the Clinton bank account. If they listened to the forgotten men and women in 2016, they'd understand the wind is at Donald J. Trump's back now with an over 50 percent approval rating.

It is time for the Republicans to start wielding power. They've got to stop their spineless finger-to-the-wind approach to running the country.

It is time for Republicans to stop fighting with

each other and start supporting the president. They let the DOJ, the attorney general, and the head of the FBI stonewall them, and they need to put on their big boy pants and use the Department of Justice and the FBI to investigate and prosecute those who violate our laws. This is not going to end well until Republicans get the guts to wield the power to run our government the way it is supposed to be run.

RINOS Spending Like Democrats

The Omnibus Spending Bill Republicans gave President Trump in March was a total betrayal of him and those who elected him.[1] It was as though they left him without arms to swim in a sea of sharks, risking our health and safety.

We know there are plenty of RINO Republicans who are anti-Trump. Remember how panicked they were when it looked as though he would actually win the nomination? The party elders were petrified because the man was beholden to no one, and despite their backslapping and glad-handing, they've proven they still are. Once Trump was elected, the establishment's mission was to make sure he failed.

Candidate Trump ran on a promise to build a border wall between the United States and Mexico. In 2017, Speaker of the House Paul Ryan and Senate

Majority Leader Mitch McConnell promised to build that wall with $12 billion to $15 billion.[2] The amount allotted for the wall in the Omnibus Spending Bill they presented was only $1.6 billion, short more than $10 billion of the minimum they had promised. They specifically precluded the use of that money for the wall prototypes the president had inspected in California. That makes them both LIARS.

That betrayal should come as no surprise. Ryan and McConnell never cared about President Trump succeeding. Ryan failed to deliver votes on the health care bill—the one that he had seven years to work on. The one that Ryan hid under lock and key in the basement of Congress. The one they finally pulled out of embarrassment because they didn't have enough votes to pass it,[3] even while controlling the House, the Senate, and the Oval Office.

So, why did the president sign the omnibus bill? Simple. The first order of government is the protection of its citizens. The bill included $700 billion to shore up the military, which had been diminished, devalued, and destroyed by Barack Obama. As Obama took our military down to pre–World War II levels,[4] North Korea was launching ICBMs with nuclear war tips, threatening Guam, Hawaii, Chicago, and all America. Meanwhile, Iran was spinning centrifuges, allegedly for "nuclear medicine," while at the same time threatening the extermination of both Israel and the United States. And Russia, now in possession of 20 percent of our uranium, thanks to Bubba and his wife Hillary, was continuing to build its nuclear arsenal.

So, faced with this triad, the president chose to put our defense into the strongest position, to protect us and our service members. There is now sufficient funding for the F-35 stealth bombers that are virtually invisible to the enemy.[5]

Any leader's success is based on his ability to take action and get results. That's what Trump does. He did it with deregulation. He did it by signing the repeal of the individual health insurance mandate in the tax reform bill.

The RINOs got things done, too, but they were all the wrong things. They funded sanctuary cities—the ones that protect illegal criminals, risking the health and safety of US citizens such as Kate Steinle, who was killed by an undocumented immigrant. They pitted federal and local law enforcement agencies against each other, and they funded Planned Parenthood, which performs more than 300,000 abortions a year,[6] at a cost to US taxpayers of $500 million a year.[7] That makes them LIBERALS, too!

Congress has allowed rogue cities to protect criminal illegals, putting Americans at risk. Congress prefers no border wall, where criminal illegals can bring in drugs that take the lives of over a thousand Americans per week. While we pay for border walls for Tunisia and Libya, Americans will suffer a plague of drug overdoses from illegal drugs that come into this country from Mexico. Ninety percent of the heroin used in this country comes in through the southern border. Although we're only 5 percent of the world's population, we use 80 percent of its opioids, which have a potency fifty times that of heroin and one hundred times that of morphine. These are the drugs the establishment is not willing to build a wall to stop—and Congress is killing more than a thousand of us a week by not building that wall.

Folks, these are double-dealing, two-faced politicians who care only about themselves, lobbyists, their contributions, and the next election. The Democrats crowed because they funded sanctuary cities and Planned Parenthood and have only $1.6 billion for a see-through wall. Meanwhile, they kept out DACA, which the president was willing to give, so they could use it against him in the upcoming election.

I want to be really clear: the shame of the spending bill was not on President Trump; it was on the leadership of the Republican Party, the RINOs—LIARS AND LIBERALS all—on whom the president should be able to rely. The truth? The president is surrounded by inept, incompetent, or disloyal warriors, and the spending bill reflected just that. It was a total betrayal by the Senate and House leadership.

How dare the RINOs play politics with our lives with all their namby-pamby nonsense about "their" security border? The president and the people who voted for him have been betrayed by Speaker Ryan and Majority Leader McConnell. Ryan has announced he's not seeking reelection in November 2018. The people in Kentucky need to make sure McConnell doesn't come back, either, so this president can get to the agenda we elected him to follow.

This isn't the first time Paul Ryan sold out the president. As the 45th president of the United States marched into the White House running on a promise to repeal Obamacare, Speaker Ryan knew very well where the hardliner, moderate, and Freedom Caucus votes stood.

Ryan, of course, knew their demands. If he didn't, why didn't he? Some demanded repeal of the Obamacare individual mandate and he couldn't figure out what he needed to do to get their support?

Ryan was aware no Democrat was going to support the bill and that he would have to rely upon the Republican vote. Was this calculated? Was it a simple misjudgment? Was it planned because he had already decided to retire?

The stench in the Republican part of the Swamp

goes all the way to the top in both houses of Congress. That certainly includes Mitch McConnell. We gave him and the other establishment bozos majorities in both houses of Congress, and they still couldn't repeal Obamacare; not even a "skinny repeal." At least they took out the egregious individual mandate in the tax reform bill.

They had no problem campaigning and voting on repealing the bill while Obama was president, knowing it would go nowhere. But as soon as they had a president with pen in hand, ready to sign the repeal, the LIARS wouldn't vote for it. In fact, they won't even put a true repeal of the awful law up for a vote. So, what was all their talk about repealing Obamacare "root and branch" in the seven years prior? It was just LIARS lying.

It was not as though the president had been dogmatic about what the bill had to contain to get his signature. He knew how much damage the terrible law was doing to the health insurance market and American families. He was ready to sign any reasonable bill the Congress sent him to get Americans some relief. As he said many times, it would have benefited both him and the Republican Party more to simply let Obamacare fail, letting Democrats take the blame.

Majority Leader Mitch McConnell led the legislative effort in the enactment of the Omnibus Spending

Bill. The omnibus bill failed to address immigration or President Trump's promise regarding the border wall. The president wanted to veto the measure but he had no choice but to sign it because he needed to fund our military.

The president is right. He should never sign a bill like that again, and McConnell should eliminate the sixty-vote filibuster that allows the Democrat minority to block appropriation bills that are passed by the majority.

Putting Obamacare repeal-replace first on the legislative agenda wasn't the politically expedient thing to do, but it was the right thing to do. The president and the honest members of Congress who haven't forgotten why they're in Washington didn't want the people to suffer any longer than necessary. All the rest of the Republicans had to do was take the same vote they had taken fifty times before.[8] The worthless stuffed suits couldn't even do that.

They draw a salary and a pension for this? It's not just Obamacare or the omnibus bill. As of this writing, the Senate slugs had failed to pass more than five of the four hundred bills passed by the House. Why can't these senators do more? What the hell do they do all day? They're either too busy drinking or eating at fancy restaurants, or maybe they just hate our outsider president so much they'll refuse to do even what they know will help their constituents. Do they hate the man we elected to drain their Swamp so much, they're willing to let the Democrats win the next election?

Don't forget, most of these parasites come to Washington as people of modest means but often leave as millionaires. Yet they do nothing for the hardworking, forgotten men and women of America who sent them there. Once they have their cushy positions, all they care about is holding on to them, their constituents be damned.

America Last

We knew that was the case the day after Donald Trump was elected, when Mitch McConnell announced to Trump's voters, as clearly as the snake believed he could get away with, that he was going to stonewall their agenda.[9] Drain the Swamp through term limits? Forget it; that's why we have elections. Act immediately on the Trans-Pacific Partnership? Not during a "lame duck" session in the Senate. Build a wall on the border? A mealymouthed answer on "whatever is most effective." He even had kind words for Crying Comrade Chuck Schumer.

When President Trump moved quickly to keep a key campaign promise with a travel ban, to stem the tide of radical Islamists using our immigration and refugee systems to enter our country, McConnell was quick to line up with the LIBERALS in pushing back on the ban.[10] He said he hoped the courts would determine whether the executive order had gone too far.

That's funny, because I don't remember him taking that position when President Obama restricted entry from the *same seven nations* just thirteen months prior.[11] Where were his sanctimonious concerns about religious liberty then?

House Speaker Paul Ryan wasn't any better. Having just witnessed an election he called "the most incredible political feat I have seen in my lifetime," admitting the reason was that Donald Trump "connected in ways with people no one else did,"[12] he nevertheless pushed back against Trump just five days after the election, on the single most important issue to the people who voted for Trump: enforcing immigration laws.[13] "We are not planning on erecting a deportation force," he said, playing into the Left's unhinged characterization.

Let me be clear: He was responding to a question on President Trump's statement earlier that day about going after illegal aliens who have committed crimes while here. In the president's own words, "What we are going to do is get the people that are criminal and have criminal records, gang members, drug dealers…"[14]

So, the president was not talking about shaking down every suspected illegal immigrant household in the United States with jackbooted storm troopers demanding "Papers, please!" He was talking about finding illegal immigrants who had committed violent crimes including drug crimes. The government is *supposed* to arrest people suspected of committing those crimes, whether they are here legally or not! Instead of putting the lie to the Fake News Media's hype, Rotten Ryan decided to signal that he was on their side, not Donald Trump's. And he wasn't just talking to them. He was talking to every American who had voted for Trump.

It wasn't just immigration. Ryan told Trump's voters the same thing about infrastructure the day after the election, saying that, "We've already decided what to do about infrastructure. We don't care who you elected or why."[15] That's a paraphrase, of course. He didn't have the stones to disagree with the president's pardon of Sheriff Joe Arpaio. He released a statement through a spokesman, undercutting the president again.[16] Just a few months ago, when the president kept another key promise to protect workers in our steel and aluminum industries from rivals and supposed "trading partners" that do not reciprocate any of our fair-trade policies, Ryan again came out against him.[17]

Supporting the Witch Hunt

It's one thing to ignore the overwhelming mandate given to the president by the voters in his party. It's quite another to openly support the coup d'état now being attempted by this anti-American coalition of bad actors.

I realize the Mueller investigation put Republican congressmen in a difficult spot. If they had come out against the investigation right away, it could be seen as not respecting the rule of law. I get it. But it's been more than a year, and enough is enough. When you have all the resources of the federal government at your disposal and several witnesses who have pled guilty and still not only don't have a case but literally don't have one piece of evidence of a crime, it's time to close the investigation. It's time for Republicans who aren't part of the "Resistance" to stop playing cover your ass and take a stand.

Every legislator promotes the interest of his or her constituency. However, faced with the usual midterm pushback after a presidential election, the Republican Party needs to stand shoulder to shoulder and make sacrifices for the greater good. Senator Grassley, along with Republican Senators Ernst and Fischer who are assisting him, have demonstrated they are up to their knees in Swamp water and controlled by the ethanol lobby.

Every time a gallon of ethanol is mixed with fuel, a credit, called a "renewable identification number," or RIN, is issued. These credits may be bought or sold and are required to be used by refiners to prove compliance with biofuel standards. Big oil and the ethanol lobby control the credits and the price of RINs is sky-high. Since small refineries have no way of producing RINs, they must buy the credits. Due to their high cost, these independent refineries cannot compete and are being forced out of business, resulting in job losses.

These small refineries operate in states such as Pennsylvania, Michigan, and Wisconsin, critical states in the 2016 presidential election and equally critical in this year's midterm elections. Rather than level the playing field in these key states, Grassley sent a communication to EPA head Scott Pruitt that if the big oil companies and ethanol lobby was disturbed, EPA nominees would be held up! So much for party initiative.

My interview with Senator Grassley, the longest serving Republican senator after Orin Hatch, was just one more example.

I asked why the Senate passes virtually no bills and yet they are considering a bill that precludes the president from firing Mueller. They propose this even though the president has indicated that he has no intention of firing Mueller or Rosenstein. Grassley's answer was "if there is a bipartisan bill brought to me I would put it out there for passage."

Say what? This is a waste of taxpayer dollars in the make-believe Russia Collusion saga and yet the Senate Judiciary wants to let it pass? Whose side is he on?

Mueller is a special hire of the Justice Department, which is part of the executive branch. Every single person who works in the executive branch ultimately reports to the president. President Trump and Vice President Pence are the only two people elected out of approximately two million employees in the executive branch, not counting uniformed military. So, no, firing a subordinate would not be "a constitutional crisis," regardless of what the bill's proponents say.

Let's not forget how this all started. Republican Senator John McCain dispatched former State Department official David Kramer to London to retrieve the infamous Russian dossier from Christopher Steele.[18] Kramer now works at Arizona State University's Washington-based McCain Institute for International Leadership. But it was McCain who handed the dossier over to the FBI and then decried release of the Putin memo as "doing Putin's job for him."[19]

Is that the extent of his involvement with the dossier? We don't know. There were rumors circulating— before the House closed its investigation—about McCain possibly being more involved, perhaps even helping to fund the dossier himself. The House Intelligence Committee subpoenaed Kramer to ask further questions, but he took the Fifth,[20] which means that he believed testifying on this subject to the House might have tended to incriminate him.

What crime was he afraid of being charged with? We'll never know. The House has closed its investigation into Russia's interference in the election, and it's unlikely that Kramer will be called by Mueller. If we ever got real justice, the conspirators trying to overturn the 2016 election would be the ones on trial.

On top of all the other reasons to thank Donald Trump for leaving a rather comfortable, happy life to run for president, saving us from enduring yet another RINO Republican nominee has to be high on the list. Let's not forget "low-Energy Jeb" Bush was once a frontrunner, at least in terms of fundraising, in the race for the 2016 Republican presidential nomination. Jeb was all set up to either be the next George W. Bush or lose to Hillary, with real conservatives having no voice in the election at all.

It's almost hard to believe at this point. But, yes, the party might have nominated another milquetoast RINO, had it not been for Donald Trump's epic destruction of Jeb's campaign in a debate in South Carolina with the audience packed with Bush loyalists.

Only Donald Trump could have pulled this off. Can you imagine any other Republican—any other politician—having the balls to say the Iraq War was a colossal mistake in front of a hostile crowd in South Carolina? When the crowd began to boo, Trump didn't back up an inch. He told the television audience, "Do you know who that is? That's Jeb's special interests and lobbyists talking." When the packed audience continued to try to shout him down, Trump confronted them directly, saying, "I only tell the truth, lobbyists."

What Jeb's jeering supporters didn't understand—what the entire Establishment has never understood—is that Donald Trump is a force of nature. The same heat that would burn others feeds him. For any other candidate, taking on the media is suicide. Donald Trump checkmated them. Whether it's real estate, entertainment, or politics, he is not afraid to jump into the fire. His message is always uniquely his own. He understands people and he sees things that other people don't see. He is not afraid to take positions that would make others cringe.

The attacks in any presidential campaign are vicious, brutal, and lightning fast, the kind of heat the average person simply can't take. What Donald Trump does, he generally does against all odds. A brash billionaire from New York City, candidate for president? "You must be kidding." So began the campaign of the most unlikely outsider presidential candidate in American history.

They all underestimated Trump, even ridiculed him. But what they couldn't comprehend was the difference between him and the other sixteen establishment candidates. This guy named Trump was fearless and had the guts to walk into a den of lions and come out the winner.

For all intents and purposes, Jeb's campaign was effectively over after that debate and the Bushes certainly haven't forgotten it. They're part of the RINO stampede from the sidelines. "Many of the Bush people are the ones on TV and in print attacking this president," says Kellyanne Conway. "They weren't well-known when working for President Bush, but they try to become rich and famous working against President Trump. It's ironic, because they know how unfair the press can be. Yet it's unsurprising. President Trump upended two political dynasties—Clinton and Bush—and is compared most with Reagan. The conservative movement was always looking for the next Reagan, and they kept picking Bushes—Jeb was out before South Carolina. Later, Hillary cratered. Out: Dynastic elections. In: Forgotten men and women."

The Bushes can yap all they want about their dislike for Donald Trump. Nobody cares. While we still have to fight to ensure a Democrat doesn't win the White House in 2020, at least we know it won't be occupied by a phony, RINO Republican, thanks to Donald Trump. Now, it's time to turn our attention to Congress this November.

CHAPTER FIVE

Liberal Sanctuary Cities

She was a pretty thirty-two-year-old, with blonde hair and a bright smile.

He was a dirtbag illegal alien and career criminal, a drug dealer with seven felony convictions and five deportations under his belt.

She was walking along a San Francisco pier on a sunny day with her dad.

He had been released from jail a few months before.

She had just met the love of her life, a handsome young lawyer whom she planned to marry.

He pulled the trigger of a stolen .40-caliber Sig Sauer handgun, the bullet piercing the pretty blonde's heart.

She had everything to live for.

He had no right to be there.

She said, "Help me, Dad," as she lay dying in her father's arms.

The day José Ines Garcia Zarate shot Kathryn

"Katie" Steinle to death, he was supposed to be in the custody of US Immigration and Customs Enforcement (ICE) or on his way back to Mexico. He wasn't. Instead, he was walking the streets of San Francisco thanks to LIBERAL San Francisco Sheriff Ross Mirkarimi. Three months before Katie was killed, the feds had asked the sheriff to keep Garcia Zarate in jail until they could pick him up for deportation. But, in the sanctuary of San Francisco, the sheriff thought it was better to let him go free.

Tell me how much of a sanctuary San Francisco was for Katie?

While the Deep State continues its assault on President Trump, LIBERAL politicians and the Fake Press continue to undermine his policies. Nowhere is this more in evidence than with so-called sanctuary cities.

Somewhere around the time that Donald Trump announced his presidency, the Fake News decided to tell you that "criminal illegal immigrant," "illegal immigrant," and "immigrant" meant the same thing.

Here's the narrative they disseminated: Do you have a problem with criminal illegal immigration? Then you hate illegal immigrants. Think illegal immigration laws should be enforced? Then you hate immigrants. Think all immigration policies should be fairly enforced? You hate immigrants and you are a racist.

The press didn't have to work hard to get their

point across. In fact, they were preaching to the choir. LIBERALS have their heads so far up their asses they care more about criminals than innocent victims. And they look down their noses at anyone who thinks differently from them. They can be holier-than-thou because most of the interaction they have with illegals is when they get their lawns mowed. You don't see a whole lot of liberals in South Texas or along the Mexican border of Arizona screaming about how unfair our immigration policies are unless they are the illegals themselves. You know why? Because if they lived there they would be helping build the wall themselves.

But let President Trump tell the unvarnished truth about illegal immigration and criminality and they go apoplectic. This has been true since the first time the president talked about illegal immigration as a presidential candidate.

The Speech That Saved Our Borders

On June 16, 2015, Donald Trump gave maybe the most memorable speech announcing a presidential run in the history of politics. The liberal press was outraged because of these words:

"They're sending people that have lots of problems…They're bringing drugs, they're bringing crime; they're rapists. And some, I assume, are good people."

In the next few days, the geniuses on liberal editorial boards predicted the shortest campaign in history. Trump is done, the headlines blared. Hollywood
blew a fuse, and stars lined up to take shots at Donald. Macy's dropped the Trump clothing line. People
couldn't wait to stomp on his campaign's grave.

But guess what? Not everybody is liberal. In fact,
most of the country isn't. Do you know what the rest
of the country thought of Donald Trump's first campaign speech? *It's about time someone had the balls to
say it.*

You think I'm wrong? Well then tell me what happened to Donald Trump's campaign following that
speech. Was he done? Was his the shortest campaign
ever? No. In fact, that speech started a movement that
blazed a trail right to the White House.

Okay, I'll give you this: Sometimes the president
isn't as politically correct as LIAR Obama. But isn't it
refreshing to finally be able to listen to someone who
says what he thinks? To hell with political correctness.
A nation exhausted after eight years of Obama's "I say
what I mean and mean what I say" doubletalk were
starving for the straight talk Trump delivered. Sometimes his wording is a little rough around the edges.
But Donald Trump feels the way much of America
feels, and that's why he was elected our president.

Does Donald Trump hate immigrants? No. Absolutely not. His wife is an immigrant who speaks with an accent. While doing a Street Justice segment, the Trump Tower employees I spoke with who have foreign accents talked about what a great employer he is. Calling him anti-immigrant is the equivalent of calling him un-American, and the American people know Donald Trump loves this country. The man had to go to court to fight for his right to fly as big an American flag as he wanted at Mar-a-Lago!

Being 100 percent pro-immigration does not, however, mean our borders should be open to people who want to break the law or take advantage of the American system.

Trump is a populist who understands the frustrations of the American people. Illegal immigration affects the least fortunate Americans more than it does anyone else. Those at the bottom of the ladder should not be undercut by cheap, illegal labor. Nor should illegal immigrants be released into the community after committing crimes against American citizens. The president understands that immigration into our country should be based on fairness, the needs of the American economy, and the safety of both American citizens and legal immigrants rather than family unification or proximity to our borders.

The Sanctuary State

There are more than three hundred sanctuary cities in the United States where government employees and local law enforcement are prevented from reporting and sharing information on illegal immigrants. When their police arrest an illegal immigrant for felonies, or fine them for misdemeanors, they don't turn them over to Immigration and Customs Enforcement—even if the illegal, like Garcia Zarate, is a career criminal.

And, now the state of California as of January 1, 2018, has passed legislation making it a sanctuary state. In response, various cities and counties in California that face problems with illegal immigration have commenced litigation against the state of California. But California is not alone. Other sanctuary states include Colorado, Illinois, New Mexico, Oregon, and Vermont. Is this a new civil war in America—the federal unity of the fifty states versus the separate interests of several states? I believe in most matters the states should decide their own fates but not where the safety of its citizens is outweighed by illegal criminal activity. Public safety is a fundamental right. The first order of government is the protection of *its* people. Emphasis *its*.

For over one hundred years, the federal government

has been entrusted with regulating immigration. But, suddenly, in cities across this country, local law enforcement is releasing illegal aliens who have committed crimes back into the community after they serve their sentences and are released from jail, as if they had any right to be there in the first place. They do this in total defiance of requests by federal ICE agents to hold the individual wanted for deportation or federal crime, and without any constitutional grounding of their own. The term *sanctuary city*, when it comes down to it, is nothing more than an official-sounding phrase cooked up by local LIBERAL politicians and members of city councils. It's never been written down in federal law or a court case of any consequence. The whole concept is a lie.

To Act Or Not To Act

If you're a cop working in a sanctuary jurisdiction, then you're being directed by some left wing LIBERAL progressive mayor, county executive, or governor to protect criminals who are illegal, who not only violated our laws in coming here but committed additional crimes while here.

You're being told not to share any information about illegal criminals and not honor federal ICE detainers. So, you've got a decision to make. And if this is a tough one for you and you can't figure out what your sworn obligation is, then I suggest you get the hell out of law enforcement.

Think back to the day you graduated from the academy, when you got a badge and a gun. You earned the right to protect us. We trusted that you understood your mission. We were proud of you—proud to count you as part of that blue wall that every day separates a civilized society from a chaotic and barbaric one.

Your job: to protect the innocent, follow the truth, arrest the criminal, be true to your oath. That oath is *not* negotiable. It is not for sale and neither are you.

You knew this when you signed up, and no namby-pamby bleeding-heart left wing socialist political whore has the right to demand that you defy that oath. If you don't have the courage to do what you know needs to be done, then you don't deserve to wear that badge.

How many innocent Americans do we need to lose to deported illegals who come back to the US and go on to kill? Every politician who ordered you not to cooperate with federal authorities has blood on their hands.

You would never allow an American criminal to roam freely in your jurisdiction if another law enforcement agency asked you to hold them. Why is it different for illegal aliens? Why do these criminals have protections American criminals don't? It's absurd.

If you release him, you guarantee fellow officers or agents are going to be in harm's way when they go out to find him.

To be clear, most are not talking about calling the illegal simply working in the fields, waiting tables, babysitting, or cleaning houses. We're talking about criminals who pose a clear threat to American citizens.

So, what to do? You notify ICE as soon as you can. And I don't care what you must do to get that done. If you must do it quietly, anonymously, behind closed doors, underground, through a special hotline, email, or carrier pigeon, damnit, just do it.

You instinctively understand danger. It's in your DNA.

If you have an MS-13 gang member whose initiation you know requires that he beat somebody to death or rape someone in front of fellow gang members and you don't tell ICE, you have blood on your hands.

Americans have the right to know when they are in danger. Why would you treat an illegal criminal different than an American criminal? Hell, maybe law-abiding states should clear out their prisons and send their own criminals to sanctuary states; since they're open to taking other countries' criminals, the least they can do is take ours. Think of the money we could save not jailing them.

Can't you see that you're being used in a political tug-of-war?

If this is a tough one for you and you are going to start listening to the ACLU or some LIBERAL mayor who doesn't give a damn about you, your contract, or your oath, when they direct you to release the wanted criminal alien out the side door, then maybe you should rethink this and go into social work.

As of this writing, the state of California is locked in a legal fight with the United States of America, trying to defend its right to ignore federal law. Only they're arguing from the opposite direction. *Sure,* they say, *the federal government has jurisdiction over immigration, but in this case, we're going to do everything we can to make it impossible for them to enforce it!*

News flash: The United States Constitution's Supremacy Clause can't be set aside because California— or Colorado, New Mexico, Oregon, Illinois, Vermont, or the Queen of England—says it should be. That's why it works. States do not get to make their own rules that fly in the face of our founding documents, so they can appease LIBERAL voters and ensure LIBERAL politicians stay in office for a few more terms. There's a new sheriff in town, who actually cares about our founding principles and won't stand by while they're ignored and mocked.

"Democrats' priority is to protect criminals, not to do what's right for our country," President Trump said recently. "My priority and the priority of my administration is to serve, protect, and defend the citizens of the United States."[1] Just as it should be, Mr. President.

But not everyone feels the same way, apparently.

LIBERAL Libby Schaaf is the Democratic mayor of Oakland, California. She's one of the people currently involved in the lawsuit between California and the United States. In February 2018, she decided that the courts weren't the only place that she and her state would go after lawful federal processes. She decided to send out a message to illegals herself. This message came in the form of a tweet—a public document, which will someday be admissible as evidence. The tweet warned that ICE was about to conduct an illegal immigration sweep throughout Northern California, including Oakland. She cried: The feds are coming; the feds are coming. The sweep, of course, was something ICE was well within its rights to do. The tweet foiled the operation, sent the immigrant community in that city into a panic, and left some eight hundred illegal immigrant criminals, including violent ones with violent felony convictions that include rape, domestic violence, pedophilia, larceny, burglary, and assault, on the streets.

Betrayal! She put her concerns for people who are in this country illegally, and who have committed crimes while here, ahead of the safety of the people of Oakland.[2]

ICE was able to detain 232 illegal immigrants over the four days after the mayor's tweet. According to Tom Homan, the acting director of ICE, out of those 232, 115 had prior felony convictions of serious and violent offenses.

But the ones that got away are still out there. In the weeks that followed the tweet, at least three of those eight hundred illegal immigrants, who had criminal records that included drug possession, hit-and-runs, and spousal abuse, committed new serious crimes. One was a robbery with gun charges.

Being a law enforcement officer is already dangerous enough, giving the criminals a heads-up that cops are coming for you should be a jailable offense.

So, the question is, do we protect illegals, who flouted our laws to come here, who committed crimes while here, or law-abiding American citizens, who should be able to live safely without sanctioned criminals in their midst?

You can march, and you can hate, and you can demonize the forty-fifth president, but mayors like

LIBERAL Bill de Blasio in New York, LIBERAL Rahm Emanuel in Chicago, and LIBERAL Libby Schaaf in Oakland, who say their policies only improve relations between the immigrant community and law enforcement, are now effectively removing law enforcement protection from American citizens and legal immigrants.

Proud To Be An American

Donald Trump has launched a new era in American history that will last for decades. It's called "Americanism." He is announcing *our* agenda of America First, the safety and security of her citizens, her allies, and her interests here and abroad. The LIBERAL Left—both here and across the globe—are doing everything they can to destroy both his vision and our way of life. We finally have a leader who understands the need to take care of us, to do what's in America's interest.

Our NATO so-called allies, acting like children refusing to leave Mommy's and Daddy's basement, should be on notice: they can no longer despise us, take advantage of us, and reap the benefits of our largesse. But like spoiled children, they continue to kick and scream. Thanks to Trump's leadership, they are finally starting to pay their way.

My Own Cases Prove Sanctuary Cities Don't Work

LIBERALS believe that if illegal immigrants don't have to fear being found out and deported, they'll be more likely to engage with the community or report crimes when they are victims or witnesses. It almost makes sense when you hear it for the first time.

But it doesn't work. Thirty-two years as a prosecutor, judge, and DA, in a county of about a million, tells me that.

As evidence, consider a case handled by my office when I was DA. It involved two illegals:

The victim, José Martinez, was an illegal immigrant from Ecuador. He was a hardworking painter who was paid in cash every Friday. Almost every Friday, another illegal immigrant would assault him and steal his cash.

One day the other guy took a rock and smashed José's head in, killing him. Like most homicide victims, I only ever knew him through the cold lens of the camera taking black and white autopsy photos. He was a small man with a big heart, who simply wanted to work and take care of his family.

Talking to José's family was a real eye-opener for me. They told me José had been afraid for his life but was too scared to come forward. There is a law intended to provide the illegal victims a safe haven and to encourage illegals to report crimes. This provides the sanctuary wacky leftists think they're creating. So, in order to protect "innocent" illegals we need to allow criminal illegals to roam freely to victimize citizens, legal aliens, and even other illegal aliens? That's what José was afraid of. In his mind, Westchester was already a sanctuary the criminal illegal was free to roam.

Even if Westchester County was declared a "sanctuary county" and hung banners that said "You're Safe, We Won't Deport You" from every building in the county, José still wouldn't have come forward. Declaring communities "sanctuary" for illegal aliens sends a message to criminals that they will be protected and you won't.

When LIBERAL politicians enact laws protecting criminal illegals from deportation, all they're doing is further excusing these people from the rule of law. They're allowing criminal enclaves to form and fester, and giving rise to all the shady codes of honor that come along with them. Why, when you are illegal yourself, would you report another illegal immigrant for beating you up and robbing you when you know he'll be right back on the street the next week, without fear of the police? Why would you say a word when the government can't send a lowlife like this guy back to where he came from?

In order to get undocumented immigrants to cooperate with law enforcement, you don't need a blanket sanctuary city. The law is already in place. It's called a U visa. It's intended to encourage illegals to report crimes and provide them and their families a safe haven in America. I used it as DA. If you're illegal and you want to report a crime, this visa will protect you and give you and your family sanctuary from deportation. It's already the law. So, in the end, sanctuary cities are nothing more than safe havens for criminal aliens and not their innocent victims, legal or illegal!

José Ines Garcia Zarate came to San Francisco, where he shot and killed Kate Steinle, because it was a sanctuary city. He knew he wouldn't be deported—that he could continue his life of crime without fear of deportation or any substantial repercussions. And just to prove California is truly a sanctuary irrespective of any legislation, a jury acquitted him of murder in spite of conflicting statements about where he found the gun.

How many parents must lose their children?

And now, Mexico gets into the mix. They say that a wall and a crackdown on illegal immigrants is an affront to Mexico. They *want* us to have sanctuary cities.

Really?

So enough of this benign-sounding sanctuary city nonsense that protects criminals. At what point do we stop the killings and the violence? Why risk it all to protect criminal illegals? Who would it be okay to lose? Your son? Your mother? Or as Jim Steinle did, his daughter, who died in his arms after asking him to help her.

To all those mayors like De Blasio in New York, Eric Garcetti in Los Angeles, and Muriel Bowser in Washington, D.C., who say they won't retreat from being sanctuary cities, my question to you is this: Who put you in office? Who did you take an oath to protect? Don't you understand that the first order of government is the protection of its citizens? American citizens? That's your job!

LIBERALS, you have a decision to make. Are you willing to lose federal dollars that help pay for the cops in your city, who protect American citizens and legal immigrants, just to resist the deportation of criminals who are here illegally? Because that is where this is going. You cannot continue to accept federal money for law enforcement while at the same time doing everything you can to undermine federal law.

Let me make one thing clear: we are all immigrants—except those of us who are Native American. But most of us came here under the rules. In fact, the happiest days for me as both district attorney and

judge were when I welcomed newly naturalized citizens who worked hard to get here and pledged allegiance to our republic. But the concept of sanctuary
cities is wrong—fundamentally flawed. Because of
this mutinous refusal to follow federal law, you and
your family are in real danger.

So, what to do? I'll tell you what to do: enforce the
law. If a city refuses to comply with federal warrants,
they get no federal money. California gets $40 million
a year to house criminal illegals until the feds pick
them up. That's our money. Don't give me this "have
a heart" nonsense! Americans are the most charitable,
generous people on the face of the earth. But don't you
dare ask us to create a zone of lawlessness and ignore
the murder of innocent victims, so some criminal here
illegally won't have to go home.

Don't tell me I have to be welcoming to people who
break the law to come here. It's bad enough I must
pay for their food, education, and medicine, but now
I must bite my tongue and pretend to like it? I don't
think so.

I continue to believe a border wall is necessary, in
whatever form it may ultimately take.

I want the wall, so we can know who is in our
country.

I want the wall to prevent drugs from entering our
country and our neighborhoods.

Most of all, I want the wall to protect American lives. Anyone in law enforcement, especially in states on the border, will tell you the border wall is imperative to the safety and well-being of our citizens. So is the enforcement of federal laws.

If you don't believe me, ask Kate Steinle's family.

CHAPTER SIX

Lying, Leaking, Liberal Leadership

If you want to understand the constitutional crisis and attempted coup unfolding before our eyes you must know how it originated. This plot against Donald Trump and every American who voted for him goes all the way to the top of the previous administration. It was conceived and planned at the top and executed by like-minded Deep Staters in law enforcement, the intelligence community, and their Swamp Party talking heads in the media. Allow me to introduce you to a few of the highest-ranking LIARS, LEAKERS, and LIBERALS involved in this scheme.

Pond Scum Brennan

I can only imagine the joy the Deep State experienced on Inauguration Day in 2009 when LIAR President

Obama was sworn in. The intel community got a craven, malleable community organizer who would go along with their globalist plans as if he wrote them himself.

Right off the bat, Obama's administration sent the message it could be talked into anything and was ready to work with anyone, regardless of the damage to our country. It all began with his "apology for being an American" speech in Cairo, Egypt, in January 2009—the first row filled with members of the Muslim Brotherhood, political arm of Hamas, picked by the Obama White House. The bottom line was Obama didn't have the balls to stand up to anyone. He was famous for boiling down his lead-from-behind foreign policy with the phrase "Don't do stupid shit!"

"If you can't beat 'em, join 'em" would have been more appropriate.

As "luck" would have it, he found a guide, someone who knew the Swamp better than anyone else. And Obama wouldn't have to compromise his far-left ideology to accept this person's help. On the contrary, he might have to double down. His eventual CIA director and Swamp guide, John O. Brennan, had once voted for Communist Party nominee Gus Hall in a US presidential election.[1] But that didn't stop Brennan from rising through the ranks of the Central Intelligence Agency. Far from it.

Make no mistake: LIBERALS control the Deep State.

Writing for *National Review* a few years back, Fred Fleitz, a retired CIA analyst, wrote how LIBERALS had taken control of our intelligence agencies. According to Fleitz, who is vice president of the Center for Security Policy, a Washington think tank, the Clinton years were like a Petri dish for the politicization of the CIA. "The liberal tilt within the CIA, especially in the Directorate of Intelligence (the analysis office), grew worse during the Clinton years as personnel were hired and promoted to support Clinton-Gore policy objectives,"[2] he wrote. Those policy objectives didn't seem to include keeping the United States safe from Osama bin Laden.

By the time George W. Bush took office, Clinton's petri dish had become a biohazard waste dump, and W didn't help matters any by retaining Clinton's CIA director, George Tenet. With the Clinton operatives burrowed in, the intelligence complex began to protect its liberal flanks. Fleitz cited several examples of the political maneuvering in the agency, including a CIA officer in Bush's inspector general's office leaking classified information about Bush's counterterrorism programs to the *Washington Post,* and intelligence officers trying to torpedo John Bolton's nomination as UN ambassador.

Corruption in the intelligence community spread like mold. That's what happens when no one's looking.

The days after 9/11, when the country was still shaken and vulnerable, presented the opportunity a career spook like John O. Brennan, waits for his whole life. He was an old boy from an old boys' club playing on the public's fear to seize powers they had failed to persuade the country to give them in saner times. In the mid-2000s, LIAR Brennan was running counterterrorism operations for George W. Bush and likely dreaming about his chance to run the entire Swamp the way most kids dream of becoming astronauts.

Having crawled from under the same, far-left rock and then been elected president, LIAR Obama liked what he saw in LIAR Brennan and named him the head of his CIA. Brennan's long and murky history in the intelligence complex made him the perfect reptile to work in Obama's Swamp.

The Brennan-Obama CIA became not only the most careless in the agency's history but the least transparent. It was Brennan's CIA that spied on the Senate Intelligence Committee while that committee was investigating the CIA's detention and interrogation program.[3] Not only did it read senators' emails; it sent a criminal referral to the Justice Department based on false information. So, the FBI was just following established Deep State protocol when it requested its FISA warrant to spy on the Trump campaign. In fact, the whole Russia-collusion delusion was cooked up to get a wiretap on the campaign.

By the time Brennan became CIA director, the post-9/11 American public had been relentlessly browbeaten into believing they had to give up their freedom for safety. To Congress and much of the public, the credibility of the CIA and NSA was unimpeachable. Exploiting this misplaced, blind trust, Brennan's CIA wasn't just a cloak-and-dagger outfit. It was looking for someone to stab in the back. Obama gave Brennan's agency a million daggers and a black cloak with which to operate.

When Donald J. Trump stormed past the other Republican candidates for president, his ascension shook the unelected career administrators, the power-hungry leadership in law enforcement and the intelligence complex, and the rest of the Deep State. The threat that a Trump victory represented to their cabal was enough to set in motion a coordinated conspiracy to keep him out of the Oval Office.

So, it's no surprise LIAR Brennan, working with another career bureaucrat across the Atlantic, James Bond-wannabe Christopher Steele, started the whole phony Russian collusion investigation. It was Brennan who pressured the FBI into investigating the Trump campaign, using Steele's comic book, cobbled together from hearsay and rumor. It was Brennan who touted the now-discredited dossier all over Washington as credible evidence. That comes as no surprise. But leaving aside for a moment that the bill for this piece-of-trash dossier was split three ways between Fusion GPS, the Hillary Clinton campaign, and the Democratic National Committee—conduct far more illegal than any Donald Trump is accused of—just think about who *wrote* the thing.

Christopher Steele might as well be the British John Brennan. He's certainly every bit a LIAR and LIBERAL. He climbed the ranks of posh British society without a hitch, went to Cambridge University, and then planted himself behind a desk at MI6 before the ink on his diploma was even dry. Within a few years, he was on the Russia desk, making "friends" in the Kremlin and hanging out—you might even say *colluding*—with Russian officials whenever he got the chance. By the time he retired and launched his private practice, he was basically a Russian citizen.

So, why did Steele take a piece of counterfeit opposition research and go to newspaper after newspaper trying to peddle it like a door-to-door insurance salesman? Why was he so insistent on it becoming a huge news story? He was supposed to be a spy. Isn't keeping your trap shut one of the core competencies of his profession? Apparently not in Mr. Steele's case, at least as far as this "research" was concerned. He couldn't wait to spill his guts to the liberal media.

At least one source tells me the FBI paid him fifty grand for the dossier. Maybe he was just in it for the money. Was that why he rushed to Michael Isikoff of *Yahoo! News* and David Corn at *Mother Jones* to tell his far-fetched story? Did he have dreams of a book deal and a Hollywood movie?

Although his motives still aren't entirely clear, one thing is certain: Christopher Steele is not who the LIBERALS say he is. He's not a top intelligence officer with impeccable credentials, a friend of the United States, and a warrior for liberty. In fact, he's the exact opposite. He's a mercenary in a Harris Tweed jacket and corduroy trousers, hired out to the highest bidder.

LIBERALS would have you believe the Russians are responsible for the political divide in our country. NEWS FLASH: the Russian Fake News stories placed on Facebook accounted for about 0.1 percent of Facebook advertising revenue. Now, compare that pop gun to the Steele dossier dirty bomb that exploded in the media and has ever since poisoned us with a phony crisis, a politically motivated investigation, and a body politic more deeply divided than ever before. Mr. Steele's dossier caused real damage to the fabric of our nation, unlike Russia's insignificant meddling.

And while our nation tore itself apart, Steele went underground in Great Britain. He lied to the Congressional committee, lied to the FBI and that's perjury. I don't care if he's from the UK or Mars—actually I do, we don't have an extradition treaty with Mars. And if Martha Stewart can go to jail for lying to the FBI and Roger Clemens can be indicted for lying to Congress, why not equal justice for the Brit? I think he needs to be brought back to the United States and prosecuted!

Meanwhile, LEAKER Brennan conducted a campaign of disinformation by leaking false information about the Trump campaign's collusion with the Russians without a shred of evidence, other than information from the discredited dossier itself. But this wasn't the first time Brennan abused the power and secrecy of his position to deceive the American people. Not even close.

It was LIAR Brennan who helped put together the Obama administration's talking points to cover its deplorable handling of the Benghazi attack and Crooked Hillary's complicity.[4] It was LEAKER Brennan who had to apologize to US senators for the CIA spying on their computers. And now LIBERAL

Brennan will go to any length to disparage, slander and sabotage the duly elected forty-fifth president.

LIAR Brennan talks a tough game, but he's a snowflake at heart. Like his FBI friends on the seventh floor of the J. Edgar Hoover Building, he's a desk cop, not a street cop. And when the shit hits the fan, you don't want a desk cop coming to your rescue. By the way, if you're a *Homeland* fan, wipe Saul Berenson out of your head—Brennan ain't no Berenson. He's been pushing papers around his desk his whole career, at least when he's not out in the hallway hoping to bump into someone to whom he can whisper his top-secret garbage—like the Steele dossier.

For months, he was hyping the dossier to just about anyone who would listen. In July 2016, he tried to get the FBI to investigate the Trump campaign, but Cardinal Comey turned a deaf ear. Back then, the Cardinal, another desk cop, was too busy neutering the investigation into Hillary's emails to buy the crap Brennan was selling. One conspiracy at a time, please. That's when everyone was sure she was going to win, remember?

That August, Brennan went over the Cardinal's head, directly to President Obama. According to the *Washington Post*,[5] a story based on leaks that just might have come from LEAKER Brennan himself, the CIA was the only intelligence agency present at that briefing. Brennan was still the only member of the intelligence community who was publicly saying that Russian president Vladimir Putin was trying to get Donald Trump elected. At that time, none of the other agencies bought Brennan's fairy tale. I don't even think the writers of *Homeland* would have been interested.

Still Brennan wouldn't quit. Like a one-man band with an accordion on his chest and cymbals on his knees, he made as much noise as he could. He next went to Congress and briefed leaders from both parties. He didn't get much traction there, either. Desperate, he took his story to the one person of any note who would believe him.

Minority Leader Harry Reid was at the end of his career in the US Senate. The 2012 midterm elections had rendered old Harry about as politically impotent as Anthony Weiner (sorry, couldn't help myself). Literally adding injury to insult, he'd smacked himself in the eye with an exercise band and was walking around with one lens of his glasses covered in duct tape.

Okay, I'm joking. It wasn't duct tape. And I don't mean to make fun of the senator's injury; I just wanted to set the scene. But it is true that Senator Reid was doing just about anything to make himself relevant. When Donald Trump became the Republican nominee and was therefore eligible to read the classified daily briefs given by the intelligence agencies, Reid wanted intel analysts to send Trump phony briefs. I kid you not.[6]

So, when LIAR Brennan cornered Harry and spewed his cooked-up tale about Putin and Trump, the minority leader swallowed it hook, line, and sinker. Reid sent a letter posthaste off to the FBI director, urging him to open an investigation. Cardinal Comey didn't open one, at least that the public knew about. He was still too busy fudging Crooked Hillary's investigation. Two months later, Senator Reid pounded the keys on his computer again, this time scolding the Cardinal for reopening the investigation into Hillary while not doing a thing about Putin's interference. Comey and the FBI responded, taking the official position that there was no clear evidence linking the Trump campaign with Russia.[7]

The Cardinal would eventually change that official position. He had a habit of doing that. Meanwhile, with Brennan as ringleader, the anti-Trump conspiracy's numbers began to grow.

Unmasking the Unmaskers

On the day Donald J. Trump was sworn in as the forty-fifth president, Susan Rice, Obama's last National Security Advisor, sat in front of her computer composing an email she was about to send to herself. Her purpose, she later said, was to create a "permanent record" of a meeting she'd had with Obama and his top national security advisors a few days before.[8] The discussion at the meeting centered on how much of their investigation into the phony Russian collusion story they were willing to share with the incoming administration.

So, let me try to get this straight. Obama's NSA chief wanted a permanent record of the outgoing president's directive to keep national security information secret from the incoming president?

However, just because it's in an email doesn't make it any less a lie. What is it with the Deep State that they think putting words on a page magically makes them true? I guess Susan learned after lying about the "spontaneous protest" in Benghazi that it would be better to put her lies in an email.

Second, Susan, the fact that you were conspiring against the incoming administration is simply more proof the shadow government was looking to control the intelligence community during the Trump presidency. In truth, your career is a testament to how one can rise in the government if lies are your stock-in-trade. What your actions say to me is that, at the very least, your allegiance to the country you swore to protect is suspect. At worst, you were plotting to take down the commander in chief.

LIAR Rice first waded into the Swamp under Bill Clinton's administration. Bill's secretary of state, Madeleine Albright, recommended Rice for a senior job in the State Department. Albright and Rice's mother had known each other for years. Rice was named the assistant secretary of state for African affairs. In that post, she stood by with the rest of the Clinton administration as the ruling Hutus conducted a mass execution of ethnic minorities in Rwanda. Rice was more worried about politics than the lives of eight hundred thousand Tutsis and other minorities. Of all people, it was Samantha Power, who would become Obama's UN ambassador and card-carrying member of the Deep State, who would expose Rice's true feelings about the Rwandan slaughter. In an article Power wrote for *The Atlantic*, she quoted Rice as saying: "If we use the word 'genocide' and are seen as doing nothing, what will be the effect in the November [congressional] elections?" It was so callous and incendiary; the comment might have stopped Rice's government career in its tracks had the article not been published in September 2001.[9] The events of 9/11 overwhelmed all other news coverage.

Rice crawled deeper into the Swamp in Obama's

first presidential campaign as a national security advisor. After his election, Obama rewarded her with a plum job as United States ambassador to the United Nations (the same job he would give Samantha Power, ironically), which turned out to be a complete disaster. Out of her depth, Ambassador Rice failed to get either Russia or China to join the US to deal with Syria or to impose sanctions against Iran.[10]

Rice's most memorable moment during her time at the UN had nothing to with her role as US ambassador.

I'm sure you remember.

On September 16th, 2012, the Obama administration needed to go on television to explain the deaths of a US ambassador and three others six weeks prior to the 2012 presidential election. The White House wanted Hillary Clinton, the secretary of state, and the natural person to comment and explain on the Sunday-morning talk shows, to tell the lie, which she would end up telling repeatedly, but that day she was nowhere to be found. Several officials, including Ben Rhodes, reached out to her, but Hillary had either gone into hiding or was busy planning a cover-up at the highest levels of government and bungling foreign policy—there's only so much you can ask from one woman.

And so, Susan Rice ended up doing what is known as the full Ginsburg:[11] interviews on all five Sunday-morning news shows. On each of those shows, she looked right into the camera and told us the September 11 attack five days earlier on our diplomatic compound in Libya was a "spontaneous" reaction to an anti-Muslim YouTube video. She told us that, and yet she knew full well it was a premeditated terrorist attack.

When the deputy chief of the Libyan mission, Greg Hicks, heard LIAR Rice on the Sunday shows, he couldn't believe his ears. Hicks was the last person to speak with Ambassador Chris Stevens before he was murdered during the attack. He had firsthand knowledge of what occurred in the Benghazi diplomatic compound. In emotional testimony in front of a congressional committee, Hicks refuted the Obama administration's version of events. "I was stunned. My jaw dropped, and I was embarrassed," he said about watching Rice's remarks on television. He was questioned for about two hours on the matter, giving a chilling minute-by-minute account of the attacks. None of it sounded anything like the minor incident Susan Rice was peddling on television. He called it a "demonstrably false narrative." The most emotional moment of his testimony came when he spoke of learning of Ambassador Stevens's death. He called it, "the saddest phone call I have ever had in my life."

Hicks told the committee that he and the others trapped in the compound expected US military reinforcements, but Washington never sent them.

"Okay, we're on our own," he recalled telling his colleagues. "We're going to have to try to pull this off with the resources that we have available."

Four brave Americans, Ambassador J. Christopher Stevens, Information Officer Sean Smith, and two CIA operatives, Glen Doherty and Tyrone Woods, gave their lives that night in Benghazi.

Despite Rice's dismal track record in international politics, and after she lied to America on national television, Obama rewarded Rice by making her his secretary of state. In one of the only good decisions she's ever made, Rice withdrew her name from consideration. But that didn't stop Obama. Six months later he named her his national security advisor. Rice was accused of "unmasking," which means revealing the names of US citizens who are incidentally surveilled during targeted surveillance of foreigners, during her tenure as national security advisor. Intelligence officers are required to follow a "minimization" policy, which directs them to leave identifying information on US citizens incidentally surveilled out of intelligence reports unless very specific circumstances warrant revealing their identities.

Initially, Rice said she knew of no such unmasking. Privately she told House investigators she unmasked the identities of senior Trump campaign officials to understand why the crown prince of the UAE was in New York.

Of course, her lying continued. Again, she went on a Sunday-morning news show and said that Bowe Bergdahl served the United States with honor and distinction. "Sergeant Bergdahl wasn't simply a hostage; he was an American prisoner of war captured on the battlefield."[12] Bergdahl would later plead guilty to deserting his fellow soldiers. What made the lie even more egregious was Obama's exchange of five high-risk detainees at Guantanamo, the "Taliban Five," some of whom have predictably returned to the battlefield, for deserter Bergdahl.

So why in God's name should we believe LIAR Susan Rice when she says she never sought to uncover the names of American citizens being surveilled for political purposes? "The allegation is that somehow the Obama administration officials utilized intelligence for political purposes. That's absolutely false," she told NBC's Andrea Mitchell.

How invested was she in the Deep State's campaign against Trump? Well, according to a former US attorney, Susan Rice put together spreadsheets detailing phone calls of many of the people who worked in the Trump organization and for the campaign—including President Trump!—which President Obama then made available to all intelligence agencies.[13]

How big is this pool of LEAKERS? No one seems to know for sure. Six people? Ten? Two dozen?

Enough to sink the *Titanic*? Flood Washington? Who knows?

One thing is certain: with each new person who gained access to the Obama administration's database of unmasked names, the chance of a leak increased exponentially. And every so-called journalist with a laptop and a cell phone was rubbing his or her hands.

The unmasking of Americans by Obama's Deep State began with General Michael Flynn. In early January 2017, just before Trump took office and just after Obama ripped up privacy protections by expanding the limits on sharing of raw NSA intelligence, the *Washington Post* published a story about Michael Flynn discussing Russian sanctions with the Russian ambassador, Sergey Kislyak.[14]

First, allow me to explain to you what's legal and what isn't in that last paragraph. What's legal, and appropriate, is for a top security adviser of an incoming president to talk with officials of foreign countries, including officials representing countries that have difficult relationships with the United States. What's not legal is leaking the name of an American citizen captured in an intelligence report.

Here's how the illegal process of unmasking can happen: analysts from the NSA are allowed to surveil the phones of anyone whose communications are even remotely tied up with a person like Kislyak. If someone happens to find him- or herself on the same email chain, that information goes straight to the intelligence gatherers. If Kislyak orders a pizza, the kid who answers the phone at Domino's is fair game. Under section 702 of the Foreign Intelligence Surveillance Act, communications of US persons can be legally captured during surveillance of a foreign target.[15] This is how a bunch of people sitting at their laptops in some NSA office would manage to justify tapping the phone lines and email correspondence of the president-elect of the United States a few months later. But I'm getting ahead of myself.

Now, try to forget that in a court of law someone can't be found guilty by implication alone. It takes work to convict someone in public, under the scrutiny of a judge and a jury, made up of fine people like you. You would at least think that these records would be kept secret, wouldn't you? That no one outside the NSA should be able to peek and make copies whenever they feel like it?

Wrong again.

Remember Obama's executive order?

Well the EO directed people like Susan Rice, in the days after Donald Trump was elected president, to spend time pilfering every page of classified correspondence she could from the NSA. She and her co-conspirators at the Obama White House decided to store it in six different servers, all in different places. (Is it something about being a liberal that makes you want to do that? I'll never understand it.)

And all of it was to build a stockpile of innocent Americans who could be cast as part of the phony Russian conspiracy.

Michael Flynn has pleaded guilty not to making the phone call, or to anything he said on the call, but to lying to the FBI. However, there are those within the FBI who believe Flynn did not intend to lie. This becomes even more troublesome when Andrew McCabe, deputy FBI director, arranged for and was present at the interview.

Michael Flynn's unmasking, however, brought no consequences to Susan Rice or any other co-conspirator, and was such a successful tactic for the anti-Trump plot that unmasking became the Deep State's signature move.

If I had Susan Rice on the stand, I would instruct the jury to take her testimony with less than a grain of salt. However, I imagine a jury could figure that out for themselves after listening to her.

Which brings us back to another conspirator I'd love to get on the stand—the former director of National Intelligence, LIAR James R. Clapper, Jr. Brennan may be pond scum, but Clapper lies for a living. Talk about being part of the Deep State! Clapper's father, his wife, and *her* father all had careers in the National Security Agency. I guess going into this line of work for Clapper was a little like taking over the family pub—one where they've got little microphones under all the bar stools and copies of everyone's credit card information in the back.

By 2001, he was head of the National Geospatial-Intelligence Agency, a little-known branch of the intelligence community that operates under the umbrella of the military. As the head of that organization, Clapper got pretty comfortable operating far outside the realm of public opinion. He wasn't being watched by the media or Congress, and he probably became accustomed to doing things his own way. How else can you explain the widespread collection of data on American citizens he oversaw as Barack Obama's director of National Intelligence? Did he not think he was going to get caught?

When President Trump named General Michael Flynn his national security advisor, the appointment couldn't have thrilled Obama or Clapper. The appointment was akin to kicking sand in their faces. Obama had Clapper fire Flynn from his post as director of the Defense Intelligence Agency (DIA) in 2014, and then went to great lengths to try to talk our current president out of hiring him, but to no avail.

President Trump undoubtedly knew why Obama

had Clapper fire Flynn as director of the DIA: it was because Flynn had already started to upend the Deep State. One of General Flynn's coworkers from that period told the *Washington Post* the reason Flynn was fired was because he wanted to move intelligence analysts "up and out of their cubicles into the field to support war fighters of high-intensity operations." In other words, he wanted to set a fire under the ass of the administrative state.

Obama couldn't have that.

Neither could Clapper.

So, when President Trump made General Flynn his NSA head, the Deep State had a conniption. Flynn was a direct threat to the status quo.

So, what did the Deep State do?

They unmasked him, leaked it, destroyed his reputation, and prosecuted him.

So, let me get this straight. Lying to the FBI is a chargeable offense, but Swamp Monsters like Cardinal Comey, Susan Rice, and Clapper can lie at will to Congress and the American people with impunity? By the way, it is not a crime for the FBI to lie to the American people, but it is a crime to lie to Congress whether under oath or not. Why is it everybody else gets prosecuted, but not them?

There is something very wrong here. But not for Comey; he gets to write a book on his falsehoods.

Clapper gets to be a paid political pundit for the same network where he leaked information!

Since he retired from his position of Director of National Intelligence, James Clapper has been a constant presence on political television. James Clapper lied when he told CNN's Don Lemon in March 2017 that he did not interact with the media prior to leaving the Obama administration in January 2017. His reputation as a LIAR is bolstered by his testifying before a House panel that he LEAKED the made up dossier to CNN's Jake Tapper while he was still serving as the Director of National Intelligence. The man is a classic LIAR who cannot keep his lies straight.

This is the man who in 2015 barred all intelligence workers from providing the press any information, to guard against leaks! Makes you wonder what happened to that little directive? So, when Obama was president, Clapper was all about plugging the leaks, but as soon as Trump is elected, it's *Open the flood gates!*

From his new perch as "news" commentator, he's belched a steady stream of misinformation designed to undermine President Trump, including the outrageous claim that our president is somehow unfit for office.

Clapper even predicted Muammar Gaddafi would prevail in Hillary's war—the rebel uprising in Libya—before the rebels dragged Gaddafi's body through the streets. He called the Islamic extremists' Muslim

Brotherhood, "largely secular." The comment came despite his own CIA labeling the Muslim Brotherhood a "religious-based" organization.

LIAR Clapper also lied to the Senate Select Committee on Intelligence when he said the NSA did not spy on Americans.

Clapper told us that very few Americans are unmasked. He later had to admit in front of the Senate committee that, in fact, nearly two thousand Americans were unmasked in Obama's last year in office alone.[16] This was an increase of 350 percent during the Obama administration.

And he has the nerve to say on national TV that President Trump is unfit for office?

Which brings us to the last of our little Deep State threesome, LIAR Samantha Power.

President Obama had a thing about hiring fiction writers like Power and Ben Rhodes, probably because he needed them to weave a believable narrative out of the web of falsehoods that characterized his presidency. The House Intelligence Committee has identified Rhodes—whose only postgraduate qualification is an MFA in fiction writing from NYU—as a "person of interest" in their investigation into the unmasking of Americans. As for Power, when it came out that she had unmasked more than one American per working day for the last year of the Obama presidency, the cleverest excuse she could come up with was *someone else did it.*[17]

I'm not kidding.

In testimony in front of the House Committee on Oversight and Government Reform, Power had the unmitigated gall to say that most of the 260 unmasking requests that had her name on them were made by someone else. "I did not make those requests," Power told the committee, according to Chairman Trey Gowdy.[18]

What the hell does that mean?

Power's explanation can mean only one of two things: either she's lying, or she's a pawn whose stupidity or naiveté was exploited by members of the Deep State. If the second explanation is true, it begs a very big question.

Who used her name?

The Samantha Power cover-up is one of the most intriguing and possibly explosive elements of the anti-Trump conspiracy.

In October 2017, Judicial Watch, the conservative watchdog group, filed a Freedom of Information Act (FOIA) request to the US State Department asking for information on Power's "unusual unmasking request." That information included, "all requests for information submitted to any intelligence community member agency by former United States ambassador to the United Nations Samantha Power concerning, regarding, or relating to the following:

> "Any actual or suspected effort by the Russian government or any individual acting on behalf of the Russian government to influence or otherwise interfere with the 2016 presidential election. The alleged hacking of computer systems utilized by the Democratic National Committee and/or the Clinton presidential campaign.
>
> Any actual or suspected communication between any member of the Trump presidential campaign or transition team and any official or employee of the Russian government or any individual acting on behalf of the Russian government.
>
> The identities of US citizens associated with the Trump presidential campaign or transition team who were identified pursuant to intelligence collection activities."

The State Department stonewalled the request, giving only a vague, boilerplate denial. Then in February 2018, Judicial Watch filed a lawsuit against the State Department. Why would the State Department go to court to keep this information secret? I can't imagine they'd go through all that trouble—hiring lawyers, paying legal fees, arguing their flimsy case in front of a judge—if they didn't have something very important to hide.

The State Department came up with an ingenious excuse. In a letter dated May 23, 2017, the National Security Council informed Judicial Watch that all records pertaining to unmasking by Susan Rice had been "removed to the Obama Library."[19]

Under the Presidential Records Act, that means they're closed to the public until 2021—or until the Obamas manage to suck enough tax dollars out of the citizens of Illinois to get their library built. If we do have to wait that long, I'd at least like to be kept up to date on the library planning. For example, will they be keeping the Susan Rice records in the fiction section, or the nonfiction section? Maybe by the time they're done filling the pages with black lines and cross-outs, they can just hang them up on the walls like pieces of modern art, since nobody's going to be able to read the damn things anyway.

It isn't the total lack of transparency that gets to me. We've all come to expect that from people at the highest levels of government. What bothers me about this are the lies.

George W. Bush went to great lengths to make sure as few people as possible could find out what he was up to in the years immediately after 9/11. He signed

an executive order that essentially gutted the Presidential Records Act, locking up who knows how many
documents and conversations. And he took his share
of beatings in the media for that.

But that was a time of war. America had just
been attacked, and desperate measures needed to be
taken—measures, like torture, that most of the American public couldn't stomach. Barack Obama took
office during a time of peace. He whipped up an
executive order that made it seem like he'd be letting
the press and the American people in on every decision he was going to make in the White House, and
every conversation he'd be having. Executive Order
13489 said that only living former presidents could
invoke executive privilege to keep documents hidden,
and made most documents of his predecessors even
more accessible to the public than they'd ever been
before.[20] Obama reestablished the post of archivist of
the United States, a government job whose occupant
would be able to decide which records were in and
which were out, and vowed to bring the records of his
predecessors to light.

The press ate it up. Suddenly, we were dealing with
the "most transparent administration in history."

Yeah, right.

Little did they know that while Obama was flash-
ing EO 13489 around the Oval Office, his cronies in

the Deep State were fudging the rules and creating loopholes so fast none of us could keep up. They knew that when it came time to answer for their high crimes and misdemeanors, the records would be long gone—some bound for a dusty library in Illinois, where they'd be chopped up and redacted beyond recognition, others deleted "accidentally" or spread among so many private servers that even the best prosecutor couldn't put all the pieces together—and the conspirators would all get off scot free.

Any documents that would indict them are long gone. Team Obama spent the years they were in power making sure of that—years when they should have been governing and working to keep our citizens safe from harm.

The Swamp King

Out of all the creatures in the Swamp, maybe the most slippery is our former president Barack Obama. Did you ever wonder to what lengths LIBERAL Obama went to get his co-conspirator, his handpicked successor, LIAR Hillary, elected to protect his legacy? Did you ever wonder what connection his administration had with the Deep State? I have news for you; his administration *was* the Deep State.

Right from the start of his political career, there

were questions about Obama. I knew nothing about him when he appeared on the political stage. With other presidents, it wasn't that way, right? You knew where they came from. If you're old enough, you knew Reagan was a movie star and then governor of California. You knew H. W. Bush was a navy pilot, a war hero, and former Director of the CIA. You even knew, with his bellbottoms, flag-burning wife, and girlfriend Gennifer Flowers, what you were getting with Bill Clinton. But Obama? Right out of nowhere. A first-term senator from Illinois, he appears in a puff of smoke, right out of a magic act. He then takes on the biggest political machine of our time, the Clintons, and blows them right out of the water! I don't know about you, but by the time I finished scratching my head, he was sitting in the Oval Office.

Things didn't get any clearer for me throughout his eight years as president.

Who was this guy? And what was he up to?

Only in looking back can we put the pieces of the puzzle together. Clue number one came during his first presidential campaign. It was then he hired the high priest of the Deep State, John O. Brennan, as a national security advisor. In the Senate, he had played his *Mr. Smith Goes to Washington* act to perfection, railing from the Senate floor about the Patriot Act "violating our fundamental notions of privacy." But once in the Oval, Jimmy Stewart turned into Joe Pesci from *Goodfellas*. He supported a law that legalized the NSA's warrantless eavesdropping and let telecom companies who aided the NSA in intruding in the lives of private citizens off the hook. By the end of his second term, he'd expanded warrantless eavesdropping on innocent Americans to the point that individual privacy no longer existed.

By LIAR Obama's second term, any pretense of adherence to the Fourth Amendment—the principle of probable cause and the judicial sanctioning of search warrants—had all but disappeared. Even the supposed sanctum sanctorum of the Foreign Intelligence Surveillance Court (FISC) had been violated. In fact, the Obama administration had so little respect for the super-secret court, his NSA was reprimanded several times for lying to FISA judges.[21] Sound familiar? If you know anything about the Steele dossier, it certainly does.

And how did Obama react to the fact that his NSA was lying to FISA judges?

He gave the agency's director, three-star general Keith Alexander, another star and as much money as he needed to erect an American spying operation that a comic book writer would have trouble imagining.

So much for *Mr. Smith Goes to Washington*.

Oh, and by the way, Former President Obama's director of National Intelligence, LIAR James R. Clapper goes to Congress and tells them that the NSA doesn't spy on Americans. Here's how that came down:

> **Senator Ron Wyden** (D-Ore.): "So what I wanted to see is if you could give me a yes or no answer to the question, does the NSA collect any type of data at all on millions or hundreds of millions of Americans?"
>
> **Director of National Intelligence James Clapper**: "No, sir."
>
> **Senator Wyden**: "It does not?"
>
> **Director Clapper**: "Not wittingly. There are cases where they could inadvertently perhaps collect, but not wittingly."

Then came Mr. Snowden. Oops! Turns out the NSA not only spies on Americans, it spies on practically every American. They even used Xboxes to spy on people! Clapper simply said he'd "forgotten" that small fact. LIAR!

After Edward Snowden exposed the breath of spying under his administration, LIAR Obama excused his violators saying, "I think it's important to recognize that you can't have 100 percent security and also then have 100 percent privacy and zero inconvenience."

During his last few months in the White House,

during the 2016 presidential campaign and Donald Trump's transition, President Obama was engaged in some very secretive stuff. I don't mean the $200 million he sent to the PLO or the Taliban Five he let waltz out of Gitmo in exchange for deserter Bowe Bergdahl, or the $104 million in cash, euros, and, Swiss francs he sent to Iran. No, I'm talking about something much closer to home.

After Donald Trump was elected president of the United States, an event that shocked the Deep State to its core, Obama issued an executive order that allowed all sixteen intelligence agencies to unmask Americans at will and without regard to any previously instituted privacy protections.[22]

Why was that Mr. Former President?

I'll tell you why: so he could unmask the names of Americans to the press. He sacrificed the privacy of countless Americans so that the names of a couple of people loosely connected to the Trump campaign who had contacts with Russians would slip through the intelligence agency sieve into the hands of the Fake Press.

The idea that LIAR Obama, as a pawn of the Deep State didn't use his weaponized intelligence-gathering capabilities against the threat of a Donald Trump presidency is ludicrous.

Donald Trump knew this right from the beginning. They were spying on him! They were listening in on Trump Tower. They had Paul Manafort, who was Donald Trump's campaign chairmen for all of three months, and who lived on the forty-third floor of Trump Tower, under constant surveillance. And if they "accidentally" happened to pick up conversations of people working for Donald Trump's presidential campaign, or Donald Trump himself, well that was purely coincidental, and they certainly wouldn't listen to them!

Give me a break.

And oh, how indignant the Obama administration was at even the suggestion they'd bugged candidate Trump. Cardinal Comey and his sanctimonious, "Aw shucks" act in front of Congress; John Brennan and James Clapper doing all the Sunday morning news shows, lying to us yet again.

The Obama mob was toeing the line.

"Neither President Obama nor any White House official ever ordered surveillance on any US citizen. Any suggestion otherwise is simply false," said Kevin Lewis, former president Obama's spokesperson.

Well, well. What a smooth answer. Only a judge can issue a surveillance warrant. But you knew that, didn't you Kevin?

Why aren't we making all those outraged liberals

eat their words? They had painted Donald Trump as a lunatic, crazy, a guy wearing a tinfoil hat. *He thinks they were tapping his wires*, they snickered. Well, guess what? They were. So, he used the wrong word. The gist was right on. In our upside-down world you can attack someone for telling the truth and there is no consequence. Drives me nuts.

Lewis's statement is misleading on its face. It's the FISA court that permits the surveillance. It's the Justice Department that asks the court to do it. The idea that LIAR Obama was somehow above the conspiracy against Donald Trump is hogwash. He has done much worse. Many believed Obama's intelligence agencies listened in, and, in fact, recorded a phone call of Congressman Dennis Kucinich because he had the temerity to stand against Hillary's failed war in Libya. So why would he have any compunction to listening in on Hillary's opponent? To say Obama didn't condone or instruct his Justice Department to petition the court for permission means either Lewis doesn't know what he's talking about, or he's lying. Guess which one I think it is?

Obama has a history of asking courts to snoop on people. Ask my Fox News colleague James Rosen.

Rosen was the chief Washington correspondent for Fox News. In 2009, he broke a story that North Korea was about to respond to a UN Security Council resolution condemning their nuclear tests by test-ing a nuclear weapon. He got his information from a LEAKER in the State Department named Stephen Jin-Woo Kim.[23] Obama's Justice Department obtained a warrant from a federal judge deeming Rosen a "crim-inal co-conspirator" and a flight risk. Armed with the warrant, they captured his phone records, his emails from two accounts, and tracked him by phone traces. Even the *New York Times*, and the *Washington Post* condemned the feds for the action.

He also had a history of manipulating intelligence for political purposes. Just ask General Lloyd J. Austin III, CENTCOM commander, who oversaw a white-wash of Obama's war against ISIS by painting it in a positive way. Guess what? Obama's war wasn't going in a positive way.

The truth is, the Obama administration was so desperate to keep Donald Trump from being elected that his Justice Department, prodded by his CIA chief John O. Brennan, misled the most secret court of the United States. The goal was simple: spy on the Trump campaign to undermine a presidential election. Mem-bers of the highest echelon in Obama's FBI, CIA, and Department of Justice, all conspired to prevent an outsider from breaking the establishment's strangle-hold on the American people.

They used a dossier of lies, paid for by a major

political party, the Democratic National Committee, and a presidential candidate, Hillary Rodham Clinton, and even the FBI, to dupe the court! But based on text messages later found between FBI agent Peter Strzok and his girlfriend Lisa Page, they wanted to forum shop for their favorite judge, Rudolph Contreras, plotting their move under the pretense of a dinner party to get their warrant. They swore to facts they knew were lies to get what they wanted to surveil a candidate they could not imagine being president. So was the FISA court duped, or was it complicit with the fraud?

The top echelon of our intelligence agencies, whose salaries we pay, decided we didn't deserve a free and fair election!

Why isn't this the biggest scandal in America today? Why isn't a sitting president's use of national security surveillance against a candidate from the opposite party in a presidential election at least as big as Watergate?

The answer is: it is!

Furthermore, former president Obama knew all along what Russia was up to. He didn't do anything because he, and the establishment pollsters, thought Hillary would win. He tells us, though, that he met with Putin and told him to "knock it off." Picture this visual: Putin, bare chested, riding his horse and

Obama riding a bicycle with his helmet on. Do you think Putin was scared? Do you even believe Obama said it?

It was only after the election that he imposed sanctions on Russia. Why not before? Maybe because it's he who had the cozy relationship with Vladimir Putin, and not Donald Trump? Let's look at the facts. Fact: in 2009, it was Obama's vice president Joe Biden who first expressed the president's wish to press "the reset button" on the US's relationship with Russia. It was Obama's secretary of state, Hillary Clinton, who met with the Russian foreign minister in Geneva where together they pushed a symbolic button on which *reset* was printed in both English and Russian. It didn't matter that Obama's advance team, or whoever oversaw the details, misspelled the Russian word for *reset* and instead used one that meant *overload*. Everybody just got a big laugh about it because it was Obama who wanted to make nice with the Russian bear.

Fact: It was Obama who was overheard speaking to Russian president Medvedev asking for time with missile defense and, in that famous hot mic, moment saying "This is my last election. After my election, I have more flexibility."

Fact: It was under Obama's watch when 20 percent of our uranium was sold to Putin with a $145 million kickback to the Clinton Foundation and a

$500,000 speech fee paid to Bill by a Kremlin-connected company.

Fact: It was Obama who put Putin in charge of over-seeing the elimination of chemical weapons in Syria. Putin pressured Obama to let him handle the situation for his ally, Assad, and Obama caved. Putting the fox in charge of the henhouse clearly failed since chemical weapon elimination deadlines were missed repeatedly. You remember that? A line in the supermarket was taken more seriously than Obama's line in the sand.

Fact: It was Obama who watched like a Cheshire cat as Russia invaded and annexed Ukraine and the Crimea Peninsula in 2014. He knew what was happening.

Fact: Long before she met with Don Jr., it was Obama's DOJ that let the Russian lawyer Natalia Veselnitskaya into the United States, without a visa, using a legal loophole called "extraordinary circumstances." Then, Obama's administration then allowed her to then sit in the front row of a congressional hearing!

So, who's Russia's pal? Donald Trump or you, Mr. Former President?

The facts speak for themselves. The witch hunt and false narrative put forth by the Swamp's propaganda machine has turned the truth on its head. The United States president who had the coziest relationship with Vladimir Putin is not the one in the Oval Office today, it's good old Mr. Former President, smooth-talking Barack, who pulled the wool over the eyes of all his fawning liberal lambs.

Obama is the best evidence that the Democrat Party who expects and relies on the African-American and Latino vote, does nothing for them.

As we go to print, while every major media source is busy fantasizing about a Trump-Russia collusion, under Trump's administration, African-American unemployment rates are at an historic all-time low.

As a presidential candidate, Trump had anticipated he could do as much when he told African-American voters, "What do you have to lose?"

In August 2015, even before the first Republican primary debate, Trump was calling out Obama for his poor record on helping African Americans.

In an interview with ABC's Jonathan Karl, Trump said, "(Obama) has done nothing for African Americans. You look at what's gone on with their income levels. You look at what's gone on with their youth. I thought that he would be a great cheerleader for this country. I thought he'd do a fabulous job for the African-American citizens of this country. He has done nothing." I agree.

Just eighteen months into his presidency, Trump accomplished what Obama couldn't do in two terms: provided concrete proof that African-Americans are legitimately better off under the Trump presidency.

The Real Deplorables: Crooked Hillary and Lying Bill

Any case against an anti-Trump conspiracy must include the high priestess of the Deep State, LIAR Hillary Clinton.

In January 2018, I took a camera crew to Chappaqua, New York, in search of Hillary. You might have seen the segment on my show *Justice with Judge Jeanine.* In it, I stand at the edge of the woods that surround the quaint town yelling her name. I peek into a local dry cleaner asking whether she ever comes in and gets her famous pantsuits cleaned. It's good for a chuckle, anyway.

No, I didn't find her. I wasn't expecting to. If she weren't so good at keeping herself out of the spotlight when she has to, she'd have been thrown in jail a long time ago. Still, in her own hometown, we thought there'd be a chance of getting some good interviews with people who know her. But none of the businesses we stopped at, from pizza parlors to nail salons, had seen any sign of her for months. As the owner of a bookstore told me, she rarely came into town anymore. While Bill would stop at the store and look around quite often, Hillary usually ordered her books—and I bet her white wine—by phone. She would then send someone into town to pick them up.

Her reluctance to come into town and mingle with the hardworking Americans who run the shops there shouldn't surprise you. She's a Clinton, after all. And Clintons don't leave the house for less than $250,000 per trip. They figure if you're going to talk to people, you might as well get paid for it.

Nice work if you can get it, right? Bill has been doing it for years and making big piles of cash for his time. It's no surprise that Hillary has decided to do the same thing. You would think that being the most famous loser in the world wouldn't look as good on an event program as "former president." Yet, Hillary has made it work for herself. She's still cashing plenty of checks on her "Boohoo Tour."

Since losing the election in the worst upset in American electoral history, Hillary Clinton has given over fifty paid speeches blaming just about everyone she can think of for the loss except, of course, herself.

The sad truth of the matter is that she's got a captive audience. There's a whole group of whiners who haven't gotten over the fact that Donald J. Trump won the presidency of the United States fair and square. They don't like that he's securing our borders, making trade fairer for Americans, lowering unemployment, boosting the economy, lowering taxes, putting North Korea on its knees and creating a strategy together in the Middle East. They just want someone to blame, and Hillary, as always, is happy to provide.

For instance, she made a speech at the India Today Conclave, which was held in Mumbai just a few weeks prior to this writing. If you thought her "basket of deplorables" remark during the 2016 presidential campaign was bad, get a load of this. I call it the "basket of deplorables, part two." LIAR Hillary, it seems, just can't help herself. In Mumbai she continued to call Trump supporters misogynists, racists, and immigrant-haters.

"And his whole campaign—*Make America Great Again*—was looking backward," she said. "You didn't like black people getting rights; you don't like women, you know, getting jobs; you don't want to, you know, see that Indian American succeeding more than you are—you know, whatever your problem is, I'm going to solve it."

While the audacity of Hillary Clinton never truly surprises me anymore—trying to list all the lies that leave this woman's mouth is like trying to count the snowflakes in a Buffalo blizzard.

Trump supporters don't like women getting jobs? *Really?* Why doesn't she tell that to Kellyanne Conway, Sarah Huckabee Sanders, Betsy DeVos, Gina Haspel, Nikki Haley, and Seema Verma—both of whom are, ironically, of Indian descent. How about the millions of women who voted for Trump? The ones who *must* have real jobs to support their families because no one's going to pay them hundreds of thousands of dollars to babble on stage?

When I first ran for county judge in 1989, my critics said, "We can't have a woman county judge. She won't be strong enough to sentence people!" That made me laugh. What a joke. The people who said that obviously hadn't met me. Still, I held a press conference where I assured voters I had the intestinal fortitude to sentence anyone to life. What they didn't know was that I had the fortitude to sentence a man to death. I made history in Westchester when I was elected the first woman county judge. My being a mother of two babies was proof of my incompetence to some of my peers.

"You can't be a judge and a good mother," one guy said to me. He was wrong.

I was a duty judge, meaning I was on call 24/7. During the week of Christmas, I was called in to work and I didn't have a babysitter. So, I took my toddler son Alex, to court with me and hid him under my bench while I arraigned a shackled out-of-state murder defendant. I thought I had gotten away with it until he started yelling, "Mommy, it's dark!" Moms do what they have to do.

In 1993, the first time I ran for DA, the concern wasn't about my credentials and whether I had the fortitude to do the job. It was about who would take care of my little kids if I couldn't get home at night. Al, my husband at the time, and I had to issue a statement that if I couldn't get home at night, he would watch the kids.

The guy I was running against, Michael Cherkasky, *had three kids*, and his wife was pregnant with their fourth. *I only had two!* No one ever asked him about who would be watching his kids! It was ridiculous, but it was classic. I was never a bra burner or ballistic about that stuff; it was just the way things were and I had to work within that context. My job was to be at least as good as any guy and just get it done, and I did.

Hillary says Trump supporters don't like working women. Let her say that to my face. Hillary also floated the notion that white women only voted for Donald Trump because their husbands told them to. I don't know about you, but the day a man tells me how I'm going to cast my vote is the day I'm dead. But maybe things are different in the Clinton household. There, when your husband tells you to go dig up dirt on the women he's been running around with behind your back, you do it. You even set up a war room in the White House for it.

In Mumbai, LIAR Hillary wasn't finished. She also called all Trump voters—wait for it—slackers. Yup, good-for-nothing, lazy slobs. That's what half of America is to Hillary. This coming from a woman who wouldn't get off her ass to go to Pennsylvania, Michigan, and Wisconsin when she needed to in the last weeks of the campaign, and ended up losing all three states. She couldn't find Wisconsin on a map, and neither could any of the "brilliant" political operatives to whom she was paying six-figure salaries to run the campaign while she spewed her hate. But she never really cared about Wisconsin or the other states in what she and the other liberal elites consider "flyover country."

"If you look at the map of the United States, there's all that red in the middle where Trump won," Clinton said. "I win the coast. I win, you know, Illinois and Minnesota—places like that. But what the map doesn't show you is that I won the places that represent two-thirds of America's gross domestic product. I won the places that are optimistic, diverse, dynamic, moving forward."

She wears her disdain for the heartland of America as a badge of honor.

Hillary, if you really want to know what happened, here's a hint: he won, you lost! You lost because you were a lousy candidate, you didn't have a message, and you lied just about every time you opened your mouth. You put our national security at risk with your email setup, and ran a foundation that was nothing more than an organized "pay to play" enterprise parading as a charity. Four men died in the attack in Benghazi under your watch as you lied about what caused it.

I could go on, but my readers might have something to do next Thursday. Stop with the *poor me* nonsense, Hillary. We've had it with you Clintons, always claiming victimhood. You say you take absolute personal responsibility? Well how does that square with blaming everyone, including just about all Middle America? The truth is you're damn lucky you're not in jail wearing a cheaper version of one of your pantsuits.

And you say it's a painful process, reliving the campaign. Think about the rest of us! Since as far back as we can remember, we had to watch you go from one lie to the next. I know how you operate from firsthand experience.

Allow me to enter a bit of background: it was 2005 and I was just finishing up my third term as district attorney in Westchester County. During my time as DA, I ran an office that prosecuted virtually every type of criminal: robbers, rapists, murderers, drug dealers, mobsters, and cyber criminals. When it came to domestic violence abuse and sex offenders, I was relentless.

It's the way I've always been, and the way I'll remain. I go with my gut. Always have. I've lived by that my entire life, with one exception: when I agreed at the insistence of the Republican Party to run against Hillary for US senator in New York.

That wasn't my first rodeo—I'd campaigned before—but it was the first time I'd run against a political machine like the Clintons. Let me refresh your memory. Hillary was running for the junior US Senate seat in New York State. Bill and Hillary had slipped into the leafy town of Chappaqua in 1999, just in time to qualify for her first run in 2000. But this was 2005, and Hillary was up for reelection even though she had no plans to stay a senator for long. Oh, no. She already had her carpetbags packed for her 2008 run for the White House. Becoming a senator was just a stepping-stone. For the record, I was born and raised in the upstate city of Elmira, New York. There I worked on a dairy farm while going to school.

I wasn't completely naive. I knew what I was in for. People always attack you when you run for office; if you don't have thick skin you should get the hell out of the race. But it was different running against Hillary. Suddenly, there were things that the press attributed to me that were just lies.

Early in my campaign, we visited a farm. When

we were leaving, one of my staffers handed me an article about the visit. That article had been written ahead of time! Most of the "facts" in the story weren't true. Although I didn't understand what it was at the time, I came to find out that it was Fake News with—surprise, surprise—Hillary Clinton's gang orchestrating the whole thing.

When I got home from the farm that night, I was a bit shell-shocked. My boots were clean, but it still felt like I had stepped in crap. I'd spent my life as DA. I'd grown accustomed to truth and justice. *This is what happened, these are the facts.* What good were facts in the world of national politics?

That night, I knew I couldn't finish the race. Politics with the Clintons in the picture became all about lies and smears. The message didn't matter, and neither did integrity. That's not a game I was willing to play. It still isn't. Later, a former Clinton adviser told me Hillary had me in her sights since I was a native New Yorker and rising Republican star with a record of accomplishment. He told me she's a powerful enemy to have.

But, I'll give you this, Hillary. You did say one thing in that Mumbai speech that had some merit. When someone asked whether Vladimir Putin might "have something" on Donald Trump, a question that is right out of the liberal conspiracy textbook, you gave the India Today Conclave this response: "Follow the money," you said.[24]

Why, Hillary, I thought you'd never ask.

As of this writing, the hardworking men and women at the FBI (and not their politicized bosses) are investigating the Clinton Foundation. What are they looking for? Donations to the Clinton Foundation that directly influenced official actions taken by Secretary of State Hillary Clinton.[25]

The old pay-to-play scheme. It's as old as politics itself. Money goes in, favors and contracts come out.

A ruthless, profit-driven woman, LIAR Hillary's attempted ascension to the presidency was all about money and power. Underneath those pantsuits were pure corruption, crookedness, and a callous disregard for morality. She covered for her sexual predator husband and her sexual predator financial supporters in that den of inequity known as Hollywood. She hated anyone in the economic class beneath her. And, she headed an organized pay-to-play enterprise parading as a 501(c)(3) charity known as the Clinton Foundation.

How big of a crime are we talking about? Well, ask yourself this: How do two people who start with nothing, without a business, without a product, without any practical business expertise, amass a fortune worth hundreds of millions of dollars? How do you go from dead broke to rolling in dough while working in government? I'll tell you how: you use your position and power to engage in a give and take.

Since the day it filed for tax-exempt status with the Internal Revenue Service—don't get me started on those wackadoos—the Clinton Foundation has been little more than the world's biggest superstore for political favors and under-the-table deals. Foreign heads of state, some of whom are antagonists to the United States, make donations, and in return, they get all the power and influence that comes with being a former president of the United States or secretary of state. And because these are donations to charity, which for Americans are tax deductible under the Internal Revenue Code, the amounts are much larger than your typical campaign contribution. It's a simple arrangement, when you think about it. But it's also easy to screw up. That's why most amateur politicians who try it get caught.

Take LIAR Hillary's buddy Bill de Blasio, for example. He's been taking contributions for favors for years, and now he can't get through a press conference without some reporter asking about it.[26] When they write his obituary, just under the line about how he caved to liberal pressure on sanctuary cities and gave safe harbor to illegal criminals, you'd better believe there's going to be a section on the widespread corruption he brought back to New York City politics.

But Bill and Hillary Clinton are more cunning than that. They're lawyers, and they know how to tip-toe through a legal minefield. Together, they've managed to operate their foundation on the very edge of legality, offering only the briefest glimpses into the operation underneath.

One of these glimpses came when Anheuser-Busch donated just over a million dollars to the Clintons. According to Peter Schweizer's explosive book, *Clinton Cash*, the beer giant gave the money to the Clinton library, and then watch President Bill Clinton, who was just a few months from leaving office, drop a bill that would have regulated beer advertising that targeted minors. Interesting timing, huh? Another of Schweizer's revelations told about Secretary Hillary Clinton's failure in 2007 to impose the strictures of a law called the Congo Relief, Security, and Democracy Prevention Act, which would have taken a Marxist dictator in Africa out of power. This wouldn't have been interesting—secretaries of state fail to impose the law all the time; just look at Benghazi—if it weren't for a $100 million donation to the Clinton Foundation that had come through a few months before. The donation had come from Lukas Lundin, who ran a corrupt mining company in the Congo, and needed the dictator to stay in power if he was going to keep his business running. So, he slipped a hundred million bucks to the Clinton Foundation, and Hillary decided to abandon the legislation—which, by the way, she had supported just a few months before the donation went through.

It's impossible to know how many other actions Clinton failed to take or how many shady deals she cut because of big donations just like that one. We can only hope that the FBI is allowed to do its job, far from the political biases of its top brass and find out.

Here's one more Schweizer unearthed: in 1998, when India conducted illegal tests of nuclear weapons, shocking the world and flagrantly violating the Treaty on the Non-Proliferation of Nuclear Weapons, Bill Clinton imposed economic sanctions. They remained in place until well into Barack Obama's first term. To combat these sanctions, the Indian government sent scores of lobbyists to the United States throughout the early 2000s. Officials in New Delhi also encouraged all influential Indians in the US who would listen to affiliate strongly with the Democrat Party. As a result, millions of dollars in cash donations flowed into the Clinton Foundation's bank account. Suddenly, just a few months after Hillary Clinton had been named secretary of state, those sanctions were gone. She became a vocal supporter of ending sanctions on the country and played a large part in lifting them.

Bill and Hillary Clinton, two people who once had

a remarkably tense relationship with India, were now being honored at dinners in that country and seeing their friends get "person of the year" awards in front of huge Indian crowds. It's amazing what a few million dollars in cash will do.

And as just mentioned, Hillary still stops by India on occasion to give a speech and pick up an extra few bucks. Any place that's given up that much cash is worth another hit every once in a while, I guess. This woman does not even have the decency to commit crimes and then stay away from her accomplices like a good criminal. Instead, she throws her criminality in our faces, knowing that no federal prosecutor in the country would ever make a move and indict her. Especially not Jefferson Beauregard Sessions.

There is a pattern with the Clintons always walking the line. Remember the Whitewater papers and the Rose Law Firm scandal? How about giving a pardon to Marc Rich after Denise Rich raised a fortune for the Clintons? (Oh, and before I forget, I was so sad to see Denise denounce her American citizenship.)

Let's look at more recent manifestations of this "enough is never enough" playbook. Let's start with Uranium One and the Iran deals. Both deals set the stage for an unbelievable sale of 20 percent of the US supply of uranium to Russia. Unfortunately, Iran—Russia's puppet state—will receive highly enriched uranium, used to make nuclear bombs, under the guise that it will use it for submarines and the production of radioactive isotopes, used to treat diseases like cancer.

Who else but LIAR Hillary Clinton could have talked the State Department into approving a deal that sent 20 percent of America's weapons-grade uranium to a state-sponsored company in Russia—a country, by the way, which has just announced a frighteningly revamped nuclear weapons program, built using uranium? Who else would have had the insane belief that she'd never get caught?

If you've watched my show you know how angry I am about this. And if you don't watch my show (I won't hold it against you), here's why I'm mad: uranium is essential to make molybdenum-99 (Mo-99). Better known as Moly-99, this isotope is used in medical nuclear imaging. Moly-99 is one of the most important weapons we have in the fight against cancer; often, it's how doctors detect cancer, as well as diabetes and heart disease, early enough to save a patient's life. I know all about Moly-99, because for me it's personal.

In 2012, I was diagnosed with cancer. I didn't talk about it. Even now, I try to avoid talking about it. I continued to do my show every week as if nothing were wrong. Toward the end, as the chemotherapy and radiation treatments progressed, I was on air talking to my audience as usual, but I was exhausted. I didn't have my eyebrows or my eyelashes. I was wearing a wig because I was bald. Like too many who've battled cancer, my doctor's initial diagnosis was confirmed thanks to nuclear imaging, That imaging and the medical isotopes used to treat disease are made from uranium. It is uranium that saved my life and countless others. But do we have enough uranium?

It seems like the Department of Energy has sipped the Obama Kool-Aid on the domestic production of Moly-99. There is no domestic production of Moly-99 as required by the American Medical Isotopes Production Act of 2012. When I spoke to the president about this, he had been advised by the Swamp, presumably by DOE Obama holdovers, that there is plenty of the life-saving isotope. Notwithstanding, there are shortages reported by US hospitals while Russia has positioned Iran as the world producer.

On its face, the Uranium One deal stunk. Not only were we off-loading one-fifth of the raw material used for life-saving medical work, we were sending weapons-grade uranium to a sworn enemy—Russia.

The Clintons' involvement in Uranium One goes all the way back to 2005. It was then that Bill Clinton met a man named Frank Giustra who wanted to buy uranium mines in Kazakhstan, a country that has

20 percent of the world's supply of uranium. Clinton, who barely knew Giustra then, traveled with him to visit the president of Kazakhstan. Two days later, Giustra signed contracts that made him a partner in three of Kazakhstan's uranium mines. Soon after, Giustra "donated" $31 million to the Clinton Foundation. A year later, Giustra sold his stake in the mines to a company called Uranium One. When the deal closed, he gave the Clintons another $100 million.[27] Later, in 2010, the Chairman of Uranium One donated millions to the foundation, and Bill got $500,000 from a Russian bank for a twenty-minute speech.

The Clintons' influence peddling is massive—global in scale. Hillary set American foreign policy to coincide with the flow of hundreds of millions of dollars to the Clinton Foundation. Bill was the fixer or bagman for the foundation.

Try to find a real audit of this alleged charitable foundation. Good luck, because there isn't one. This is astounding when you think of the money the Clinton Foundation spends on expenses, salaries, and airfare for mostly Clinton comrades and former Clinton campaign members.

On November 14, 2017, *Newsweek* published an article titled: "Fox Host Told Trump to Appoint Special Counsel to Investigate Clinton at Private Meeting with President." Here's what they wrote:

"Fox News host Jeanine Pirro told Donald Trump he should appoint a special counsel to investigate Hillary Clinton during a private meeting in the Oval Office." Even though they had their facts wrong (no surprise there)—I'm keenly aware that a president doesn't appoint a special counsel, the attorney general does—the reporter did manage to capture the essence of what happened.

"At the November 1 meeting between Trump and Pirro, the TV host also hit out at Attorney General Jeff Sessions for failing to investigate the former secretary of state, including her role in the Uranium One deal," the *New York Times* reported.

"Shortly after the conversation Pirro and Trump had in the Oval Office, Sessions announced the Department of Justice would be looking to 'evaluate certain issues' outlined by Republicans, including the Uranium One deal."[28]

The House Judiciary Committee had already requested the Justice Department appoint a special counsel to investigate these matters. Under their chairman, Bob Goodlatte, R-VA, they made this request, twice, on July 27, 2017, and again on September 26, 2017. They never got a response.

Then, I had my meeting with the president on November 1, 2017, when Jeff Sessions was due to give testimony to the committee, and "suddenly" he acquiesces.

In other words, it took a lot of pressure for Sessions to even consider a special counsel was merited. What exactly is so difficult to understand here, Jeff? How many more fact patterns do you need to see? You certainly figured out quickly that you needed to recuse yourself from Russia, when all you did was sit across the table from a guy you barely knew, but you can't figure out whether we need to look at the selling of our uranium to a foreign government?

When Sessions did finally cave in and agree to investigate Uranium One, he said, "I'll have my smartest lawyers take a look." That's nice talk, but a second-grader could make this case. And meanwhile, it's July 2018, and LIAR Hillary is still out there and thumbing her nose at all of us.

Now she's out raising money to fund the "Resistance" and smugly thinking she's gotten away with everything.

CHAPTER SEVEN

Lying, Leaking, Liberal Law Enforcement

O f all the elements of the coordinated attack against our president, perhaps the part that infuriates me the most is the corruption that exists at the top in federal law enforcement. They did the lying, leaking, and spying necessary to cook up the dishonest investigation of nonexistent collusion between the Trump campaign and the Russian government. In addition to amounting to a coup attempt against the president, their actions represent a betrayal of all the men and women who dedicate their lives to fighting crime.

Clean House at the FBI

T he FBI needs a complete overhaul. A complete cleansing. Cut off its head. When a company in the private sector stops serving its shareholders or is tainted by politics, the board of directors fires the CEO. Sometimes the shareholders fire the board of directors *and* the CEO. That's what needs to happen at this government agency, whose leadership has become so corrupt and politicized that it has rendered the agency completely incapable of performing its core functions.

Gone are Director James Comey, Deputy Director Andrew McCabe, General Counsel James Baker, FBI Chief of Staff James Rybicki, Assistant Director of Public Affairs Michael Kortan, and Lisa Page, FBI attorney and love interest of Peter Strzok (who has been demoted). The upper echelon of the FBI has become ground zero for LIARS, LEAKERS, and LIBERALS. Perhaps at no time and place in US history has this much lying and leaking occurred in so short a time, all for one nefarious purpose: to whitewash Hillary Clinton, nullify the election of Donald Trump, and see that nothing the voters elected Trump to do ever gets done. This is the Deep State and the heart of the Swamp; and it's a heart of darkness.

FBI agents, some of whom are on the Mueller special counsel team, chase Russians to create a nonexistent Trump-Russia collusion narrative and work the fake Hillary email investigation—or should I say "matter"?—while ignoring credible tips loaded with probable cause. As Peter Strzok and Lisa Page carry on their affair, thinking they're going to change the course of history, Andrew McCabe, handling both the Clinton "matter" and the Trump "case," collects hundreds of thousands of dollars from a Clinton political ally for his wife Jill's campaign. Meanwhile, real justice is thwarted.

The FBI made several major errors, many on James Comey's watch. Jim, were you too busy trying to concoct a Russia collusion case? You screwed up the Boston Marathon bombers' case. Four people died, and many others lost limbs or eyesight, thanks to your BS excuse that the threat wasn't specific enough. The Fort Hood massacre, the Orlando Pulse nightclub shooting, the San Bernardino massacre, and the attacks of 9/11 are all among FBI spectacular failures.[1] You were involved in most of them. But you're so territorial, so selfish, so politicized, so focused on headlines, so full of yourself that you refused even to share information with other agencies.

It's not as though the Parkland, FL school shooting was the first time the FBI failed to prevent a mass shooting by an unstable person it had already investigated. It investigated Pulse nightclub shooter Omar Mateen prior to his mass shooting, with similar results. And just as in Nikolas Cruz's case, the FBI had multiple warnings Mateen was dangerous and likely to harm others. For heaven's sake, even his mosque had told the FBI he was dangerous![2]

All of this seemed to have slipped LIAR Jim Comey's mind when he was questioned about the FBI's previous investigations of Omar Mateen, going back years before the shooting. All we got from Comey was the usual set of excuses for why an obvious threat was ignored while the agency was busy rummaging around for Russians.

The *New York Times* says that even pervert Dr. Larry Nassar was on Comey's radar almost three years ago.[3] And what did Comey do? Nothing. Whom did he notify? No one. As a result, an estimated forty more young women were victimized by Nassar. And when confronted with this atrocity and blatant disregard for our children, the FBI public relations team said, "The safety and well-being of our youth is a top priority."

Of course, there are good men and women in the FBI; I have worked with a lot of them. But they're marginalized; they're not advanced. The power is in the clique at the top. It was FBI leadership that handled the Hillary "matter," not the field offices. This FBI has been stained and politicized by Comey.

It's time to stop this charade. It's time to return the FBI to its original mission.

In March 2018, FBI Deputy Director Andrew

McCabe turned over notes he had kept on President Trump to Robert Mueller, just hours after he was officially fired from the FBI.[4] He then claimed "victim status," claiming his downfall was the result of a series of attacks designed to undermine his credibility and reputation.

Andy, I don't know how to break this to you, but the only reason you're even in the news is because you're a LIAR. And when you lie under oath or even to the FBI when not under oath, you've committed a crime, whether you're convicted or not.

Consider this: General Michael Flynn, who put his life on the line for all of us when he served in the military, admitted to lying to the FBI about something that wasn't even criminal! And now he's a convicted felon. Martha Stewart lied to the FBI, and now she is a convicted felon who spent time in prison. McCabe lied not only to the FBI but to the inspector general and under oath,[5] even after being given an opportunity to take the lie back. Flynn and Stewart are crooks and McCabe isn't? The *Wall Street Journal* called McCabe "the new 'Deep Throat.'"[6] Just like the original, Mark Felt, McCabe abused his power, leaked information about an ongoing investigation for his benefit and lied about it. Lest we forget, Felt was convicted on felony charges for his behavior, although he was pardoned by President Reagan in 1981. As far as

I'm concerned, McCabe's actions warrant prosecution far more than Felt's did.

McCabe is out of a job because the FBI's Office of Pro-fessional Responsibility said, after the inspector general's investigation, that McCabe had made unauthorized disclosures to the news media,[7] and that he had "lacked candor." Translation: he lied. He lied about the investigations into the Clinton Foundation and leaked information to the *Wall Street Journal* and the *New York Times*, neither of which he was authorized to do.

Cardinal Comey

We shouldn't be surprised. McCabe's boss, Jim Comey, also leaked information,[8] seeking to get it into the *New York Times*, because he didn't have the guts to stand up and say what he wanted to say himself. Comey and McCabe are Gold Members of the LLL Club. They're LIARS and LEAKERS. They both lied and leaked in direct violation of federal laws. And McCabe has the audacity to cry about being targeted?

I have a message for you, Andy: you're not that important. No one's looking to bring you down personally. But your wife gets almost $700,000 from the Clinton cash machine, and you handle the Clinton email investigation?[9] A five-year-old could see the conflict of interest. We entrusted you with the power of the greatest law enforcement agency in the nation, and you not only used it to your own advantage, you used it to your political and financial advantage.

Every FBI employee knows that lying to the FBI results in automatic dismissal. That's only if you're a privileged government employee. Regular folks who lie to the FBI go to jail. But McCabe wants us to believe his termination is part of an effort to undermine the special counsel's Russia investigation. He's lucky he's not in jail.

The only Russia investigation that should be going on at this point is one looking into Hillary and that whole gang for the shady sale of our uranium to Russia.

It's going to get worse for McCabe when his sidekick Peter Strzok and Strzok's girlfriend are called on the carpet for their undertaking to create an "insurance policy" to take down Trump. If Comey and McCabe are Gold Members, Strzok is definitely Executive Platinum. He's a LIAR, LEAKER, and LIBERAL. He hit the Traitor's Trifecta. Platinum cuffs for him unless, of course, he decides to rat on his comrades.

McCabe also lied about his relationship with top counterintelligence agent Strzok, who worked for him while McCabe, Strzok, Comey and others tried to affect the presidential election, and later the presidency of Donald Trump, by starting the Trump-Russia inquiry. They opened that investigation even though the only person who had colluded with the Russians was Hillary.

There were three pending federal inquiries into McCabe's actions while he was still at the FBI. He was removed from his post only after the new FBI director saw evidence regarding his misdeeds.

While McCabe threatened Jim Comey, saying he would "torch the FBI" if forced out of his job,[10] Comey wrote a conciliatory tweet, saying "Special Agent Andrew McCabe stood tall over the last eight months, when small people were trying to tear down an institution we all depend on. He served with distinction for two decades. I wish Andy well. I also wish continued strength for the rest of the FBI. America needs you."

Comey is clearly hoping that McCabe won't testify against him. Who is going to rat on whom? If this were the movie *The Godfather*, Cardinal Comey would be the *capo di tutti*, Andrew McCabe the enforcer, Lisa Page both the consigliere and the *goumada*, and Peter Strzok the button man. And it looks as though Strzok, who may have signed the warrant application to the Foreign Intelligence Surveillance Court (FISA Court), was a close friend of Judge Rudolph Contreras, who signed the warrant.

Since Comey's book came out, the intrigue has

deepened. McCabe says Comey gave him permission to leak information. Comey, in a rare moment of clear recollection, claims he didn't. McCabe insists Comey lied to Congress. McCabe said he not only had authority to share information with the media about Hillary, but he did so with Comey's knowledge.

His former coworkers at the FBI called James Comey "Cardinal Comey" behind his back. It wasn't meant as a compliment. They were referring to the exasperating sanctimony with which he cultivates his false image as an incorruptible, morally superior servant of the people.

In one way, it's fitting. That's because he may be more revered today by liberals than the Pope by Roman Catholics. But it wasn't so long ago that those same liberals considered him the Devil incarnate for supposedly stealing Hillary Clinton's certain victory in the 2016 election. That was before they bought into an even less realistic theory: that "the Russians" had somehow turned the election for Trump, simply by disseminating nasty (and often true) stories about Crooked Hillary.

Now Comey is selling a book about how he and others of his ilk within the agency are patriotic heroes, defending the republic against a supposedly authoritarian and illegitimate president, Donald J. Trump. As I said recently on my show:

"Don't you love it when arrogant egomaniacs are

hoisted with their own petard? FBI Director James Comey and Deputy Director Andrew McCabe now know the pain of that petard. The Department of Justice is investigating Andrew McCabe after an Obama-appointed IG made a criminal referral against him. And pompous Cardinal Comey is now being investigated for leaking classified information."

When Comey›s memos were released, they were supposed to lay out the real reason for his firing—that Donald Trump was colluding with Russians and looking to obstruct justice. Unfortunately for Comey, the Democrats, and the mainstream media, they prove just the opposite.

Because he didn't trust the president, Comey made notes of his presidential meetings. The memos were written contemporaneously with the meetings (one within five minutes of the meeting). Contemporaneous notes carry great legal weight, because they are made almost immediately after the event, when the memory is fresh.

But unfortunately for Jim Comey, they don't support his narrative. In fact, they prove three things. One, the president encouraged the FBI to investigate the issue of collusion between anyone on the Trump campaign and Russia. Two, he encouraged the FBI to investigate the Steele dossier. Three, the president wanted to make sure his administration was free of leakers.

Here's the rub. The meeting was a setup to allow CNN to go forward with a negative story about the president and to create the illusion of Russia collusion. Comey himself admitted to the president that CNN wanted to go forward with the dossier story because some LEAKER gave it to them. But there needed to be a news hook. The meeting Comey set up to inform the president about the dossier was the hook. Four days later, CNN ran the story Comey told the president about the dossier. Comey's hook worked. But it gets even better. James Clapper, the man Jim Comey said he admires most in government, whom we already know is a LIAR based on his "we don't spy on Americans, well not wittingly at least," told Comey to meet with the president to speak about the dossier. Comey is dumb enough to admit this.

"I then executed the session exactly as I had planned. I said the Russians allegedly had tapes involving him and prostitutes in Moscow so that they could lend credence to a hyped-up Russia collusion investigation."

Trump, however, interjected—saying there were never prostitutes. Comey lied and said the FBI was keeping a close hold on the dossier so that there would be no excuse to expose the story.

So, to make it simple:

Clapper told Comey to meet with the president to alert him about the prostitutes, which was a pretext to create a news hook for CNN to leak the story.

Once Comey is fired, he decides he will leak information through a friend to the *New York Times*. Now the Department of Justice is investigating that leak of classified information.

Jim, you're the head of the FBI. You told the president he wasn't under investigation. You get fired, and now you need to put things in the public square to get a special counsel to put him under investigation? Why would you need to do that?

Your first memo was actually sent to the FBI—to your Deputy Director Andrew McCabe, your Chief of Staff James Rybicki, and your general counsel and closest advisor, James Baker—and who knows who else? Since there clearly wasn't anything criminal evidenced in the memo, what's with the hogwash that you need to get the information into the public square to get a special counsel appointed?

Comey says the release of his memo to his liberal Columbia University professor friend, now "lawyer" Daniel Richman, was done with the intent to get it to the *New York Times* and generate a "special counsel." He denies he "leaked" it, saying it was not a "leak."

Both Fox News Channel's Bret Baier and CNN's

Anderson Cooper were incredulous at his response. He responded by saying it was his "personal diary," as if anyone at the FBI, routinely, if ever, sends his or her diary to the deputy director of the FBI, his chief of staff, and legal counsel.

Comey relies upon Clintonian language to evade legal jeopardy and defend sharing a classified memo. He says he was sharing an unclassified document to get out to the media. The memo says "secret" on its face, which means it's classified! That leads to the next question: Why was Daniel Richman given a special government employee status and why isn't he being questioned about his role in leaking information? In order to obtain special government employee status, he would have been required to have training on federal records and federal information. He knew it was illegal to leak federal records and had an obligation to report Comey for leaking.

Although Comey admits leaking to Richman a memo that doesn't implicate the president of anything, anyone would have to ask if he did it before. Did Comey use Richman on other occasions to leak information meant to gin up a fraudulent, illegal, immoral Russia investigation? After all, Comey was clearly a Clinton political ally. He absolved her of criminal liability in the email scandal. What few know is that Comey investigated the Clinton Foundation and

Hillary in particular for the failure to file from 1999–2004 annual legally required audits. The case abruptly ended. The players? US Attorney James Comey, FBI chief Robert Mueller, and the one who had final tax fraud prosecution oversight, Rod Rosenstein. The Swamp hard at work.

Jim, you are a LIAR. And a LEAKER. You are pompous. Egotistical. Condescending. And you violated the laws that you swore to uphold because you want to make news, because you want to write a book. Because you want to be a hero. And because you don't think the rules apply to you.

And because you are like your friend McCabe, you do it for personal gain.

Newsflash: once you took those memos out of the building to leak to the *New York Times* you committed a crime. You had no right to do that. They were federal records. They were not personal notes. They were not memos to self. They were memos to other FBI agents. If Donald Trump needed investigating why didn't you investigate him when you were the highest-ranking law enforcement official in the country?

Why? The investigation was secondary. It was phony. You needed to make yourself the protagonist. Now we know that but for those memos and your illegal leak to the *New York Times*, Robert Mueller wouldn't be tearing at the fabric of this country. Isn't it a bittersweet irony Jim, that both you and McCabe are being looked at for the same thing Hillary did? You're in the same boat as she. You said she didn't intend to have classified information on her server. But you, Jim, made it clear you intended to release those memos so that you could get even with the president. You had the intent you say was missing in Hillary's case.

Jim, the FBI is not proud of you. You're a former FBI director out there discussing matters presently under investigation by the special counsel. Where do you come off publishing a book about issues under investigation? You even admitted what you leaked was secret and, therefore, classified.

But you protest that you don't do sneaky things, Cardinal. You don't leak. You don't do weasel moves. Jim, are you schizo? On the one hand, you lie to the president that you don't leak but the whole point of the memo and the meeting with the president was to leak it. And now on your book tour you say, *It's true; I'm a LEAKER.*

And Jim—you're a political operative, too. You wanted Hillary Clinton to be president. You even skirted the law to let her get away with it. And you played along with Loretta Lynch so she could help.

But Jim you must keep your facts straight. During your book tour, the same day you said Hillary would be a better president, you demurred and said it's too hard to go back in time and answer that question. Jim, do your answers depend on the time of day or who's interviewing you?

Jim, it isn't working. You're trying to look like an objective individual until you again admit you're not.

So, you're not sneaky. You're not a LEAKER. She'd be a better president. Jim, be very careful. You knew from the get-go you would cut Hillary loose, and you knew from your time in the Obama administration you would go after Donald Trump. You've deceived the American people. As a result, you're under investigation for leaking classified information, theft of government property, obstruction of justice, and a clear abuse of power. If I were a betting woman I'd lay odds your friend Clapper is another one soon to be under investigation. The bittersweet irony for all Americans is we will be able to watch you fight each other— Andrew McCabe who says you told him repeatedly that it was okay to leak to the *Wall Street Journal* and Loretta Lynch whom you accused of pressuring you to not call Hillary's case an investigation.

So now folks, as the whole idea of collusion with Russia by the Donald Trump campaign fades into obscurity, we now see the Deep State doing what it does best—state actors protecting each other and like-minded members of the system. But if there's any justice, and the DOJ is dutifully run, you'll all be made accountable. It's no accident everyone Comey sent his original memo to has either left or been reassigned away from Mueller's witch hunt. That should raise questions for anyone with an open mind.

Here's a question that may not have occurred to you: Why haven't we heard anything from or about assistant director of the FBI Counterintelligence Division Bill Priestap? Priestap was Peter Strzok's boss while this whole anti-Trump conspiracy was being perpetrated. Certainly, we would expect to hear his name mentioned when everyone else on the seventh floor of the J. Edgar Hoover Building—above and below him—is making daily news.

I suspect we haven't heard about Priestap because he's cooperating, either with Mueller's investigation or investigations into the FBI's leadership. I don't have any inside information on this, but my experience as a prosecutor tells me this is the most likely explanation for Priestap's silence. We'll have to wait and see.

Or is it J. Edgar Comey?

Because his mission was to change the course of American presidential history, Jim Comey has done more damage to the FBI as an institution than J. Edgar Hoover. The only difference between him and J. Edgar is that we know he wore dresses.

The truth is Comey was the chief architect in tainting and politicizing the FBI. When I say "partisan hacks," I don't necessarily mean Democrats or Republicans. But that doesn't really matter, because the 2016 election wasn't about Republicans versus Democrats. It was about the Establishment versus the people.

I am the eternal optimist. There have been rough patches in the FBI's history, but the rank-and-file men and women of the FBI have done wonders over the years to restore the agency's reputation. Starting with its very first director, J. Edgar Hoover, there was corruption at the top. While Hoover is credited with taking down high-profile bank robbers during the 1930s, developing counterespionage work during World War II, and modernizing law enforcement technique in some areas, he's also notorious for abusing the power vested in him to wage personal and political vendettas. They started during Hoover's first years with the FBI's predecessor, the Bureau of Investigation.

According to Boston University professor Alston Purvis, son of the legendary special agent Melvin Purvis, who brought down the notorious criminals John Dillinger and "Pretty Boy" Floyd, Hoover persecuted his father relentlessly. The younger Purvis wrote in his book *The Vendetta: Special Agent Melvin Purvis, John Dillinger, and Hoover's FBI in the Age of Gangsters*, that Hoover "blocked him [Melvin Purvis] from getting jobs, ordered agents to dig up dirt on him, invented stories that impugned his character, and deleted him from official FBI histories."[11]

And why? Because Purvis was receiving too much of the credit for stopping Dillinger and Floyd, credit Hoover believed should be bestowed solely upon himself. Forget that it was Purvis and his men who had risked their lives in two spectacular gunfights with the gangsters,[12] eventually killing them both, while Hoover sat on his ego in a cozy office in Washington.

Hoover pioneered the practice of wiretapping politicians and other political opponents on behalf of the presidents he served under.[13] Meanwhile, he repeatedly denied the existence of the Mafia. Rather than doing the hard work of investigating it, he preferred the relatively easier glory of designating lone bandits "Public Enemy No. 1" and taking the credit when real law enforcement officers like Purvis hunted them down. So, the Mafia ran wild, even establishing a quasi-corporate organization called Murder, Inc., while Hoover was busy abusing his power for personal and political ends.

The good people within the FBI worked for decades to reform the agency's reputation after Hoover finally abdicated his dark throne and this world.

Until Cardinal Comey, the Bureau had for the most part convinced the public that it was an apolitical law enforcement agency. Unfortunately, as with the IRS and EPA, President Barack Obama sought to politicize the FBI. He couldn't have picked a better man for the job than James Comey. Comey eventually surrounded himself with like-minded individuals, Andrew McCabe and Peter Strzok, both of whom figure significantly in the conspiracy to bring down the Trump presidency.

Letting Crooked Hillary Off the Hook

While the upper echelon of the FBI focused on politics, it ignored the Clinton Foundation, Uranium One, and it's own protocols in the Hillary email investigation. Let me tell you the whole story on the crooked Uranium One deal.

The Fake News Media have done everything they can to spin and downplay this egregious betrayal of US national security, but there are several facts not disputed by anyone. One, in 2010, the Russian government–owned ARMZ Uranium Holding Co. acquired a 51 percent stake in Uranium One, a Canadian uranium-mining company with significant operations in the United States.[14] The acquisition gave the Russian government control of a company with rights to mine up to 20 percent of all US uranium deposits. It would eventually buy out the remaining shares and assume complete ownership of the company in 2013.[15]

Two, for ARMZ to acquire that stake in Uranium One, it needed approval from CFIUS, the Committee on Foreign Investment in the United States. That committee is chaired by the secretary of the Treasury and includes representatives of several government agencies, including the departments of Commerce, Energy, and State. Secretary of State Clinton's representative approved the deal, as did several other agency representatives of the Obama administration.

Three, while the Russian government was acquiring Uranium One, which it did in three separate transactions between 2009 and 2013, Uranium One's chairman made four separate donations to the Clinton Foundation, totaling $2.35 million.[16] Secretary Clinton did not disclose those donations to the Obama White House, breaking a previous agreement to do so, based on the obvious potential conflict of interest the foundation represented for a sitting secretary of state.

And as if the millions funneled to the Clintons by Uranium One's chairman weren't enough, a Russian investment bank linked to the Kremlin and promoting Uranium One stock paid Bill Clinton $500,000 for a single speech in Moscow right after ARMZ announced it would acquire a controlling interest in Uranium One.[17]

None of those facts is in dispute. Now, the liberal media can make all the excuses for Hillary they want to. They say there is no direct proof of a quid pro quo, as if a scam artist with Hillary's decades of experience would allow herself to be video recorded taking the money from Uranium One's chairman and, with a wink and a nudge, telling him to let the Russians know they wouldn't get any resistance from her.

Another excuse offered by the mainstream media is that several other federal agencies also approved the sale. I thought "what-aboutism" was a cardinal sin. Besides, the State Department is the big dog in this decision, and seven of the CFIUS members are connected to the Clinton Foundation. Put those puppies under oath and watch them squirm. They want to put the president under oath, but not Hillary Clinton. The Deep State wants to checkmate the president.

Obama and the Clintons sold our uranium and with it the security of our nation. How did it happen?

In 2008, the Russians were frantic. They were desperate to buy uranium, the key ingredient to making nuclear weapons. The Obama administration was more than willing to accommodate. In fact, the whole upper tier of the Obama administration, those paragons of globalist virtue, approved the deal.

As far back as 2009 the FBI and the DOJ had an active, large-scale criminal investigation into Russia and Kremlin connected individuals who were conspiring to access America's uranium. The plan included bribery, money laundering, and kickback schemes.

In all, the Clinton Foundation received approximately $145 million yet it failed to disclose major contributions from entities involved in this Uranium One deal.

Why is this important?

Folks, context is everything. The backdrop of the sale of 20 percent of America's uranium to the Russians was Putin's ongoing racketeering enterprise that the Obama inner circle knew about and the FBI and DOJ were monitoring and investigating. And yet they subsequently allowed the transfer to Russia. You know the players. Follow the names.

The DOJ, headed by Eric Holder, was in charge not only of this investigation, but also on the committee that approved the sale.

The case was handled by Rod Rosenstein. You know him. He's the same man who told Jeff Sessions to recuse himself and get out of the way of the Russia investigation so Rosenstein could appoint Bob Mueller to try to connect Trump to Russia. If that isn't the irony of all ironies.

Who was head of the FBI at the time? It was Bob Mueller, the man now appointed special counsel to connect Donald Trump to Russia.

How about the FBI agent handling the case? It was none other than Andrew McCabe, who was handling the Clinton email investigation. You may remember his wife got $675,000 dollars from Clinton pal Terry McAuliffe, who is also connected to the Clinton Foundation. McCabe's wife lost, but under Virginia law she could keep whatever cash was left from that generous contribution.

At the time of the approval of the transfer, Republicans in Congress vociferously objected based on national security. They worried because they knew Russia helped Iran build its nuclear reactor and the takeover of US nuclear resources by a Russian government–owned agency would be against our national security interests.

At the time the Obama administration greenlighted the deal, Republicans in Congress objected and they didn't even know about the criminality and the money laundering.

The fact that other appointees of the Obama administration joined Crooked Hillary in selling us out to the Russians is not a very strong defense. Now, let me give you the clincher. The FBI knew there was something rotten going on during the whole time the Russians were acquiring Uranium One. It knew the Russians were engaged in bribery, kickbacks, extortion, and money laundering to expand Vladimir Putin's uranium holdings in the United States. They knew that before the Obama administration approved the second Uranium One deal in 2010.[18]

The FBI's covert informer, who we now know was William Campbell, was inside the Russian nuclear industry. Campbell provided direct evidence to three congressional committees that Moscow had compromised a US trucking firm with bribes and kickbacks. The Russian government also expected the lobbying firm APCO, to apply a portion of its $3 million annual fee to support the Clinton Global Initiative whose incorporation was approved by Lois Lerner. The purpose was to have the Obama administration make favorable decisions for Russia on Uranium One and the US-Russia Civilian Nuclear Cooperation Agreement. More importantly, the FBI had first-hand evidence, including an eyewitness account and documents to back it up, that Russian nuclear officials had directed millions of dollars to the Clinton Foundation while Hillary was still Secretary of State and before her State Department approved the Uranium One deal.[19] You read that right. It had hard evidence of real "collusion with the Russians" by Hillary Clinton. Yet Justice Department officials sat on the information and allowed the Obama administration to approve the purchase anyway. And Hillary was right in the middle of it.

So, what happened to the criminal case? The criminal case was plea bargained to a lesser crime on a Labor Day weekend; the sentence a slap on the wrist meted out at Christmastime with none of the bells and whistles that normally accompany an international racketeering case. The informant who brought the case to the FBI's attention? Initially he was gagged by Eric Holder and then Loretta Lynch due to a nondisclosure agreement where the sanction is a criminal penalty. I have never heard of such a thing. As a result of public outcry, the informant was released from the nondisclosure agreement.

As Secretary of State, Clinton sat on the Committee on Foreign Investments in the United States (CFIUS). It was CFIUS that okayed the sale of the uranium and the Obama administration was providing cover from the start. I spoke with Victoria Toensing, the former prosecutor and experienced and respected criminal defense attorney who, along with her husband Joe diGenova, knows the Washington criminal circuit as well as anyone, about the case. She reminded me what an FBI informant named Doug Campbell had to say about the deal.

"Doug Campbell provided the United States government crucial information about Russia's plan to control our uranium supply and about the massive corruption within that country's nuclear industry.

Campbell began his reporting well over a year before the CFIUS decision to sell Uranium One to those corrupt Russian companies. He also heard continuous bragging by the Russians that the fix was in for the sale because of their connections to the Clintons. When he brought a civil suit to regain the $500,000 he paid the Russians from his own funds—under the direction of the FBI—the Obama Justice Department threatened him with prosecution unless he dismissed the case."[20]

The Obama administration was so adamant the American public not find out about this that it threatened Campbell for attempting to reveal the information he had gathered during the 2016 election, citing the confidentiality agreement he had signed with the government.[21] The Senate obtained permission from the Trump Justice Department to hear Campbell's story and submitted a written statement in February, confirming the facts as I've related them above.[22]

Still, even in the face of Campbell's eyewitness testimony, the lying liberal Democrats have the audacity to defend Crooked Hillary, saying Campbell didn't provide evidence of a quid pro quo.[23] But even if you somehow conclude that there isn't enough evidence to prosecute Clinton for corruption in this case, despite the glaring evidence of her guilt, you really have to ask yourself this question: If all of the above isn't enough to prosecute or at least investigate Hillary for criminally "colluding with the Russians," how can you possibly justify the ongoing investigation of President Trump, a one-and-a-half-year investigation that has turned up no evidence at all?

A major player in all this was Victor Pinchuk. The largest individual contributor to the Clinton Foundation, Pinchuk builds steel pipes in Ukraine, in violation of US law.

Don't forget Special Counsel Robert Mueller was Director of the FBI while all this was going on. It was Mueller's FBI that opened the investigation into the 2012 Benghazi attack, also on Secretary Clinton's watch, that resulted in the first death of a US ambassador in more than thirty years. At the very least, Secretary Clinton was guilty of an extreme dereliction of duty, as her State Department denied repeated requests for additional security from Ambassador Christopher Stevens himself and other officials stationed in Benghazi in 2012.[24]

Clinton's motivation was unclear. But we know Clinton was lying through her teeth when she said the attack was born out of the spontaneous protest of a poorly made anti-Muslim video. After offering that explanation to the public shortly after 10 p.m. on the night of the attack, she emailed her daughter, Chelsea, at 11:12 p.m. saying the attack had been perpetrated by an "Al Qaeda–like [*sic*] group."[25] On a phone call the next day, Hillary admitted to the Egyptian prime minister that the attack had had nothing to do with the film. Yet she went on publicly saying it did for ten days after the attack, including while attending the return of the coffins in Delaware two days later.

The simplest explanation is that she was simply covering for her State Department's earlier denials of requests for additional security. Or was there something else she was covering up? There was some evidence that she might have been running guns from Libya to Syria,[26] hoping to do there what she had done in Libya: support radical jihadists to overthrow a dictator. Even as Libya descended into chaos, she couldn't seem to learn from the mistake of deposing Muammar Gaddafi and leaving a power vacuum for the jihadis to fill. Five years later, she was still defending that decision,[27] ignoring the chaos she had unleashed across the entire region.

Whatever she might have been up to, there was one thing that was certain: the FBI's investigation wasn't going to shed any light on the matter. One consistent theme throughout the tenures of directors Mueller and Comey was the FBI would find no wrongdoing by Hillary Clinton, no matter how much smoke poured from the barrel of the gun.

And remember, this isn't because they necessarily

liked Hillary Clinton. They weren't RINOs in that respect, secretly working on behalf of the Democrats. As I said at the beginning of this book, the real partisan divide isn't Democrat versus Republican; it's the Swamp Party versus the people.

I started this time line long after the scandals that plagued Hillary Clinton while she was First Lady and don't want to spend the time and space reviewing those here, except to point out one interesting little fact:

Back in the 1990s, more than two decades before he became deputy attorney general of the United States, the man who appointed Robert Mueller special counsel to investigate Russian interference in our elections, Rod Rosenstein, was part of another special counsel investigation. He was one of a team of prosecutors working under Kenneth Starr to investigate Bill and Hillary Clinton's Whitewater real estate scandal.[28] The investigation found no evidence of wrongdoing by the Clintons.

A Foreign Policy for Sale

So how do I really feel? Here's what I said about Hillary before the election:

Hillary Clinton would be without a doubt—hands down—the absolute best CEO of a public company.

Ruthless.

Profit driven.

And all about the money.

But if you're looking for a different kind of CEO, one to run the greatest nation on earth and bring back America—now teetering on the brink of socialism—to be president of the United States, Hillary Clinton is the worst possible choice.

She is the person to run away from!

She has never cared about you. This woman only cares about herself, money, her next step up the political ladder, and if president, will only care about her legacy.

Her influence peddling on a global scale and the setting of American foreign policy to coincide with the flow of hundreds of millions of dollars to the corrupt Clinton Foundation and millions directly to Bill Clinton (and ultimately Hillary) in speaking fees has no parallel in American history.

There is no question that Bill Clinton's speaking fees tripled and quadrupled when Hillary was Secretary of State. Contributors who stood to profit from Hillary's influence at the State Department looked to hire Bill.

Historically—prosecutors have looked for quid pro quos from politicians when they deliver to constituents or contributors. Politicians doing business for themselves—lining their own pockets—is the essence of public corruption.

Not only were contributions to the foundation and speaking fees to Bill made but in many of these deals both Hillary and Bill were in the subject foreign country at the same time—wheeling and dealing. She wielding American diplomacy. He receiving speaking fees of a half a million to three-quarters of a million dollars. And their foundation—the huge beneficiary of hundreds of millions of dollars. Some reported, some not.

Prosecutors have convicted politicians for things as simple as a free cab ride in exchange for favors. It's called bribery, conspiracy, and violation of theForeign Corrupt Practices Act.

Whenever an American government official accepts gifts intended to curry favor—he crosses the line.

Bill and Hillary started with nothing. Bill is now the wealthiest ex-president in the United States. Might it be because Hillary greased the skids after which Bill accepted massive gratuities? Many think we may never know because she refuses to give up her email server.

How do you go from dead broke to filthy rich? Why would you not recuse yourself as Secretary of State when there is a conflict of interest or even the appearance of one?

Hillary Clinton's life has always been about money. From Whitewater to cattle futures to leaving the White House with whatever she could take. As a prosecutor,

I can tell you that it's always about money or women and the Clintons have both. When I hear things like 'oh everybody does it' I get aggravated. I am tired of people condoning corruption when it's committed by a member of their party. My back goes up when I hear that Russia, because of the Clintons, now controls a great deal of America's uranium. There is a name for people who are willing to sell out their country for cash.

CHAPTER EIGHT

Lying and Leaking to Fix an Election

In 2016 Andrew McCabe leaked information to the *Wall Street Journal.* He lied about this in congressional hearings. McCabe, I guess, never thought he would get caught.

The *Wall Street Journal* did a follow-up story regarding McCabe's issuance of a "stand down" order he issued to FBI staff who were looking into Hillary's email server. In brief, it goes like this.

The FBI field office was investigating the improper use of Hillary's email server where classified information was disseminated. McCabe heard about this while he was on a trip overseas. He then told his field office he was not happy and directed them to stand down. That is, stop the investigation of Hillary immediately! Was this another effort by FBI bosses to get Hillary elected? Do you think?

Hillary received significant cooperation from her longtime Deep State friends in the DOJ and FBI.

Changing of the Deep State Guard

On February 1, 2013, eighteen days after the Russian government completed the aforementioned acquisition of rights to 20 percent of US uranium supplies, Hillary Clinton stepped down as secretary of state. In addition to brushing off scandals that suggested unethical, if not criminal, behavior, as she had all her life, she had presided over one of the most disastrous foreign policies of any secretary of state in US history.

Her reckless advocacy for intervening in Libya, where she supported the Muslim Brotherhood and other known terrorist groups seeking to overthrow Gaddafi,[1] was a direct cause of the refugee crisis engulfing Europe and spilling over into the United States. Back in 2011, Gaddafi himself warned of precisely that outcome if he were deposed.[2] He was right. But Hillary's policy in Libya was just one example of a pattern: supporting the toppling of oppressive regimes in the Middle East without regard to who would replace them or whom the United States would be supporting in doing so. She left a classic vacuum.

The same year Hillary stepped down, President

Obama appointed James Comey to replace Robert Mueller as FBI director. There is plenty of reason to believe the relationship between Obama and Clinton never really improved after their bitter fight for the 2008 Democratic nomination. But even when the players don't like each other, they close ranks when it comes to protecting their fellow Swamp creatures. Comey, a convenient Republican at that time, was one of them. He could be counted on to defend the status quo and the Deep State against any external threats.

Just as Hoover would spy for Democratic or Republican presidents when it suited his personal agenda, "J. Edgar" Comey's abuse of power crossed party lines. And, like Hoover, Comey seems to have an insatiable appetite for public acclaim, whether deserved or not. His press conference on Hillary's emails wasn't the first time he elbowed his way into the spotlight.

Way back in 2007, when Attorney General John Ashcroft was on his back in the hospital, Comey made a spectacle of himself by rushing to the hospital, sirens blaring, to "save America." White House Counsel Alberto R. Gonzales and President Bush's chief of staff, Andrew H. Card, Jr., were in the intensive care unit trying to get Ashcroft to reauthorize President Bush's domestic spying program. Comey wanted to prevent this because the power of the attorney general had been transferred to him while Ashcroft was ill.

Once appointed FBI director by President Obama, Comey was the good little Deep State soldier any sitting president would hope for.[3] When the Uranium One story broke in 2015, did Comey let anyone know about the FBI's informant and the evidence of money flowing directly from the Russian government to the Clinton Foundation? No.

When Attorney General Eric Holder ordered an investigation into the IRS's targeting conservative groups to unfairly revoke their tax-exempt status, the results of the investigation sounded eerily like those of the Clinton email investigation. There was nothing that rose to the level of criminal behavior, as far as the FBI was concerned.[4] Could the FBI have put together a case against a member of the Obama administration for any one of several illegalities? Their answer was apparently no, even if they had caught one crook red-handed.

The intent was to defend the machine, the apparatus, made up of millions of federal government employees who retain their jobs, regardless of who is elected by the people. After residing in the Swamp for so many decades, their goal is to guard the Swamp and protect each other.

God forbid Lois Lerner from the IRS is prosecuted, especially since Lois is the one who approved the 2009 Clinton Global Initiative for tax exempt status. The same goes for state department employees. That just might lead the great, unwashed masses to doubt whether the Washington Establishment selflessly serves the public as it claims. As much as they might have disliked the Obama administration, letting Toto expose the man behind the curtain was a much bigger threat than enduring a president with a few policies they didn't like.

From that perspective, what Comey, Andrew McCabe, and Peter Strzok did during the 2016 election year makes much more sense. No, they didn't like Hillary. Strzok said he was worried about her becoming president. He thought everything Bernie Sanders had said about her during the fixed primaries was true.[5] But he preferred her to Donald Trump.

Comey's intent was recently made clear when he announced during his book tour that he also preferred Hillary to Trump for president.

The Bogus Clinton Email Investigation

They didn't love Hillary Clinton, but they liked Donald Trump even less. Clinton might have been a LIAR, a crook, and a Democrat, but she was also one thing Donald Trump wasn't: a member of the Establishment. They disliked Clinton, but they feared Trump and what a Trump victory might mean for the parasite class that had fed so long and so voraciously on the American body politic. Trump was talking about busting up their racket, as more honest federal agents had done to Al Capone's mob. Trump was an existential threat to the Establishment, and had to be stopped. But if that's true, why did Comey make so many damaging statements against Hillary Clinton? Why not just quietly conclude the investigation with a recommendation that no criminal charges be brought, or at least follow the rules and say nothing.

The first answer is arrogance. Comey and his co-conspirators were so arrogant they didn't even think Trump would win. Has there ever been a guy from real estate and then television to become president of the United States? They all thought it was a joke. They believed they could inflict some damage on Clinton without seriously jeopardizing her chances of winning.

Why would they want to damage her at all?

I believe they needed to maintain their own credibility. A recurring feature of Donald Trump's campaign rallies was the thunderous sound of thousands of Trump supporters chanting "Lock her up!" It even broke out at the Republican National Convention, if you remember. President Trump graciously responded instead, "Let's defeat her in November." The animosity toward Crooked Hillary was not limited to the

Republican Party. A good many Democrats believed she and the Democrat Party had colluded to steal the nomination from Bernie Sanders. Now, we know they were right.

The FBI couldn't just blow off the email controversy. They were going to have to come up with a way to appease the many millions of people who thought Clinton should be prosecuted for something, without exposing her to the justice system. So, they came up with the story that she had been "extremely careless" with classified information, but not grossly negligent. There was a reason for that.

We now know that the first draft of Comey's statement clearing Clinton said she had been "grossly negligent" with classified information. It was none other than our Trump-hating suspect Peter Strzok who changed those words to "extremely careless."[6] Why? Because the statute criminalizing mishandling of classified information stipulates that a crime has been committed if the suspect is grossly negligent in handling the information, *even if there was no intent to commit a crime.* Mishandling classified information is one of the few crimes on the books that doesn't require intent, as Comey himself acknowledged in the aforementioned statement.

"What is the difference between 'grossly negligent' and 'extremely careless?'" Congressman Raúl

Labrador asked the irreproachable Comey under oath. Comey slithered out of answering the question twice by splitting hairs over the way the question was asked.[7]

That exchange confirmed for me that Comey was dishonest. He went to law school, just as I did, and he knows full well that any legal definition of gross negligence contains the word *careless* or words to the effect of *failure to exercise reasonable care.* Strzok's sly little line edit didn't change a thing. Comey's statement proclaimed Crooked Hillary guilty and then proceeded to say that the FBI wouldn't recommend prosecution, when that wasn't even his job.

He wasn't just getting Hillary off the hook; he was sending a message. He was sending a message to millions of Americans who wanted the woman prosecuted that the rules don't apply to her. Not only would she not be prosecuted, she would ascend to the highest office in the land.

I believe he was also sending a message to Hillary Clinton, just as his predecessor J. Edgar Hoover might have. He was telling her "We know what you did. We could finish you if we wanted to, but we'd rather have you in the White House. And once there, don't you dare cross us, because we can take you down anytime."

It was a classic Deep State move, and it would have worked if it hadn't been for one little detail: she didn't win.

CHAPTER NINE

The Liberal Insurance Policy

Peter Strzok, the FBI's deputy assistant director of the Counterintelligence Division, who led both the investigation into Hillary Clinton's emails and the investigation into possible Russian interference in the 2016 US presidential election, hated Donald Trump much more than Bernie Sanders or Hillary Clinton. Yes, he texted his mistress Lisa Page that Bernie Sanders was such an idiot that seeing his bumper stickers made him want to key the owner's car.[1] But his loathing of Donald Trump went far beyond even that.

Strzok seems to share Cardinal Comey's affectation about being a selfless servant of the people (even though he seems to simultaneously hold them in contempt). One of Strzok's anti-Trump text diatribes claimed the president "appears to have no ability to experience reverence which I [*sic*] the foundation for any capacity to admire or serve anything bigger than self to want to learn about anything beyond self, to want to know and deeply honor the people around you."[2]

Can you believe the arrogance, hypocrisy, and self-delusion wrapped up in that one statement? And I love the Freudian slip of apparently mistyping *is* as *I*. Perhaps Mr. Selfless just couldn't get *I* out of his mind while expounding about Trump's personal shortcomings to the woman with whom he was cheating on his wife.

Despite the assurance he shared with everyone in that corrupted organization, Peter Strzok still feared what he ostensibly believed to be the impossible: a Donald Trump victory. And that's when the idea of an "insurance policy" was born.

For the record, here is what Strzok texted:

"I want to believe the path you threw out for consideration in Andy's office—that there's no way he gets elected—but I'm afraid we can't take that risk. It's like an insurance policy in the unlikely event you die before you're 40 . . ."[3]

There are Strzok's words, as clear as day, and no amount of Fake News Media spin can change them. What could an "insurance policy" mean other than a way to derail or incapacitate the Trump presidency in

THE LIBERAL INSURANCE POLICY   209

the unlikely event he won? Think about the insurance policies you yourself carry. Why do you have them? Not to *prevent* something bad from happening, but to be able to better deal with something bad if it *does* happen.

You have fire insurance on your house in case there is a fire. Do you expect to have one? No. There's a very low chance your house will catch on fire. That's why fire insurance is so affordable. But you carry it just in case, so you can replace your possessions or your home, if necessary, if the unthinkable happens. Buying fire insurance doesn't do anything to prevent a fire. It only helps you deal with the consequences after you have one.

So, no, Strzok wasn't trying to prevent Trump from winning. What he was doing was even worse. He was talking about having a plan to effectively disenfranchise the voters who elected Trump should he win. Forget democracy. Those voters whom Strzok doesn't like are idiots, remember? He said so himself in one of the texts to his mistress. If his candidate of choice didn't win, he was going to abuse the power entrusted to him to ensure that it didn't matter. If the unthinkable happened, his insurance policy would help deal with it.

The insurance policy was the Russia collusion investigation.

Who Really Hacked John Podesta's Email?

You may have trouble remembering how this all started. It began with the WikiLeaks release of a trove of emails from John Podesta's account, which contained emails from Hillary Clinton or email chains containing emails from Hillary Clinton, which among other things showed what a phony, LIAR, and hypocrite she was. The important thing to remember is that everything WikiLeaks released was a primary document. It was Hillary Clinton in her own words, in context, firsthand. To date, there has been no proof WikiLeaks accounts were doctored.

Regarding WikiLeaks, at least one credible source says it wasn't even the Russians who hacked Podesta's emails. As reported by *The Nation*, a hard-left progressive publication, Veteran Intelligence Professionals for Sanity (VIPS) has independently analyzed the forensic data and concluded there was no hack at all.[4] VIPS is made up of veterans of the CIA, the FBI, the NSA, and other agencies. This isn't a group of bozos on the Internet. They're serious people, and they pointed out that the data in question had been copied at too high a rate of speed for it to have been done over the Internet. They said the speed with which the data had been copied was typical of copying data directly to a thumb drive. They also said that evidence showed the data had been copied on the East Coast.

Now, I'm no computer expert, and I certainly don't intend to imply Vladimir Putin and the Russian government weren't up to no good regarding our elections. There is other evidence that they have been at it since 2014.[5] But I will say this: *The Nation* offers the only evidence to back up any conclusion about what happened to John Podesta's emails. All the anti-Trump intelligence community has said is "Trust us." Sorry, boys. I'm going to need more than that.

Even if the Russians did indeed hack John Podesta's email account and give the information to WikiLeaks, no Russian interference affected the outcome. That bring us to "the dossier."

Fake Intelligence: The Dossier

We now know, thanks to the memo by the chairman of the House Intelligence Committee, Devin Nunes[6] (which wasn't substantively refuted by the Democratic attempt to spin the same information a different way[7]) that the FBI requested and received a FISA Court warrant and three subsequent renewals to electronically surveil Trump campaign volunteer Carter Page. This was based on a dossier compiled by a foreign agent, funded by the DNC, and the Hillary Clinton campaign that was so outlandish that even most of the Trump-hating Fake News outlets excoriated BuzzFeed for publishing it.[8] Although the dossier was not credible enough even for the *Washington Post*[9] it was somehow credible enough to obtain a warrant from a secret court to spy on a private US citizen, Carter Page.

Suffice it to say, it was an unsubstantiated narrative to imply the Kremlin might have leverage in the event Donald Trump was elected president. The basis for that implication? That Trump had been set up with prostitutes during a visit to Russia. Not content to leave it at that, the author(s) threw in that prostitutes peed on Donald Trump, a known germaphobe. Cardinal Comey said he didn't know of the story's accuracy, but he believed it was possible. As I've said before, it's possible, and it's possible Martians were in that room peeing on the prostitutes, too. Maybe we should start a new investigation: are Martians colluding with the prostitutes to make the president look bad?

No major media outlet published the dossier besides CNN and BuzzFeed, amid condemnation by all their anti-Trump media colleagues.

I'm not going to bore you with a lot of legalese but allow me to take you into the courtroom with me for a moment. There is a rule of evidence, "Rule 403" in federal court, which deals with this kind of information being admitted as evidence into a court of law.[10] It says the court may exclude evidence if its probative value is outweighed by, among other things, its prejudicial value. What does that mean? It means that if the evidence would tend to prejudice the jury against the defendant much more than it would tend to prove he committed the crime, the evidence can be excluded. Whenever extremely salacious evidence is offered in court, the defense attorney will object. And for anything as outlandish-sounding as what was in that dossier, that objection would be sustained every time.

Now, it's true that the burden for obtaining a warrant is much lighter than for getting a conviction in court. An investigator need only show probable cause to believe that a crime was committed. There is no need to prove guilt beyond a reasonable doubt. But obtaining a warrant still puts a rigorous burden on the applicant. The judge starts from the fundamental position that a wiretap warrant is at the very least an assault on the fourth amendment which must be overcome.

The FBI must truthfully present evidence and not mislead the court. Here it failed to fulfill that responsibility. It withheld a most important piece of information in obtaining the FISA warrant: that the dossier, compiled by a former foreign spy was paid for by the Hillary Clinton campaign and the DNC.[11] That was

important information the court needed in making
its determination that the representations made in the
dossier were credible. The FBI intentionally withheld
that. All it told the court, in a footnote no less, was
that the material was "politically motivated" and had
been "paid for by a political entity."[12]

No unbiased law enforcement agency would ever
present such an application to a judge, especially the
top echelon. The FBI didn't have responsible leadership in 2016 and 2017. FBI head James Comey, along
with Andrew McCabe and Peter Strzok, all had a political agenda.

Fruit of the Poisonous Tree

The whole house of cards should have collapsed
the moment the FBI knew the Clinton campaign
and the DNC had paid $12 million for their chief
piece of evidence. To circumvent election laws, the
campaign had paid a law firm, which had then paid
a research firm, which had then paid a former British spy to get dirt on Donald Trump from Kremlin-
connected Russians.

The FBI had previously worked with that former
British spy Christopher Steele. But when it came to
the dossier, it not only ignored the political motivation behind his research, it paid him an additional

$50,000 to continue. Not only was this dossier used to smear the president politically, it was used to create the special counsel, as the basis of congressional hearings and the reason for wall-to-wall anti-Trump media coverage. But worst of all, this known piece of political fiction was used as the excuse for further investigation, wiretaps, unmasking, and the FISA warrants in question.

That makes whatever was developed because of the warrant classic "fruit of the poisonous tree," meaning it is inadmissible in court. When police illegally conduct a search without a warrant, any evidenceis inadmissible in court.

According to news breaking at the time of this writing, misleading the FISA Court and getting a warrant to spy on Carter Page wasn't the most egregious act in furtherance of this conspiracy. Although the details are not all confirmed, my FBI sources are telling me there was indeed an FBI informant working inside the Trump campaign. They also say attorney general approval is required for this type of operation in a national campaign.

That means either Loretta Lynch was directly involved, or the FBI went rogue spying on a presidential campaign. Either way, it's one of the most egregious abuses of power in our lifetime if not American history. The president is calling it "bigger than

Watergate." The media writes it off as hyperbole, It isn't.

So was there a spy in the Trump campaign? Of course there was! Comey denies a spy was used, instead calling it a confidential human source. Clapper as much as said so on *The View*, suggesting that Trump should be happy they were spying! He then admits that unfortunately the confidential name of the informant is out—and that's reported to be Stefan Halper. Comey follows suit, saying there was no spy—and the term they use is a confidential human source—so he doesn't answer if there was a confidential human source.

As Andrew McCarthy of *National Review* astutely observed about the investigations. The investigation of Hillary Clinton was a criminal investigation; the investigation of Trump's campaign was a counterintelligence investigation.[13] That's an important distinction.

They opened a counterintelligence investigation because there was no evidence of a crime by any Trump campaign official. Yet, even with all the additional powers a counterintelligence investigation gave them, including wiretaps, covert informants, and prosecutions of Trump campaign officials on unrelated charges in an effort to get them to testify against Trump, there is still nothing for Robert Mueller to bring into court.

But the "Trump-Russia collusion" farce is never going to any court. First, there isn't any law on the books making the supposed collusion illegal, unless you're talking about anti-trust. Second, it never happened. From the very beginning, this has been a charade, a wag the dog, where the agency makes up a crime and accuses the other side of committing it, then calls in its friends to prosecute it. Meanwhile, said friends collect the cash flowing out of rotten deals made as part of creating the crime in the first place.

It's all smoke and mirrors to cripple the Trump presidency. It's the claim payment for the FBI's rotten "insurance policy." If it couldn't keep Donald Trump from becoming president, it was going to ensure he couldn't get any of his agenda accomplished. It would paralyze his administration with its spurious investigation of a noncriminal act that had never happened in the first place. Trump and his administration would be so busy defending themselves that they wouldn't be able to keep any of their campaign promises.

That was the plan. It failed. A little over a year after Trump took office, unemployment is at historic lows, the economy is booming, and ISIS has been defeated. Yes, the president might have accomplished more if this antidemocratic conspiracy hadn't fought him every step of the way. But at the end of the day, the president is advancing the agenda he was elected to advance, despite the best efforts of the Swamp to defeat him.

Different Rules for Liberals

One of the reasons this charade has been allowed to continue so long is the ingenious move Swamper Rod Rosenstein pulled off early in the scheme: getting Attorney General Jeff Sessions to recuse himself from the investigation. I understand the motivation behind it: to remove any appearance that Sessions's support of President Trump would influence his decisions, and that he might be compromised by Russians he met. It's the same honorable intention that has motivated the president to allow this baseless investigation to continue as long as it has. Neither Eric Holder nor Loretta Lynch recused themselves, but the rules are different for Republicans.

It's time to stop giving dishonorable people the benefit of the doubt. Mueller, McCabe, Rosenstein, and their frenemies in the Democrat Party have no desire to get to the truth. They don't care about protecting our republican institutions. They're out to destroy them by taking down the duly elected president of the United States and overturning the decision of millions of voters who put him in the White House. Their agenda is to get Trump out, reverse his policies, and replace him with someone who will resume the failed Establishment policies so resoundingly rejected at the polls in 2016.

The FBI director is not elected. He is appointed by the president, one of only two elected members of the executive branch, and reports directly to the attorney general, also appointed by the president. It's time to stop playing nice with these miscreants. If Jeff Sessions won't prosecute the conspirators, then the deputy Attorney General Rod Rosenstein needs to call for a special counsel. Since he won't do that because he wrote the memo saying Comey should be fired, how can he run an investigation into the president for the firing of Comey, which he recommended? He should be a witness in the case. The only way out is for Sessions to be fired by the president for taking a job he knew ahead of time he couldn't do. Comey, McCabe, Strzok, and, of course, their fellow Swamper Hillary Clinton should all be under investigation. And, since Rosenstein signed off on the FISA warrant application, he should be a defendant, too.

Unlike Mueller's current witch hunt, the facts already made public about these conspirators call for a serious grand jury investigation. I think you already know what my recommendation will be when the evidence is in and their guilt proven:

Take 'em out in cuffs!

The Lying, Leaking, Liberal Swamp's Secret Court

Many Americans today may not realize this, but the FISA Court was created out of outrage over the intelligence community spying on US civilians. After Watergate, the Church Committee was formed in the Senate to investigate the Central Intelligence Agency, National Security Agency, Federal Bureau of Investigation, and Internal Revenue Service[1]—in other words, to investigate all the same agencies Obama weaponized against conservatives—and determine how much evil they had been up to under Nixon.

Yes, the Swamp existed back then, too, and it was just as out of control as it is now. I don't begrudge the original intentions of the committee being honorable, but you just can't ask big government to reform itself. That's one of the reasons we elected Donald J. Trump.

Somebody from the outside had to come in and take on the establishment. Reform is just another word for *cover your ass.*

The Secret Rubber Stamp

So, after a lot of grandstanding, bloviating, and camera mugging, what the Swamp really did was *legalize* domestic spying. It created a secret court where the FBI and other Deep Staters could bring evidence to a judge and get a rubber stamp to spy on whomever they wanted. If you think that's an exaggeration, just look at the numbers. Between 1979 and 2014, that star chamber reviewed more than thirty-five thousand warrant requests to engage in electronic surveillance.[2] And do you know how many were denied? Twenty percent? Ten percent? Five percent?

Twelve. Not 12 percent. Twelve *total* applications out of more than thirty-five thousand were denied. If that's not a rubber-stamp court, what is? It makes you wonder: Is the FISA court really catching terrorists? Or simply invading the privacy of American citizens?

Don't forget who is writing this book. I was a prosecutor for most of my professional life. I also served on the bench as a judge. I'm not some law enforcement–hating hippie. Far from it; if anything, I'm inclined to be biased the other way.

But I also respect and understand the reasons for the constitutional protections we have under the Bill of Rights to our Constitution, especially the Fourth Amendment. The adversarial process I referred to earlier is intended to protect the innocent. The reason the Fourth Amendment was written was to prevent searches and seizures without probable cause.

Why Is the FISA Court Secret?

There is no reason the FISA Court needs to be secret. Of course, we must protect "national security" and "sources and methods" when appropriate. But a secret court is not necessary. We have just witnessed what happens when politics and Deep Staters use that court for their own benefit. The secrecy of the court cannot be used as an excuse by people trying to cover up their abuses. As a judge presiding over narcotics cases, if I had an undercover officer who was still on the street, I would order the courtroom closed to prevent disclosure of an undercover status and to make sure that the testimony was private. That way I could get to the bottom line and still protect the safety, security, and life, literally, of the undercover cop. But we didn't have to set up a secret court system to do so, one that is unaccountable to the public and most of the public's elected representatives.

The same is true of the FISA Court. It could use the same methodology. But it doesn't, because it is really a circumvention of public accountability whereby the same players keep supporting each other, get their warrants, and do whatever they want.

Why did the FISA Court judge who was presented with the Steele dossier, simply accept it without establishing its reliability? There's got to be a reliability test, a credibility test. When considering a warrant application, there is no defense attorney present to make that objection, which is why the judge must be especially attuned to it.

The Fake News Media tell us the FBI is off the hook because it told the FISA Court judge the report was "politically motivated" and "paid for by a political entity." Okay, who? Have you ever heard such question begging? How could any honest judge hear or read that and not ask the warrant applicant who the entity was? Who paid for the information to be gathered? What was the political motivation?

Knowing now the Hillary Clinton campaign and the DNC paid for the farcical hit piece, it's hard not to conclude the court was engaging in willful ignorance when reviewing the warrant application. And don't tell me the FBI was protecting "sources and methods" by withholding the identification of the parties involved.

We now know that Strzok, McCabe, Comey, and Rosenstein were part of the application process. So why was there no more probing into the source of the dossier? Why didn't the FISA judge inquire further regarding the dossier? And even after all the publicity about the dossier, why is the FISA judge who signed the warrant not demanding answers? Could the answer be in the text messages between Strzok and Lisa Page, where they discuss the need to connect with a federal judge under the cover setting of a dinner party? Isn't it curious that US District Court and FISA Court Judge Rudy Contreras, who took Michael Flynn's guilty plea, was recused almost immediately afterwards?

Dinner and a Warrant

I can't read the mind of the judge who issued the Carter Page warrant, but I certainly can read Peter Strzok's texts about his relationship with Judge Contreras. We found out in March that not only did Strzok and his mistress hate Donald Trump enough to want an "insurance policy" against his presidency, but Strzok knew Contreras was on the FISA Court and discussed setting up a meeting with him while still actively involved in the investigations of Hillary Clinton and Donald Trump, six months before his fateful interview of Michael Flynn.[3]

I point out that we found this out in March because those were texts that had previously been hidden from the congressional committees investigating the FBI's activities. Here we have the life and career of a decorated general ruined for lying to the FBI about something that isn't even a crime, while the agency he is convicted of lying to defies a congressional subpoena. The FBI redacted the text messages between Strzok and Lisa Page in which they discussed setting up a meeting with the judge, acknowledged the clear impropriety of such a meeting, and conspired to set up a dinner or cocktail party to deflect attention from the clear conflict of interest.

Contreras was recused from the case within a few days after Flynn took his plea. Why? We don't know. We're not even sure, as of this writing, if he recused himself. There are too many questions surrounding what went on leading up to the surveillance orders that underpinned the special counsel's investigation. And we may never get answers, not when it concerns the Swamp's secret court.

CHAPTER ELEVEN

The Lying, Leaking, Liberal Witch Hunt

President Trump has called Special Counsel Mueller's investigation a "witch hunt," almost from its very first day. And, as on so many other issues, time has proved him right.

Our ancestors used to hunt and burn "witches" for a variety of reasons. Some believed the victims, usually women, had occult powers they used to cast spells on their enemies and do evil upon the community. Others merely used the charge of witchcraft to settle scores or eliminate competitors.

That the crime the witch hunt was investigating wasn't even real didn't help the victims. Once the hysteria started spreading, the mob would have its blood, regardless of the evidence. I couldn't imagine a more perfect analogy for Mueller's investigation.

Fall Guy Flynn

Perhaps the most tragic development in this witch hunt is the conviction of former national security advisor Michael Flynn, who lied to the FBI about a conversation he had with Russian ambassador Sergey Kislyak.

Why Flynn lied, only Flynn knows. Whether his answers even amount to lying to a federal agent may also have been a matter of debate before he took the plea. Flynn has been a government employee for virtually all his life and can't afford the attorney fees Paul Manafort can. They may have advised him to just plead guilty and end it.

If that's true, it's very sad. The double standard is so striking, when comparing Flynn's case to Andrew McCabe's. For McCabe, there are members of Congress saying, "Call me, Andy. I'll put you on staff for a couple of days, so you can get your pension." Andy McCabe gets the sympathy of the nation, while a guy who put his life on the line and fought for all of us gets a conviction. It's crazy. And there are FBI agents who don't think Flynn lied.

Flynn may also have been trying to protect his son, Michael Flynn, Jr., who has also found himself in the crosshairs of the special counsel. Flynn Jr. worked for his dad's consulting firm and the special counsel is interested in him for—you guessed it—not complying with the Foreign Agents Registration Act (FARA).[1] Suddenly, this law that has produced a few dozen convictions in the entire eighty years of its existence figures prominently in the investigation of four different people associated with the Trump campaign or administration. Meanwhile, the rest of the lobbyist class in Washington effectively ignores it.

Going after Flynn Jr. is just another standard prosecutorial tactic in trying to pressure a defendant to give up information on a person in the prosecutor's crosshairs. Judge T. S. Ellis said as much in the Manafort case. "You don't really care about Mr. Manafort's bank fraud. You really care about getting information that Mr. Manafort can give you that would reflect on Mr. Trump and lead to his prosecution or impeachment or whatever," the judge told federal prosecutor Michael Dreeben.[2]

Prosecutors in federal cases are known for pitting brother against brother, father against son, family members against loved ones—it's how they do their dance. It's a very dirty dance.

Up to that point in Mueller's witch hunt, we'd had a nobody punk, George "Pipsqueak" Papadopoulos, drunk in a bar, talking out his backside, who was completely ignored by the Trump campaign and later pleaded guilty to lying to the FBI about what he said in the bar. Then, we had Manafort, who is under investigation for activity regarding his consulting with foreign governments, but completely unrelated to his work with the Trump campaign. Finally, we have a war hero who was railroaded into a guilty plea for doing precisely what Andy McCabe did, the latter on a much larger and more sinister scale. And not even one of these three had pleaded to anything remotely related to colluding with the Russians to undermine the presidential election.

The Thirteen Russians

That's when Rosenstein announced the indictment of thirteen Russians who allegedly tried to influence the election with phony Facebook ads and posts.[3] And what does the indictment allege? That the Internet Research Agency used deceptive means to buy social media advertisements and eventually organize rallies in the United States that almost no one attended.

The left-wing blog *Moon of Alabama* has long maintained[4] the campaign was little more than a for-profit venture seeking to make money on "clickbait" media—provocative headlines that induce people to click on the link and thereby be exposed to advertising and other revenue-generating content—rather than a serious attempt to influence the election. Right-wing blogger and former director of the Office of Management and Budget for the Reagan administration, David Stockman, called it a "comic book indictment" that "nailed a great big nothingburger,"[5] citing the ridiculous, broken English wording of many of the ads and the infinitesimally small number of people who attended the rallies.

Most importantly, Rod Rosenstein himself stated during his news conference announcing the indictment, "Now, there is no allegation in this indictment that any American was a knowing participant in this illegal activity. There is no allegation in the indictment that the charged conduct altered the outcome of the 2016 election."[6]

As with all these "reveals," this was timed perfectly. This announcement was on less than forty-five minutes notice. Now, for the special counsel, especially in a case of enormous political and national interest, to alert the press that in less than forty-five minutes they were holding a press conference for an indictment like this is more than unusual.

So, they indict thirteen Russians whom they know will never stand trial, let alone be extradited, arraigned, or even arrested. Putin will never allow them to be sent here to be part of Robert Mueller's sideshow. The special prosecutor's office admits that even this has

nothing to do with the Trump campaign or administration. There is no evidence any American, much less
anyone in the Trump campaign, knowingly partici-
pated in any of this.

Now, as a prosecutor deciding whether to continue
to pursue a case, you weigh priorities, resources, and
interest. The interest here is high, I'm not sure what
the priorities are, but the expenses don't matter. And
there is no time limit. They can go on investigating
and spending forever, even though in this case there
is no little blue dress, no cigar, no love book, nothing.

There's No "There" There

Regardless of all the hysterical Fake News trying to
rev up American voters, the investigators, by their
own admission, have found no evidence of collusion
or any related crime committed by anyone associated
with the Trump campaign or administration. There's
just nothing there. But still, Adam Schiff comes on
television every other day repeating, like some kind
of wind-up robot, "It's there, it's there," without being
able to say what it is. He wants us to believe Mueller
can't say what it is. But it's there.

Is he kidding? Everything gets leaked in Washington. It's the city of leaks, and we haven't heard a thing.

The year 2018 is halfway over. Most of the key

players from the Trump campaign were interviewed by the Mueller team in 2017. Jeff Sessions was interviewed in January 2018. With all the power of the federal government behind them, the most intensive investigation one can imagine, and grand juries at their disposal, they would have something by now if there was something to have. At some point, call it a day, guys.

But that's not their mission. Their mission is to find anything they can on Trump. These people are investigating an individual named Donald Trump and trying to attach any crime they can to him. It's disgusting. It's coming from the haters who can't believe he's president. And they're joined by the Establishment who would rather he not be president.

Mueller is supposedly restricted to investigating crimes defined in the attorney general's order appointing him special counsel.[7] Remember, because Attorney General Jeff Sessions recused himself from the investigation, the order was signed by Deputy Attorney General Rosenstein. The order empowers the special counsel to investigate "any links and/or coordination between the Russian government and individuals associated with the campaign of President Donald Trump; any matters that arose or may arise directly from the investigation; and any other matters within the scope of 28 CFR § 600.4(a)."

The statute section referred to says that every special counsel investigation will have a defined scope, but that the special counsel also has "the authority to investigate and prosecute federal crimes committed in the course of, and with intent to interfere with, the special counsel's investigation, such as perjury, obstruction of justice, destruction of evidence, and intimidation of witnesses; and to conduct appeals arising out of the matter being investigated and/or prosecuted."[8] That means the special counsel can investigate whether the subject of the investigation committed any crimes in reaction to the investigation, such as obstruction of justice.

According to the latest reporting, it appears that's where Mueller is going.[9] If true, it suggests there is no evidence of a Trump-Russia collusion. He is specifically interested in questioning the president on the firings of Jim Comey and Michael Flynn. And it appears Rosenstein amended the special counsel mandate to allow Mueller to continue.

Although Comey repeatedly said the president was not under investigation, he decided he should be *after* Trump fired him. Enter Special Counsel Bob Mueller. Comey testified under oath before a Congressional panel that he leaked memos (for which he is now under investigation) to a friend to leak to the *New York Times* to get a special counsel to investigate the president. His pettiness, evident throughout his book, seems to know no bounds. Since Rod Rosenstein convinced Sessions to recuse himself from anything campaign related, Comey's dream came true with the appointment of his friend and fellow Deep Stater Bob Mueller, who ironically is now in the position of assessing his own friend's truthfulness.

They have a few people who have taken pleas. In any case where the government is going after a "big fish," and have someone low on the totem pole that did something wrong and is being offered his freedom, they can usually get some damaging testimony. When you're trying to incriminate a president, then there are plenty of people who would step up to do it, especially to save their own behinds. And let's not forget the immortal words of former chief judge of the New York State Court of Appeals, Sol Wachtler, who said, "A grand jury could indict a ham sandwich." Despite the later behavior of the source, the observation is nevertheless an accurate one.

It's up to the prosecutor to exercise good judgment to ensure the evidence he or she has justifies an indictment. If they want to charge the president with something, they'll be able to do it.

We saw that when the special counsel referred information they dug up on President Trump's attorney, Michael Cohen, to the US attorney for the Southern

District of New York. Mueller's team did this to provide a veneer of propriety to what they were doing, which was using the power given them to investigate Russian interference in the election to find anything and everything they could possibly hang on the president, including guilt by association for anything improper his lawyer may have done.

Not only does this prove the president has been right to call Mueller's investigation a witch hunt all along, but it represents a threat to a fundamental protection against prosecutorial abuse.

Attorney-Client Privilege and Abuse of Its Exceptions

Attorney-client privilege and work product doctrine are vital. These privileges encourage persons, without fear of legal jeopardy, to consult openly, frankly, and freely with counsel of their choosing. Both privileges are generally of paramount importance and safeguarded by the courts and "promote broader public interests in the observance of law and administration of justice."[10]

There are a couple of exceptions. As for example when the client relays the information to third parties or divulges the communication in the presence of any person other than the attorney. The most relevant exception is the "crime fraud" exception, where a communication between a client and an attorney is made with an intent to "further a crime, fraud or other misconduct." In that situation, this privilege is lost.[11]

The Russia collusion investigation seemed far off in the rearview mirror when the feds received a search warrant for the attorney-client communications between Michael Cohen and the president. Mueller, no fool, had to make it look as if he had nothing to do with the seizure of these records since they were not Russia-related. He would lose support from Republican lawmakers, in particular Senator Grassley, if it looked like the raids on Cohen's law office and hotel room were his doing. So, Mueller sends materials that he received voluntarily from Cohen, to the US attorney for the Southern District of New York. To his misfortune, the president's effort to cooperate with Mueller included information about the payment to Stormy Daniels. With that information, the Southern District of New York applied for a search warrant to have Cohen's attorney-client records seized.

But requests for attorney-client records must be approved by the assistant attorney general or the deputy assistant attorney general of the Criminal Division. Don't forget the assistant attorney general is our old friend, Rod Rosenstein, who appointed Mueller. The plot gets even thicker.

Rosenstein would have had to decide if the information sought was privileged; whether other attempts were made to get the information; whether there were grounds to believe a crime had been committed; and whether the need for the information outweighed the risk that the attorney may be disqualified from representing his client. So, how does this evaluation take place? Right in the DOJ itself! In other words, the very people who make the assessment are the people looking for the information. A bit of a conflict, you think?

Once the records are seized the DOJ has everything between attorney and client. The risk to the client of course, without getting into specifics, is that they can use that info to form the basis of a new investigation.

Guess what? There was, surprise, surprise, no outcry from the ACLU or the leftist liberal groups. But if this had been an attorney representing Obama or Hillary, there would've been hell to pay. Civil libertarians only want justice for some, not all.

So now the US attorney for the Southern District of New York will be able to ask Michael Cohen:

Who were the sources for each of the specific factual representations made by Cohen that the government contends were false or misleading;

What did the source tell the attorney about specific factual representations;

When and how did the attorney receive communications from his client, source, or other purveyors of information;

Regarding the factual representations that the government claims were false and misleading, did the client raise any questions or corrections?

Did the witness review with his client any or all the written submissions forwarded to a governmental agency?

So, the Mueller investigation is not only investigating a phony conspiracy theory cooked up for purely political reasons, it's also inadvertently threatening our basic freedoms. When you look at all the wrongdoings of Hillary Clinton, with the emails, destroying evidence, deleting evidence, and not even a grand jury was impaneled—all they had to do with Hillary was ask her one simple question: Did you put classified emails on a personal server? If she said yes, she'd have admitted to a crime. If she said no, she would be committing perjury by lying to an FBI agent.

But they didn't want to indict her, which is why they didn't ask her the question.

CHAPTER TWELVE

The Real Trump Presidency

My Friend the President

It would be hard for anyone who believes even half of the anti-Trump propaganda put out by the liberal media to support the president. But once you see through the dishonesty, once you understand the agenda that propels this trash, orchestrated by dishonest people who aren't interested in your well-being; you know the country couldn't be in better hands than those of Donald J. Trump.

As I mentioned earlier, I'm a friend of the president. I first met Donald Trump in the '90s when my then-husband, Al Pirro, was Donald Trump's legal representative on many of his real estate deals. During that time, Al's famous client would call our house at all hours. Although I thought it strange at first, I would later come to know that Donald Trump never stops working. I started to look forward to his calls. He was always polite and made me laugh. I guess it's natural for people to think, because he's so rich, that Donald Trump is out of touch with regular people. Nothing could be further from the truth. He loves to interact with everybody: cops, construction workers, the guys selling hot dogs on the sidewalks. People love him, and he loves them right back.

Still, back then all I knew about him was what I had read in the magazines and newspapers. I knew he was very wealthy, I knew he built amazing apartment buildings and hotels, and I knew he was quite a character.

Then one day Al came home and told me that Donald had offered to fly us to Florida on his plane since we had just bought a house in Palm Beach. Donald also had a home in Palm Beach. You might have heard of the place.

I think that Marjorie Merriweather Post, the cereal heiress who built and lived in the mansion as a summer home, would have been thrilled that Donald Trump bought Mar-a-Lago. Both saw life in its grandest form. It took 600 workers to construct the 110,000 square foot, 58-bedroom, 33-bath estate complete with gold bathroom fixtures. It has a 75-foot tower that offers breathtaking views. Ms. Post, who was then married to the financier, E. F. Hutton, hired Joséph Urban to do much of the design of the home. Urban had been the scenic designer for the Ziegfeld Follies and the Metropolitan Opera. After they finished construction, Hutton reportedly remarked: "You know, Marjorie said she was going to build a little cottage by the sea. Look what we got!"

Along with being kindred spirits, there was another reason Ms. Post would have been happy to have Donald Trump own her home.

In 1972, at the end of her life, she donated the property to the US government with a specific wish in mind. Though the government accepted Post's gift, it did little to fulfill her desire for Mar-a-Lago. In fact, by the time Jimmy Carter was in office, plans were in the works to give the mansion back to the Post family, which the government did in 1981. Donald Trump bought the mansion in 1985. Thirty years later, in November 2016, Marjorie Merriweather Post's dream of Mar-a-Lago becoming the Winter White House had come true.

One year, Donald invited us for Thanksgiving dinner at Mar-a-Lago. He hadn't had the place long and it wasn't fully furnished yet, but he set up a large, round table with a white linen cloth in the middle of the expansive dining room.

The Thanksgiving dinner invite was sort of a

last-minute thing, and I remember being nervous about what to wear. After all, furnished or not, Mar-a-Lago is one of the most glamorous properties in the entire world. I went to Saks and spent more money than I should have on a black cashmere shawl. The wrap was worth every penny—perfect for the evening and I felt great in it.

I still have that shawl. Every time I see it in my closet, a distinct, vivid memory of that evening at Mar-a-Lago returns. It was an exciting time. Al and I had worked long and hard, and it seemed the whole world was opening up to us. And Donald made us feel so welcomed.

Of course, we had our children, Kiki and Alex, with us, and Ivanka, Donald Jr., and Eric were there. We had a traditional turkey dinner and somehow it was both intimate and grand.

At the time, Donald was married to Marla Maples. While we waited for dessert, Marla took me on a tour of the massive kitchen. Ms. Post was known for entertaining guests (she once had the Ringling Bros. Circus perform at Mar-a-Lago), and especially for her lavish dinner parties and her prized collection of tableware and china.

I love dishes and Ms. Post's collection lined the pantry in the kitchen. It was spectacular. There were ladders on wheels you could climb up. I climbed up on one and Marla pushed me down the row on it. There were dishes of every theme and style: all the different holidays, summer dishes, winter dishes, antique crystal, glass, some made of gold, some ornamented with real coral. Marla and I had a ball in that pantry.

When Mar-a-Lago opened as a private club, we became members and for years we'd fly back and forth with Donald and his family on most weekends.

I loved those trips on Donald's jet. A lot of times we'd all watch a movie together and I'd make popcorn for everyone. When I'd bring it out, Donald would say, "Jeanine, did you see any meatloaf in the kitchen back there? Could you heat some up for me?"

We were like an average American family, except we were miles in the sky. That's what makes Donald special. Though he takes his wealth seriously, it doesn't define him. I know they'll be people who'll scoff at that last line. But I'm telling you it's true.

One Sunday afternoon aboard the plane coming home, I got it in my head that I wanted to fly the plane since I'd been taking flying lessons in a Cessna 152. The guys flying the jet were real sweethearts. The captain let me into the cockpit, and the copilot gave me his seat. After being at the controls for a few minutes, Donald knocked on the cockpit door.

"Jeanine," he said, "Eric's feeling a little sick. It's a little bumpy."

"Okay, Donald, I'll give up the controls. I guess my horizon wasn't level."

For some reason, that particular trip sticks out in my mind and for reasons other than my short-lived jet pilot career. I remember that Donald was reading an issue of the *New York Times* magazine. I'd already read it. There was a particularly nasty letter to the editor about Trump in it. The particulars of the story are less important than the tone, which was thoroughly mean spirited.

Out of the corner of my eye, I watched Donald as he flipped through the magazine. I saw him get to the page and begin to read. He didn't even flinch. His demeanor didn't change in the slightest. He could have been reading *Family Circle* for all he cared. He put the magazine down and called for the kids.

"Write down everything you need for school; we're going to Kmart later on to get supplies."

Kmart?!

Though I must admit, the image of Donald Trump pushing one of those big Kmart carts still shocks me a bit. That moment was telling. Here he was getting called all sorts of names in the *New York Times* and he cared only about his kids. Out of all things in Michael Wolff's book that made me angry, what really popped my cork was when he called Donald an "absentee father." He knows nothing about Donald Trump.

Like many in the United States, the Trump children had parents who were divorced. Notwithstanding, the president respected and preserved his children's relationship with their mother. Though Donald has always been surrounded by the press, he kept his children away from the spotlight until they were adults. It was Ivanka, Don Jr., and Eric's decision to join their dad on the campaign trail. And Donald welcomed them aboard.

Though he loved and sheltered them growing up, he did discipline them now and then. I remember him telling the boys to stop ganging up on Ivanka for something or other or he was taking away their allowance. I never asked how much he gave them, but, knowing Donald, I don't think it was a whole lot. Donald did everything he could to make his children understand the importance of work. Just because their name is Trump doesn't mean they were born with silver spoons in their mouths. Believe me, they weren't.

My ex, Al, calls Donald "a flatterer," and he means it as a compliment. The president has always been interested in what's going on in my life and is supportive. Long before I was on television, Donald was promoting me. I remember walking down the street in Manhattan with Donald. Every time we'd pass a cop, a hardhat, or someone gawking at him, he'd point to me and say, "You know who this is? It's Jeanine Pirro! She's the DA from Westchester!"

It bothers me that the president has become such a target of LIBERALS for his treatment of women.

The Fake News won't tell you much about the amazing women who hold senior positions in the Trump administration. They include Ambassador to the United Nations Nikki Haley; White House Press Secretary Sarah Huckabee Sanders; Secretary of Eductation Betsy DeVos; Secretary of the Air Force Dr. Heather Wilson; CIA Director Gina Haspel; Administrator of the Small Business Administration Linda McMahon; US treasurer Jovita Carranza: Senior Communications adviser Mercedes Schlapp, and administrator of the Office of Information and Regulatory Affairs Neomi Rao. Those are just a sampling. "There's plenty of sexism, latent and blatant, even in the Republican Party," Kellyanne Conway told me recently. "I've never experienced that with Donald Trump. He enjoys women in the workplace, our advice, company, the perspective we have. And as a working mom—who is used to working for herself for twenty-one and a half years—he is a great boss to have."

I first met Melania Knauss in late 1998 while flying on Donald's private plane. It was the regular Friday night to Sunday Palm Beach trip. I was stuffing my face with popcorn and candy while watching her delicately eat apple slices. I remember saying to myself, *That's what you should be eating, Jeanine* as I continued with the handfuls of popcorn.

I moved to a seat closer to her, to see what her deal was. I was even more impressed with the woman after I spoke with her.

At one point the friendly conversation turned to jewelry. I asked Melania if Donald had given her any fabulous pieces. She said that stuff was not important to her. It was clear to me that their relationship was real.

Later, I saw that same confidence in an episode during the first season of *Celebrity Apprentice*. Trump had the contestants in his home atop Trump Tower. Their eyes were as big as saucers as they took in the extravagant furnishings and world-class views. Melania, who was dating Donald at the time, came down the stairwell and greeted the cast.

"How do you clean a house like this?" one of the contestants asked.

"You hire people to clean it!" Melania smiled elegantly.

"You're very, very lucky," another one said.

"Oh, thank you," Melania said with a smile. "And he is not lucky?"

I remember I almost choked on the water I was drinking as I yelled, "You tell them, girl!"

Melania Trump understands Donald Trump. She doesn't have to be the center of attention, and Lord knows she could be if she wanted to. Despite what so-called feminists might tell you, this does not make her subservient.

She doesn't need to be in the limelight, which is good because one person in the limelight is more than enough for a relationship.

An astonishing beauty, five-foot, eleven-inch Melania had a successful modeling career in Milan, Paris, and New York. Quiet, but thoughtful, engaging without being overly solicitous, she owns an inner attractiveness that matches her stunning features. She also has a deep love for the United States.

Her upbringing was modest, with parents who worked hard in Slovenia. While Melania and Donald were still dating, the future president made living arrangements for Melania's parents in New York.

She and Donald had been dating for several years and something told me that she might be the one. Pretty quickly, it seemed others in his family thought so, too.

On one trip down to Palm Beach, Donald's sister Maryanne Trump Barry, who is a federal circuit court judge, and I sat next to each other. We started talking about Melania.

"Well, what do you think?" I asked her.

"I think she's the one," she said.

"I'll bet you're right." I remember thinking that strong, beautiful and independent Melania would be the perfect woman for Donald.

Sure enough, in 2005, we received an invitation to the wedding.

Al and I attended the ceremony at the Episcopal Church of Bethesda-by-the-Sea and then the reception at Mar-a-Lago. It was spectacular. We drank champagne out of crystal glasses; we ate caviar and beef tenderloin. The Grand Marnier wedding cake was five feet tall.

Melania stopped the show. She wore a Dior gown with a sixteen-foot veil. The gown was bejeweled with 1,500 tiny crystal rhinestones and pearls. *Vogue* magazine called Melania's wedding gown, "the dress of the year." She could have worn a plastic trash bag and she still would have been the most beautiful woman there.

Of course, the guest list was filled with Donald's famous friends. Everywhere you looked, there was someone you knew. Paul Anka and Tony Bennett got up and sang. Billy Joel serenaded and hammed it up. Even Bill and Hillary were there (it was a different time).

Melania and Donald also invited several media

personalities, including Matt Lauer, Katie Couric, and Anna Wintour. My, what a difference a decade makes.

No one knows the true nature of the press better than Donald Trump. And no one can call them out as liars better than he can. He works every day to penetrate the disinformation that surrounds him to get the truth to the people. He sees it as a necessary part of his job.

But it's not Melania's job, and yet she's subjected to much of the same abuse as her husband.

During the campaign Melania tried to stay out of the spotlight. Her preference was often portrayed by the paparazzi of the Left as self-conscious or aloof. They tried to disparage Donald's and Melania's marital relationship at every turn. She pushed his hand away! He's walking too far in front of her!

Give me a break.

In August 2017, Melania traveled with her husband to Texas to tour the aftermath of Hurricane Harvey. You would think the media's focus would be on the devastation the people of Texas were experiencing. Instead, all they could talk about were Melania's shoes.

As she boarded a plane from the White House, Melania wore typical pumps that she often wears, shoes she wears as easily as some of us wear slippers.

The press pounced. *Vanity Fair* published a piece titled, "Who Wears Stilettos to a Hurricane? Melania Trump." The *New York Times* called the high heels "a symbol for what many see as the disconnect between the Trump administration and reality."

Arriving in Corpus Christi, Melania deplaned wearing sneakers. She had changed her shoes on the plane, completely oblivious to the media thrashing she'd been receiving.

Did that change the narrative? No. That *New York Times* quote was written after the fact. The reporter knew Melania changed her shoes on the plane, and still couldn't help but write something nasty about FLOTUS.

It is liberal institutions that continually write about women this way. It is the liberal media that only want to write about Melania when they can trash what she wears. These are the same people who accuse conservatives of waging a "war on women."

When Melania spearheaded the decorating of the White House for Christmas in the winter of 2017, the headlines were vicious. The *New Yorker* published a piece called "With the White House Christmas, the Image of Melania Trump Transforms from Fairy Tale Prisoner to Wicked Queen."

What an abhorrently sexist and Scrooge-like way

for a liberal publication to refer to the First Lady. The article called her "mostly mute" and blamed her poor English for her "unusual silence."

Hey, dummies, the woman speaks five languages. How many do you speak?

People like the *New Yorker*'s Jia Tolentino and Chelsea Handler, who go after Melania Trump with a vicious ferocity, do not compare to her in any way. (Tolentino also couldn't help but make a quip that Americans liked Melania as First Lady because of her "whiteness")

Still, Melania is one of those women who takes a lot in stride. She's very European. European women have a different approach. They're not as thin-skinned. Melania has handled the role of First Lady with style and grace and a whole lot of guts.

Donald and Melania have a loving relationship. He loves her. He admires her. He confides in her. They laugh together all the time. During the debate, whenever Donald's eyes met Melania's, you could see that he was at ease. Smart, sophisticated, and beautiful, and with a strong sense of family, she will prove to be a great First Lady.

Once Donald Trump became president I wondered if our friendship would change. It hasn't, because he hasn't. Of course, now I call him Mr. President and his shoulders do carry the weight of the office he holds. But the Donald Trump I've known for all these years is still very much the same. He makes me laugh. His priorities remain his family and his country, and I suspect he sleeps even less than before.

There is a video that has been circling the Internet for a while now. It's of an interview Donald Trump gave to the gossip columnist Rona Barrett in 1980. If you get the chance, look it up. The clip is fantastic. Not only does the thirty-four-year-old Donald Trump look like a movie star, but he also talks about his love for his country with such passion, it stirs the emotion in you. The things he says to Barrett are the same policies he campaigned on and is implementing from the Oval Office. Toward the end of the interview, Barrett tries to get him to say he would run for president. The young, unassuming Donald shrugs off the question, but he does talk about the need for a president who is outside politics as usual.

"One proper president could turn the country around," he says. "I firmly believe that."

So do I.

He's in the Oval Office now.

The Inner Circle

The Trump family is the president's inner circle. President Trump thrives on loyalty, and who could possibly be more loyal than his own family?

Who better to trust? And when each family member is blessed with a first-rate education, intellectual acumen, and unique pride of country, who better to look to for support?

Eric Trump perhaps said it best:

"No one has ever done what we did as a family. The first rule of politics is normally, 'keep the family away from the spotlight.' Most of the time, family ends up being an impediment versus being an asset. Our family has always fought together and the notion that we would sit on the sideline was almost unthinkable to us. I was on the road in 'swing states' for eighteen months straight, not because I had to be, but because I believed in my father and wanted to fight on his behalf. When you do that, you subject yourself to a tremendous amount of scrutiny but to all of us, it was worth it. Everything we've ever done we've done together as a family. Whether it's build our company, grow our company, or sit by our father's side on *The Apprentice*. We have always fought together—we have always won together.

"Don and Ivanka are two of my best friends in the world and together we worked incredibly hard. Through ups and downs, we stood on the same stage and fought, always as a collective.

"I think that you see a very stark contrast between the way we handled ourselves as a family and that of the other candidates' families. They weren't doing three hours of radio every morning, driving tens of thousands of miles in a car from rally to rally and they certainly weren't living in thirteen swing states. In many cases, they wanted nothing to do with the campaigns and while I understand that, given the viciousness of politics, we were all in this together.

"We always protect each other. That's what families do."

President Trump is not the first president to value loyalty. Abraham Lincoln demanded it and returned it. So did Andrew Jackson.

President Trump first learned about loyalty from his father, Fred. Besides being uncommonly brilliant, Fred acquired an education in hard-fisted New York politics. Loyalty was the key to trustworthy business dealings and respect, and no one is closer or more trustworthy than family.

Donald Trump, Jr. attended the Wharton School of Business, earning a bachelor of science degree in economics in 2000. Don Jr., as he is generally known, joined the Trump Organization in 2001 and immediately began managing multimillion-dollar projects, including the successful completions of 40 Wall Street, Trump International Hotel & Tower, and Trump Park Avenue.

Don Jr. worked tirelessly on the campaign alongside

the rest of his family. But instead of praising his positive work on the campaign trail, the media have focused on his infamous June 2016 meeting with a Russian lawyer, in which they said he was being offered dirt on Hillary or the Clinton Foundation. So, what? I've never heard of a campaign that didn't do opposition research!

Don Jr. is more brutally honest than Eric about the lost opportunities the Trump Organization has endured because of his father's election. The Trump Organization faces restrictions on new international transactions. However, Don Jr. has made it clear that the sacrifices were all worth the policies his father's administration is implementing. America will reap the benefits.

Like her brothers Eric and Don Jr., Ivanka Trump is brilliant; she, too, loves her father, her country and her wonderful family—Jared and her three beautiful children.

Ivanka attended an elite boarding school in Connecticut, was a model at age fourteen, graduated cum laude from the prestigious Wharton School of Business, began her real estate career with the Forest City Ratner organization, and then joined the Trump Organization.

To overcome the fact that she is an offspring of the Trump dynasty she became extremely motivated and worked harder and longer than most. She aptly negotiated large acquisitions for the family business with a unique grace and incisive analysis. In 2009, Ivanka married Jared Kushner.

Ivanka was active in the Trump campaign from the beginning. She introduced her father when he announced his candidacy for President of the United States, and again at the Republican National Convention where he accepted the party's nomination.

As a member of the administration, she has helped secure the diplomatic relations with the Japanese prime minister Shinzo Abe and the Chinese delegation. Ivanka often served as an elegant, charming liaison for her father.

Jared attended the Frisch School, a modern Orthodox Yeshiva High School. His six-foot, three-inch frame made him a natural in basketball and other sports. He enrolled at Harvard University where he graduated in 2003 with a degree in government. After Harvard, Jared graduated NYU with a dual JD/MBA degree and later become an assistant district attorney in Manhattan.

Fast-forward a few years, Jared became CEO of the Kushner Companies, a diversified real estate organization in 2008. He piloted the company through the recession.

Jared's purchase of the *New York Observer* and his subsequent immersion in the news media came in handy later during the presidential campaign.

If you know Jared Kushner, you know he is thoughtful, soft-spoken, and locked in tight on helping the president achieve his goal to make America great again.

Like Ivanka, Eric, and Don Jr., Jared learned about campaign primaries with on-the-job training. With initially no real help from the RNC and no field organization to speak of, Jared did what he does best—study the terrain, plan, and execute. He called friends near and far and implemented an online campaign. Using the president's charm, charisma, and natural oratory skills, he set in motion a series of stadium-filled speaking engagements the likes of which have never been seen before and hammered home candidate Trump's agenda across the Internet.

As a young man from a successful real estate family where loyalty was also prized, he became like another son to the president—a young visionary who could be trusted.

Jared has been rewarded with one of the most powerful positions in the White Houseand works closely with the president. In fact, his office at the White House is right next door to the Oval Office. He has been entrusted with the president's greatest goal—peace in the Middle East.

He planned the president's first foreign trip with the first stop being Saudi Arabia, where the king convened 54 leaders from the Muslim and Arab world in a historic summit to affirm their commitment to join the US in fighting terrorism in the region and around the world. During the visit, he orchestrated the sale of $100 billion in arms to Saudi Arabia.

In addition, Jared opened and headed the White House Office of Innovation. Through this program Jared has worked diligently on modernizing information-technology in the government.

During my interview with Jared in April 2018, I learned of yet another mission: prison reform. Jared believes those who have paid their debt to society should have the opportunity to rejoin it as participants and contributors. "The best solution to recidivism is a job and I am committed to ensure ex-convicts get the training and support they need to begin contributing to society again," he said.

Eric and Lara Trump are fun-loving and sports oriented. Each is committed to charitable endeavors. Lara is a huge animal lover who rescues abandoned, neglected, and often abused animals and raises money for them. She told me, "I've always loved animals. It's been my passion since I was a kid. They need our help to survive. We will never buy another dog. My dog Ben knows he's a rescue and he thanks me every day."

I can attest to that. Ben comes to my house and plays with my standard poodle, Sir Lancelot. They're happy campers.

Eric's charity, the Eric Trump Foundation, has been renamed Curetivity and is being run by cofounder and executive director Paige Scardigli. Eric stepped away from the foundation after his father's election to avoid any appearance of impropriety. Eric's interest is in supporting the pediatric cancer unit at St. Jude's Children's Research Hospital. He has raised close to $20 million for this cause. Oh, by the way, he started this campaign at age twenty-one!

Eric attended the prestigious New York City Trinity School, boarded at The Hill School in Pennsylvania, and graduated with honors from Georgetown. By 2012, he was receiving recognition as a leader in business.

Lara Trump graduated from North Carolina State University and worked as a producer at *Inside Edition* and *Real News*. Also strongly independent and a family loyalist, Lara, an avid equestrian, can often be seen on Instagram with her rescue dogs, Charlie and Ben.

She is a strong supporter of her husband and not afraid to "mix it up" in support of the president. During the campaign, she was on the road for months burnishing her credentials as an engaging, articulate public speaker.

Like Don Jr., Eric worked non-stop on the campaign from the moment his father announced, raising funds, speaking at rallies across the country, and doing whatever was necessary for his father to win the White House. Since the election, both sons have taken over running the Trump organization.

Eric speaks of his father as admiringly as does Don Jr. "He is an amazing man—there is nobody I admire more. I consider him my best friend and could not be prouder of my father."

Eric has given several interviews discussing the implosion of the Democrat Party. He recently told me many Democrats seem to have a policy of hate and obstruction without any real message of their own. I agree.

Tiffany Trump is the daughter of President Trump and Marla Maples. Tiffany, twenty-four, graduated from the prestigious University of Pennsylvania and is now studying law at Georgetown University Law Center.

In May 2016, she joined her siblings on the campaign trail. Tiffany has for the most part ducked the spotlight, but she gave a speech about her father at the 2016 Republican National Convention, and quoted her favorite advice from her dad: 'If you do what you love, hold nothing back, and never let fear or failure get in the way' then you'll succeed.

Barron William Trump is the youngest of the Trump children, and the child of the president and the First Lady. Like his mother, Barron is multilingual.

He attended the Columbia Grammar and Preparatory School in Manhattan, and now attends St. Andrew's Episcopal School in Potomac, Maryland. With the help of his siblings and strong encouragement—as well as fierce protection from the First Lady, he is surviving cruel comments from the liberal Left.

Nicknamed "Little Donald," he has his own views and a a penchant for fine suits. He is tall, smart, and, like the rest of the inner circle, will in time make great contributions to his country.

Melania understood the viciousness of the campaign and focused on maintaining privacy for her son, Barron. During the campaign Melania preferred to remain out of the spotlight and she was often portrayed by the media as being aloof. They went so far as to make fun of her accent. As First Lady she puts them to shame as she speaks five languages fluently. She is an extreme asset to President Trump during special dinners and social events. Finally, another Jacqueline Kennedy by the president's side. Anyone who has observed her and the president as a couple can easily see what I saw when they dated: that she is her own person, with a clear sense of who she is and this is reflected in her role as First Lady.

Melania Trump would rather help children around the world, provide hurricane relief, and address the opioid crisis than participate in the hand-to-hand political combat other first ladies like Hillary did.

General Kelly on the Real West Wing

Not too long ago, I met with the White House chief of staff, General John Kelly, in a conference room in the Eisenhower Executive Office Building. As he walked in, I noticed the general was wearing a splint on his right hand, his fingers swollen to twice their size. I asked what had happened, but he shrugged off the question.

What really commanded my attention wasn't his injured hand. It was his eyes. Anyone meeting John Kelly for the first time would be struck by them. Not so much the steel-blue color, but the clear sense these are eyes that have seen man's inhumanity to man in the worst of all settings, the battlefield. He has the look of a man who has spent his life defending the rest of us, the grateful and the ungrateful. Those eyes betray a hint of sadness one might explain by his being a Gold Star father who lost his son in war. The experiences that left their mark on that powerful visage have given him a quiet steadiness that is not likely to be disturbed by anything thrown at him in politics.

As a four-star marine general, a rank that is about

as rare as a snowstorm in July (there have only been fifty-one active-duty four-star marine generals in the history of the Marine Corps and only one—Kelly— in the last quarter century), General Kelly isn't prone to chitchat. He talked at length about his relationship with President Trump. Many would think the relationship incongruous—a marine loyal to a Manhattan billionaire—with love of country as the common denominator.

The media wants us to believe General Kelly merely tolerates President Trump out of a sense of duty. Nothing could be further from the truth. One of the stories the general told me was about the president's experience at Arlington National Cemetery on Memorial Day in 2017, his first year in office. The president gave a speech and then accompanied the general to an area of the cemetery called Section 60. It's in that section of Arlington where the deceased from the wars since 9/11 are buried.

That day, because of the holiday, Section 60 was filled with families of the fallen armed service members. They sat in lawn chairs and had coolers with drinks and picnic spreads. Many of them, holding special photos—from prom and high school photos to formal military photos of their children, brothers, and sisters—came up to talk to President Trump. They just wanted to share their memories, and the president listened to every one of them. "Nothing affects this president more than when a member of our military dies in service of our country," the general told me. "He's a very sensitive and appreciative guy," General Kelly said.

One of the duties the general has taken on is to deliver news of the deaths of service members to the president personally. And when he does, he told me, President Trump becomes quiet, and then often asks the same question: "Why did they do this?"

I know as I write these words there will be people who will twist that quote to put the president in a bad light. But if those LIBERAL haters would stop and think, they would realize the words the president uses are more than appropriate. Most of us can not comprehend what gives someone the courage it takes to die for one's country. That we have a president who realizes that says all you need to know about President Trump.

"At the end of it all," General Kelly said. "I would tell you that this president lives and breathes doing what's good for America and Americans. And his greatest frustration is when he can't do that."

The general also conveyed a genuine sense of respect for the people he works with in the West Wing. Leaks were a major problem when he was brought on board, a problem he had to solve. This is a man for whom, as he put it, "security is a way of life; it's a religion." He understood coming into the job that not everyone had his experience with classified information, determining what is or isn't classified, and deciding with whom one can or cannot share certain information.

One of the first things he did, with help from Zachary Fuentes, deputy assistant to the president and senior advisor to the chief of staff, was to try to get his arms around that inexperience. "We brought people in for briefings to say, 'this is what your responsibilities are when handling classified documents.' So, we've raised people's awareness. So, I think a lot of the leaks just went away. Because a lot of the people who had access just talked about it. And didn't realize that no, you're not supposed to talk about it."

The general spoke to the staff about their oath to the Constitution, reminding them they would likely never have to put their lives on the line to defend it, as so many young people he had served with and commanded had. He asked them to think about that when they were tempted to violate their oaths. "I had people come up to me afterward and say, 'I was the one.' I said, 'I don't care what you did in the past. This is a new kind of world,'" he said.

General Kelly showed the kind of leadership tackling this problem that earned him his rank. One of the ways he earned his staff's respect was having genuine respect for them. "These are good people," he told me, "overwhelmingly good people. Great Americans. Some of them old, some of them young. Some of them experienced, some not so experienced. But they're good people."

Because they are good people, the leaking problem all but took care of itself, once Kelly imparted the proper understanding of security. But no administration is ever completely free of leaks and this one is no exception. Now that Bannon and so many others are gone, we must ask: Who are the hidden LEAKERS in the White House?

A Traitor in the People's House

Back in May 2017, I called on the Trump administration to spare no resources to find the member of the White House staff leaking to the media everything from innuendo and non-stories to classified information. Since then, President Trump has cleaned house and General Kelly has assisted by training White House personnel new to security procedures on the importance of properly handling sensitive information.

The leaks have decreased, but they haven't stopped.

Somehow, information that should remain behind closed doors at the White House is finding its way to the front pages of major newspapers. Whoever is responsible is an enemy of the United States.

We know anything said over the phone at the White House is recorded and neither the intelligence community nor federal law enforcement have hesitated in the past to leak information from those calls. That was confirmed when the president's calls to Mexican President Enrique Peña Nieto and Australian Prime Minister Malcolm Turnbull were leaked to the Washington Post in April 2017, less than three months after Trump's inauguration.

We don't have evidence, however, that anyone outside the White House staff can listen to or record in-person conversations. If two or more staff members are in a room talking in the White House, we must assume no one else is privy to what is said. So, if it shows up in the *New York Times* the next day, one of the participants in that conversation must have leaked it.

There are several published reports that I went to the White House on November 1, 2017, to meet with the president about the lack of an investigation of the Clinton-Russia connection in the Uranium One deal. General Kelly and Don McGahn were the only people present in the Oval Office besides the president and me.

During the meeting, I clearly voiced my views on Attorney General Sessions' lack of prosecutorial balls, as well as on Mueller's "find-a-crime" mission. The president was annoyed, but not with me, and left the room. The *New York Times* reported that General Kelly said I was not helping things, according to their LEAKER. I probably wasn't helping General Kelly keep order, and I clearly wasn't helping McGahn. The president had showed his displeasure with McGahn's namby-pamby approach to things. But who leaked this?

When the *New York Times* called for a comment, I was shocked that anything from a closed-door meeting in the Oval Office with the President of the United States, had made it to the *New York Times*. I called the president and General Kelly about the leak. Certainly, I didn't leak it and the president didn't leak it. I trust General Kelly didn't leak it, either.

Don McGahn was the only other person there. A well-placed source tells me McGahn leaks information when he believes it suits his purposes.

And people still wonder why Donald Trump must keep cleaning house.

Nevertheless, General Kelly has helped smooth out the bumps every administration experiences in its first year. And once this one found its sea legs, it was full speed ahead.

Making America Great Again

This is the Trump administration I've seen first-hand. It's quite different from the fictional one you've been told about by the twenty-four/seven anti-Trump hate campaign. Let me tell you something, if one-tenth of the lies you've been told about the president, his family, and his administration were true, I wouldn't have been friends with Donald Trump for over thirty years. I wouldn't have put up with the boogeyman the media have created. Luckily, that boogeyman doesn't exist, least of all in the Oval Office.

Just as egregious as all the distortions, mischaracterizations, and outright lies being published about Donald Trump are all the things not being published. Most Americans have no idea that less than two years after his inauguration, Donald Trump has accomplished more than most presidents accomplish in their entire presidencies. The media might as well be writing for Trump-hating Hollywood, as accurately as they've reported what's really happened over the past year and a half. Out here in the real world, Americans are more prosperous, less likely to be unemployed, and live in a far safer world than they did on January 19, 2017.

Yes, the media grudgingly reports when the Trump

administration accomplishes something, putting a negative spin on that accomplishment whenever they can. But they bury the positive news, which is all true, under a mountain of negative coverage, which is mostly false. It's the equivalent of a hard-copy newspaper putting an innocent man's indictment on page one and later reporting his acquittal on page thirty-six of one of their least-read sections.

So, let me take a moment to tell you about the real Trump presidency, the one that is, as Donald Trump promised, making America great again. Since President Trump was elected, the economy has added three million jobs. In fact, today there are more jobs available than there are unemployed. That's resulted in the lowest unemployment rate in seventeen years. The stock market has roared to new highs despite the Federal Reserve raising interest rates five times since Trump's election.

By the way, do you know how many times the Fed raised rates between Obama's election and Trump's? Once. After announcing they would set a course back to "normalcy," having kept interest rates near zero for over seven years, the Fed raised rates in December 2015 and the stock market plunged. They never attempted to raise them again until after Donald Trump won.

Building a Real Economic Recovery

That the market went up over 25 percent despite one rate hike after another shows the difference between the state of the economy under Trump versus Obama. President Obama was inaugurated just after a historic market crash and at the beginning of a deep recession. There was nowhere for the economy or the stock market to go but up. Yet, despite literally coming in at the bottom, Obama managed to hamper the economy badly enough to preside over the slowest, most anemic recovery in modern US history. The economy needed monetary stimulus from the Fed under Obama. As soon as it was decreased ever so slightly, the market crashed. Since Trump has been in office, it has soared despite regular rate hikes.

That's because President Trump has implemented policies that make this country hospitable to business again. The Tax Cuts and Jobs Act, the largest tax cuts and reforms in US history, lowered rates for American families and businesses. And guess what? Despite all the baloney about these merely being "tax cuts for the rich," those cuts merely brought the United States in line with the world average. The United States' 39 percent corporate tax rate was the third highest in the world. Do you know what the corporate rate was in every lying liberal's paradise, Sweden? Twenty-two percent! The Trump tax cuts merely brought our corporate tax rates in line with Sweden's.

This tax reform bill wasn't just good for business. It will save the typical American family of four more than $2,000 in taxes each year by doubling the standard deduction, creating the child tax credit, and lowering individual rates for average income earners. And let's not forget the bill repealed the totalitarian Obamacare individual mandate.

Speaking of the Left's fascination with Scandinavia, I'd also like to point out another inconvenient truth the Fake News never tells you about: Those countries may have larger welfare states, but they have much freer economies as far as regulation is concerned. While they'd do even better with less welfare, they are able to pay for it because their economies are not nearly as strangled as ours was under President Obama.

On the campaign trail, Donald Trump promised to address this problem by instituting a rule for regulatory agencies to repeal two regulations for every one new regulation put in place. Well, the Trump administration didn't just keep that promise. They kept it more than tenfold, issuing twenty-two deregulatory actions for every one new regulatory action since January 2017.

The president hasn't just taken executive action, either. Unlike President "Pen and Phone" Obama,

President Trump has worked with Congress, successfully getting resolutions passed to repeal fourteen onerous Obama-era rules and regulations.

Also unlike his predecessors, President Trump isn't satisfied merely to see the stock market boom and corporate earnings improve—although both have occurred under his watch. This president promised American workers they'd have their fair share of the prosperity as well. Before his seat in the Oval Office was even warm, the president withdrew from the harmful Trans-Pacific Partnership (TPP) and began renegotiating NAFTA.

Using the negotiating skills that made him a billionaire in the private sector, he secured new concessions in the Korea Free Trade Agreement (KORUS) that will benefit American automobile, pharmaceutical, steel, and agricultural producers. And he's taken a tough, but respectful, stance against China, fighting back against unfair Chinese trade practices and intellectual property theft. He announced $50 billion in new tariffs on Chinese goods and levied tariffs of 25 percent and 10 percent on Chinese steel and aluminum imports.

"Yet, all we hear from the media is Stormy Daniels and Mueller's never-ending search for nonexistent collusion. We have important issues in this country and we have important accomplishments by this president," said Kellyanne Conway. "The five million Americans who received raises or bonuses, the millions more who live in communities that directly benefit from the jobs and opportunities created by corporate tax cuts—all those people have a right to say they're tired of this. They want to know when it will end."

Foreign Policy Miracles

One might be tempted to discount President Trump's stunning economic accomplishments because he's such a successful businessman. You'd expect economic policy to be his forte. But what he's been able to do with foreign policy in such a short time might even be more impressive.

Remember ISIS? We don't hear much about them anymore, do we? That's because President Trump has accomplished in a matter of months what the Obama administration couldn't do in years. By simply working with allies and lifting unnecessary restrictions on America's military, ISIS has been effectively decimated. Nearly 100 percent of its territory has been liberated since President Trump took office. How often has the media congratulated his administration on this decisive victory? Crickets.

Even worse, they've tried to spin one of his most stunning accomplishments into a negative. As of this writing, North and South Korea are engaged in peace talks, after North Korea's dictator, Kim Jong-un, suspended the nuclear weapons testing that had threatened stability in Asia for most of this century. President Trump's maximum pressure campaign against North Korea, excoriated by the media as reckless and dangerous, has brought the country to the negotiating table and secured one-sided concessions from North Korea.

Amazingly, three American hostages have been returned. The comparison of the Trump presidency and the Obama presidency, as reflected in this one example, couldn't be more stark. It was during the Obama presidency that student Otto Warmbier was taken hostage, tortured to the point where he would never recover, and finally released under President Trump's watch. Unfortunately, it was too late for Mr. Warmbier. We watched in horror as he returned home and died shortly thereafter.

President Trump also officially recognized Jerusalem as the capital of Israel, fulfilling a promise other presidents failed to keep, and strengthening ties with our closest ally in the Middle East. And for all those so-called allies who opposed the move at the UN, the president put them on notice that his administration would remember that when they later come with their hands out for aid.

While maintaining his anti-regime-change policy, President Trump has twice launched limited, targeted strikes against Syria's Assad regime for its illegal use of chemical weapons against its own citizens, letting Assad and the world know the United States will not stand by while international law is flouted in brutal fashion. As for Assad's ally Russia, the Trump administration has stood up to Russian aggression, announcing several sanctions packages against Russia and expelling Russian diplomats.

An "America First" Plan for Syria and the Middle East

The liberal left claims the recent air strike on Syria's chemical production facilities was another "one and done" by a president who has no plan there.

The conflict in Syria is based upon centuries-old religious differences, going back even before the Crusades. As long as different religious views vie to steer a nation's politics, the battle within will never end. Trump knows this and has no intention of keeping the U.S. in Syria.

However, Assad's second use of chemical weapons on his own people within a 12-month period was in violation of the Chemical Weapons Convention

(CWC), which Syria acceded to in 2013, during the Obama administration, under the not-so-watchful eye of Russia. Russia and Iran had long been attempting to meddle and spread their influence in Syria and throughout the region. There was widespread agreement that the threat of Iran in Syria was a clear and present danger to all concerned. When it became clear chemical weapons were again being manufactured and storage facilities built in Syria, President Trump made the decision to attack those facilities with the help of British and French forces.

Since Iran's sworn mission is to destroy Israel, they intentionally kept Israel out of the strike.

A clear message had been sent to Russia, Iran and North Korea: "If you violate international law, there will be consequences."

The aftermath: Not one civilian was killed. Syria's chemical weapons manufacturing has been set back years, and North Korea announced it was shutting down its nuclear testing.

President Trump has designated his trusted senior adviser Jared Kushner to work on bringing peace between the Israelis and Palestinians. Jared, along with Assistant to the President Jason Greenblatt, Ambassador David Friedman and Jared's "right hand," Special Assistant to the President Avraham Berkowitz, began working on this difficult task. Berkowitz is a Harvard

Law graduate who shares Jared's calm demeanor. He is particularly conversant with the situation in Israel, having spent two years in Israel before college studying at Yeshiva Kol Torah in Jerusalem.

The team Jared headed visited the region and listened to important stake holders. They worked methodically on a plan that is feasible, given the current realities on the ground.

In March 2018, Kushner hosted over 20 countries at a White House conference, including Israel, Bahrain, Saudi Arabia, Egypt, the United Arab Emirates and Qatar. It was the first time in many years that both Israel and its Arab neighbors were in such a high-level meeting together. The Palestinian Authority chose not to attend. Nevertheless, Kushner's ability to assemble all those countries in the same room is, in itself, an important diplomatic achievement.

The message the conference sent was that progress waits for no one. If the PLO wants to be part of the solution, great. If they are unwilling to help their fellow Palestinians, the Trump Administration will move forward without them. The Palestinians must get on the bus or be isolated.

Syria, North Korea and Israel are just a few of President Trump's foreign policy accomplishments, using his promised strategy of peace through strength. And while he secured the much needed $700 billion in funding to rebuild the military, he has not recklessly plunged America into new conflicts, as his predecessor did. He's also employed some "tough love" on our NATO allies to start paying more of their fair share of their own defense, as required under the treaty.

Using American power judiciously as leverage, he is on his way to brokering peace on the Korean peninsula after almost 70 years of conflict, an honorable end to the war in Afghanistan, and a contained Iran. That's what you can achieve in world affairs when you put America First.

Restoring America at Home

A booming economy and a more stable, peaceful world are wonderful accomplishments, but they are means, not ends. We don't become more productive merely to produce for its own sake, but to live more comfortable and enriching lives. And we don't fight wars and negotiate peace merely for its own sake, but so every American can live in the free society that is their birthright. Nothing we accomplish in the workplace or on the international stage means anything if it doesn't result in our being able to rebuild the America we deserve here at home. No one understands this more implicitly than Donald Trump.

The very first building block of that America is

the rule of law, which was under all-out assault from the Left when Donald Trump assumed office. That's why President Trump is reshaping the judiciary and appointing conservative judges who will stand up for our constitutional rights, including Supreme Court Justice Neil Gorsuch, fourteen Circuit Court judges, and seventeen District Court judges. This doesn't mean simply ruling according to conservative preferences. Justice Gorsuch has already voted with the liberal justices on the Supreme Court on an immigration case, because the Constitution called for that vote.

While appointing justices like Gorsuch with the Second Amendment in mind, President Trump also recognizes the need for sensible regulation of the right to bear arms. He has issued an effective ban on bump stock sales and has signed into law critical pieces of legislation designed to better enforce existing gun laws, including the Fix NICS Act, which strengthens federal background checks.

As candidate Trump said many times on the campaign trail, you don't have a country without borders. Neither do you have the rule of law without effective enforcement of immigration laws. Republican and Democratic presidents have ignored the problem of illegal immigration for decades. The last president encouraged it. But there's a new sheriff in town.

Working with states, President Trump is deploying

the National Guard to the southern border to help ICE and border patrol agents. And let me remind you, he is taking this step because the Swamp in Washington refuses to give him the tools he needs, including building the wall he promised the millions of voters who want to see it built.

Nevertheless, President Trump did secure $1.6 billion in funding for 110 miles of physical barriers on the southern border, and the Department of Homeland Security has contracted and is testing border wall prototypes. Meanwhile, during the first nine months of his administration, ICE made 110,568 arrests of illegal aliens, a 40 percent increase over the same period in 2016. The president is working with agencies to fight the vicious criminal gang MS-13, which he calls "animals", leading to the arrest of more than 4,000 gang members last year.

One of the most serious problems facing American families is the high cost of health care, which was exacerbated by President Obama's signature health care law. With the individual mandate eliminated by the tax reform bill, President Trump signed an executive order designed to offer greater choice, increase competition, and bring down health insurance costs by expanding association health plans (AHPs), short-term limited duration insurance plans (STLDI), and health reimbursement arrangements (HRAs). He also terminated Obamacare's unlawful cost-sharing reduction (CSR) payments that gave unauthorized money to health insurance companies.

If the health care system was crippled and expensive for average American families, it was downright broken for our veterans. Fulfilling another campaign promise, President Trump signed legislation that offers new protections to VA whistle-blowers and has allowed the VA to fire 1,298 failing employees, as of this writing. He also ordered the development of a plan to provide transitioning veterans access to mental health care, achieving same-day mental health care at every single VA facility. In addition, the Trump administration launched a new twenty-four-hour White House VA hotline to help veterans.

The tragedy of heroin and other opioid overdoses is one more glaring problem politicians have paid lip service to and done nothing about. That's the Swamp for you, always ready to grandstand, but never ready to deliver. President Trump declared the opioid crisis a nationwide public health emergency, released his Initiative to Stop Opioid Abuse and Reduce Drug Supply and Demand in March 2018, and is mobilizing his entire administration to address this problem and drug addiction in general. The omnibus funding bill signed by President Trump contains approximately $4 billion to combat the opioid crisis.

The President's Bipartisan Push for Prison Reform

In 1993, I was elected District Attorney in a county of approximately one million people. I was re-elected and then re-elected again. I ran an office of prosecutors where our daily fare was to deal on the battleground where the fight between good and evil unfolded every day.

Our job was to settle scores for victims, the ones who never chose to be a part of the system in the first place. They didn't do anything; they didn't ask for it. Yet, out of the blue, like a thunderbolt, criminals made the decision to turn their lives into a living nightmare. As prosecutors, we could not take away their pain or turn back the clock to undo the damage, but we could seek justice on their behalf.

When I looked at the criminal justice system then, I didn't see many shades of gray. My philosophy was that it was the criminal who made the choice to commit a crime, and no amount of namby-pamby whining would excuse the wrongdoer. It didn't matter what the excuses were—broken home, down on their luck, too drunk or high to know, or a rough childhood. There was so much focus on the defendant and their rights that I felt the system should be called "the victims' justice system," to support the victims, rather than the criminals.

As a county judge, my thought process was different. The purpose of sentencing was fourfold:

- deterrence
- retribution
- rehabilitation
- incarceration

Today, many are convinced prison reform is necessary for the criminal justice system to work. They believe balancing overcrowding, costs and recidivism should influence sentencing. As part of that, they also see a need to assess the risk of re-entry into society.

To me, the first duty of the criminal justice system is to obtain justice for the victim. Once that has been accomplished, and the offender has been held accountable, then it's time to talk about prison reform.

A 2013 Rand Corporation study concluded that inmates participating in educational programs exhibit a 43% lower recidivism rate than those who don't, and a 13% higher chance of employment. All these programs represent productive early steps in decreasing recidivism rates and thus helping address overcrowding in prisons and the high cost of incarceration, but they are only pilot programs that affect a small percentage of the prison population.

Enter Donald J. Trump.

The President campaigned on a platform of helping the forgotten men and women of this country, and
many believe none are more forgotten than ex-convicts.
Once a convict has served his sentence, the punishment
should end.

Prison overcrowding with nonviolent offenders
allows violent criminals to be released earlier than they
should be. That's a problem. And we must do whatever we can to see that a life of crime is not the only
thing ex-convicts know, making it inevitable they'll
be back to re-offend, at the expense of new victims.
The president believes that and so do I.

Jared Kushner agrees and like me has a special
connection to this issue. His first priorities after the
election were helping the President transition from
successful businessman to successful President, the
day-to-day operations of the White House, and helping promote the President's key priorities. But as the
administration became established and key objectives
were accomplished, Jared was able to devote some of
his attention to prison reform.

In September 2017, Jared held the first round of listening sessions on prison reform at the White House.
He invited a bipartisan group to ensure diversity of
ideas and opinions. The meetings were attended by

senior officials at the state and federal levels, including cabinet secretaries, Governors and U.S. Senators.

Around this time, Jared decided to back the bipartisan First Step Act, a bill sponsored by Congressmen Doug Collins and Hakeem Jeffries, to reduce crime by better preparing inmates for life outside of jail.

By November 2017, momentum for Jared's initiative began to build. The President held a roundtable with Governors, the Attorney General, conservative activists and faith leaders from around the country, following up with the bold statement, "We will be very tough on crime, but we will provide a ladder of opportunity for the future. We can help break this vicious cycle," the vicious cycle being high recidivism rates. A prison system that leaves former prisoners unprepared to join society helps neither former inmates who want to make a new start nor the rest of society, who suffer the repeat offenses and pay for the repeat incarcerations.

After the president's roundtable, Republican Governor Matt Bevin of Kentucky praised President Trump's efforts to USA TODAY, saying, "It takes someone to stop blowing smoke on it, which is what liberals have done for years. This has the ability to be something transformative, something like Nixon going to China and turning the world on its head."

Jared continued to build a strong coalition of bipartisan support and in January 2018, during his State of the Union address, President Trump gave the initiative strong support, saying, "As America regains its strength, this opportunity must be extended to all citizens. That is why this year we will embark on reforming our prisons to help former inmates who have served their time get a second chance." As Kellyanne Conway said, the President's policies are positioned to give "equal opportunity for all."

On March 7, 2018, the President signed an Executive Order creating a council to make recommendations on ways to reform prisons. The administration also publicly backed the First Step Act, which made it to the floor of the House for a vote on May 22, 2018. While the bill had bipartisan support, some Democrats opposed it. Jerry Nadler, a congressman from New York made a plea on the House floor to Democrats (and Republicans) to vote against the bill. Despite that resistance, the bill passed the House overwhelmingly by a vote of 360-59.

Senate Democrats are already signaling they will try to obstruct the bill. They don't want President Trump succeeding at anything, no matter who much it might benefit the Americans they represent. They certainly don't' want him succeeding where they failed to help a population disproportionately composed of people of color.

There are some who oppose the bill because it doesn't go far enough. Senator Lindsey Graham wants reduced mandatory minimum sentences for non-violent offenders included. The ACLU and the NAACP Legal Defense and Educational Fund are concerned that a narrow, first step approach would delay sentencing, understaffing, confinement and other concerns. Senator Chuck Grassley (R. Iowa), Chair of the Judiciary Committee and Senator leader on criminal justice reform recognizes the need for prison reform but is concerned that the First Step Act will not pass without sentencing reform, which does not yet have enough bipartisan support the Senate.

Some of the Republican hesitance in the Senate may be due to Attorney General Jeff Sessions' strong criminal justice position, which emphasizes the punitive approach. I agree with that for violent criminals, but Sessions doesn't seem to consider the total cost to society of recidivism, including monetary costs to taxpayers, the social cost of the repeat offenses, and the opportunity costs of all those services better-prepared former inmates may have contributed to society through gainful employment.

Whatever their reasons, it's time for Republicans to

stop dragging their heels on this and not let the perfect be the enemy of the good. I'm not saying sentencing reform isn't needed, but this bill will start chopping away at the overall problem immediately. Pass the First Step Act and then continue the debates on sentencing reform.

Are you listening, Mitch McConnell? You have a chance to do something that will help your country and your party in this November's mid-term elections. Yes, it will also reflect positively on the president, but you'll just have to put your RINO instincts aside for a change. Order this bill to the floor of the Senate for a vote.

Even Kim Kardashian has done more than RINO Mitch to move this bill forward. She visited the White House and met with the President and Jared Kushner to discuss ways she could get involved in the prison reform effort. Kardashian instantly brought a national spotlight to this important issue and helped put pressure on the Senate to bring the bill to the Senate floor.

The implementation of risk assessments could help overcome resistance to this bill. Risk assessments collect information on behavior and attitudes associated with lower rates of recidivism. This is generally known as the Risk-Needs-Responsivity (RNR) model. The concept is often criticized for being correlated with race and therefore discriminatory. If the assessments are discriminatory, fix them. But they should be used extensively throughout the criminal justice system, from pre-trial detention through release consider-ations. Not only will the success rates be higher, but those with legitimate concerns about this approach will know we aren't just releasing anyone and every-one to cut costs and address overcrowding in prisons.

The president has led on this issue. His administra-tion has reached across the aisle to get a bill through the House and into the Senate's hands. It's time for senators in both houses to stop playing politics and for Mitch McConnell to bring this forward for an up or down vote.

Rebuilding America First

One issue that should be bipartisan, even in today's polarized political environment, is national in-frastructure. The United States is the richest, most powerful country in the world, but its roads, bridges, airports, and other infrastructure often look more like a third world country's. And with the enormous debt his predecessor ran up, rebuilding our country might seem like a very uphill battle.

It probably would be for most politicians, but not for a billionaire real estate developer. Drawing on the distinctly American history of private infrastructure development, President Trump has outlined a plan to rebuild America's infrastructure with $200 billion in federal funds that would spur at least $1.5 trillion in private investments across America. To streamline the federal permitting process for infrastructure projects, federal agencies have signed the One Federal Decision memorandum of understanding (MOU). The president will make getting his plan through Congress a key part of the second half of his first term.

The president removed a major obstacle to energy independence and new jobs by approving the Keystone XL and Dakota Access pipelines, expediting pipeline approval and production, and improving the permitting and approval processes for liquefied natural gas (LNG) terminals and exports. He also ended the Obama administration's war on coal, rolling back harmful regulations and policies, including the Clean Power Plan and Stream Protection Rule.

Empowering Women in America

When the so-called Women's March descended on Washington, DC, on January 21, 2017, I was out on the street with a microphone. I'd been interviewing people since early in the morning, hoping to get a few quotes for the "Street Justice" segment that runs at the end of my show. I'd brought along two Navy SEALs, just in case. I really did. Wherever I went, the SEALs stood on either side of me. My camera crew, as usual, was in front, getting it all on film. For the most part, the interviews went fine. I got to argue with a few people with whom I didn't exactly see eye-to-eye, and tried my best to learn what the heck this "movement for all women" was about.

Not much, as it turned out.

There were some women who believed the march had been organized to impeach Donald Trump, others thought it was one big abortion rally. One woman told me she didn't care what happened as long as the Democrats took the midterm elections.

At some point, after we'd been out for a few hours, the feeling in the streets shifted. The crowd was getting bigger and the signs were getting angrier. I've been in protests that turned to riots, back in the '70s when I was in Europe. I knew when a crowd was starting to become hostile. I moved a little closer to my SEAL friends, hoping we could get out fast. Before long, people were hurling insults my way. They called me and my crew names I don't care to repeat in print—and I'm not exactly a shrinking violet. A mob mentality had taken charge, for certain. It was as if their human brains shut down and something primitive took over when they saw the Fox News logo on my microphone.

By that afternoon, every Fake News station in the

country had fawning coverage of the marches, making them seem like peaceful little knitting circles rather than open rebellions against our newly elected president. I was on the streets. I knew different. I saw the march for what it was. These people were militant. They were marching for women, all right, just not the ones who believe human life is sacred and begins at conception; not the ones who want a strong military; and certainly not the ones who think illegal immigration is out of hand. In other words, not for any of the millions of women who had cast their votes for Donald Trump a couple of months before. Yet, they had the audacity to tell the world that they spoke for all women.

It wasn't until I got home that the irony of it all dawned on me. If you had told me when I was a little girl that I would become a prosecutor, a judge, one of the first female district attorneys in the state of New York, and then the host of a television show, only to be spit at and ridiculed during a march "for all women," I'm not sure I would have believed you. In those days, the goal was equality of opportunity. It was making sure everyone had a fair shot. The women who raised me and the women I grew up with only wanted the same opportunities and the same rights as their male counterparts. They weren't easy to get, but they fought hard. And my generation carried the same torch.

Before I was the DA of Westchester, I was an assistant DA. It was during that time that I started one of the first domestic violence units in the country. To do that I had to convince the police chiefs from forty-three municipalities in Westchester County—all men—to allow us to work with their departments. Back then, many of them didn't think domestic violence cases even belonged in the criminal justice system. They felt they were social problems, not criminal justice problems. The DA scheduled a breakfast meeting, so I could lecture on the legal requirements of the domestic violence legislation to a roomful of hardened, armed cops. Just when I was about to begin, one of chiefs said to me, "Hon, before we start can you get me a cup of coffee?" Inside I was burning. I wanted to grab him right by the throat, but an angel on my right shoulder calmed me. *Jeanine*, it said, *you've got a mission, and this meeting is not about this S.O.B. It's about victims.* "Cream and sugar?" I asked, just as sweet as can be. Then I sat down and told them what we expected and what we wanted them to do. We got their cooperation, and my unit became a national model for the prosecution of batterers and set records for convictions.

When I marched in the middle of the protestors in Washington with a cameraman in tow, I asked what they were protesting. Between curse words, they said they want equal rights for women. I asked what rights they were fighting for. None of them could come up with a straight answer. "What right does a man have that you don't?" I asked. "Just name one." My questions were met with nothing but stammering and blank stares. All along, they'd been pretending they were marching for something, when their march was nothing more than a hissy fit, thrown because someone they didn't like managed to win an election.

All they knew about Donald Trump is what the Fake Press fed them. So, they didn't know him at all. Since he was a real estate developer in Manhattan, the president has promoted the causes of women—and also promoted women. In the '80s, at a time when very few women were working in construction and development, Trump had several female development and construction project managers. while other women, if they were in the industry at all, were working in sales and marketing. He created opportunities for women in the male-dominated construction industry long before it was fashionable or socially responsible to do so. In the Trump Organization, a woman who started as a secretary or a low-level office worker could have a reasonable expectation of rising through the company's ranks within a few years. All it took was hard work and a few good ideas.

In fact, it was a woman who handled much of

Donald Trump's day-to-day business when he had too much to do. Norma Foerderer, one of Trump's most-trusted employees, started with the Trump Organization in 1981, when it was only seven or eight people in a room, and ascended the corporate ladder all the way to the boss's right-hand side. During the campaign, a former representative for Donald Trump told the *Washington Post* that Foerderer would advise Trump on everything "from what color tie to wear to whether or not he should purchase a building." When Foerderer died from a heart attack during surgery in 2013, Donald was devastated.

He hired Deirdre Rosen as a VP of human resources, Jill Martin as assistant general counsel, Louise Sunshine as an executive vice president, and Amanda Miller as head of marketing. And, of course, there's Rhona Graff, his treasured longtime personal assistant. Today, according to company representatives, there are far more women than men working in the Trump Organization. That's better than most Fortune 500 companies. It's certainly better than most of the law firms I've dealt with, and it's not the kind of thing that happens overnight. In business, Donald Trump cared about the advancement of women long before there were hashtags and half-assed marches to bring the issue into the public eye. In the years when I, as a young prosecutor, was fighting to convince judges and juries that a man didn't have the legal right to beat his wife, women at the Trump Organization were able to lead fulfilling lives at home and in the office. Equal opportunity is bred into the culture of the Trump Org, and it comes straight from the top.

For the past decade, the Trump Organization's largest deals were spearheaded by another woman, his daughter Ivanka Trump who oversaw the acquisition and development of their largest projects.

Trump had a famous line in the '80s, which I always found a little funny. Someone had asked him whether men were better than women in business. "Men are better than women," he said, going along with the joke. "But a good woman is better than ten good men." His daughter Ivanka fits this bill.

Nowhere does President Trump show more respect for women than in his relationship with his daughter, while no one is treated with more hypocrisy by the press. Let me give you an example. In March 2015, less than three months before her father announced he would run for president, *Vogue* published a flattering feature in their magazine power issue on Ivanka subtitled: "Full-speed at work and hands-on at home, Ivanka Trump knows what it means to be a modern millennial—the exact demographic she wants to dress."

Almost immediately after her father announced,

the same magazine began to publish one negative article after another about her. Where Ivanka was the poster girl for Millennials before the campaign, she was a "faux feminist" after; where she had been an entrepreneur before he announced, she was an "opportunist" after. Previously described as true to herself, once her father announced his presidency, the media claimed her views were, "hypocritical bullshit."

I'll tell you what's bullshit. Anything *Vogue* has written about Ivanka since June 16, 2015.

I've known Ivanka since she was a teenager, before she got her degree at Wharton or joined the Trump Organization, and long before she had to deal with the press. Even when she was a kid, you could tell she'd be better than a few hundred good men. When Ivanka joined her father's business in 2006 at the age twenty four, and she proved her competence every day. She'd already worked two years at an outside firm to learn the ropes of real estate, not wanting to seem as if she was taking handouts from her father and had learned a few things of her own. Within just a few years, she worked with her brothers to oversee the expansion of the core real estate business and co-found her own branch of the business, a successful management company for luxury hotels called the Trump Hotel Collection.

By the time she was a co-judge on *Celebrity Apprentice*, the press had fallen head-over-heels in love with her. She was everything a successful woman should be, they said at the time.

Fortune magazine named her one of its "40 under 40"—the magazine's famous list of the most influential young people in the business world. She helped found the Girl Up initiative at the United Nations foundation, which provides adolescent women and girls in the developing world with opportunities to succeed and thrive as leaders in their communities. She was described at the National Women's Summit as a woman "with a drive to support other women." She won the Diamond Empowerment Fund's Good Award for helping promote education in diamond-producing African nations.

In business, she received the prestigious Joseph Wharton Award For Young Leadership from the Wharton School at the University of Pennsylvania, and was given the Young Global Leader Award from the World Economic Forum, the Ace Breakthrough Award for Excellence in Accessories, and the FABB Achievement Award from the Fashion Accessories Council for her innovative brand.

Ironically, the Left most shows its bias and hypocrisy in its treatment of women—well, certain women.

While they saw Hillary Clinton as an independent woman and not held responsible for the actions of her husband Bill, Ivanka Trump was ostracized for being Donald Trump's daughter. Recently, in a *Vogue* article about fashion designer Georgina Chapman, the magazine says that she shouldn't be judged by her monster husband Harvey Weinstein. But if you're a conservative or a Trump, the rules are different. In February 2017, one month after Donald J. Trump took office, a female Nordstrom's executive proudly trumpeted that Nordstrom's would be dropping Ivanka Trump's fashion line.

The genesis of this was an online campaign started by a marketer, Shannon Coulter (no relation to Ann), who didn't much like the president. So, she decided to take it out on his daughter, creating the hashtag "grab your wallet." Her campaign sought to punish the Ivanka Trump brand for the supposed misdeeds of Ivanka's father. It was clear this was a political hit job because Ivanka's brand revenue went up 21 percent from 2015 to 2016. Six months before Donald Trump announced his candidacy for president, Ivanka was invited to open Nordstrom's new flagship department store in Vancouver where she appeared alongside the Nordstrom family and Anna Wintour of *Vogue*. If the brand had not been selling well in Nordstrom's, they wouldn't have ordered more products for the spring 2017 season.

Ironically, Ivanka is not political. Ivanka clearly cares about policy, just not Swamp politics. She admitted as much at the Republican convention saying that she was neither Republican nor Democrat. She became involved in the campaign with the intention of talking about women and their advancement; including what her father taught her, how he advanced women in his company, and what he would do to empower women in the American workplace. This has been proven to be true now that we see the lowest female unemployment rate in eighteen years.

After her father became president, she left the family business she'd been groomed to run from the time she was a little girl. (Yes, a woman groomed to run what most see as a male-dominated business by the very man these hashtagging women despise.) She left to continue to advocate for women in the workforce. She left her own business and its talented team of women, leaving her home and a comfortable life for the Washington shark tank.

Ivanka continues forging ahead in her decade-long effort to empower women in the workplace. So, to all the hashtag haters and classless women, as well as the stores that capitulate to them, I have news for you. She is stronger than you and, amazingly, is every bit as strong as her dad.

The very so-called feminists who marched to advance

strong independent women are the ones rallying to suppress a woman who epitomizes everything these women claim to champion.

I challenge them to explain their blatant hypocrisy asking Ivanka to answer for her dad, when Chelsea Clinton never has to. Chelsea is currently making the rounds for her book, *She Persisted*. Is anyone asking her about her father's many accusers, one of whom accused him of rape, as well as his consensual sex in the Oval with an intern while in office? I don't think so.

I challenge them to tell you why Melania Trump, one of the most beautiful women in the world, has been on the cover of only one women's national magazine, while Michelle Obama and Hillary Clinton were featured extensively.

Recently, one early spring Sunday, I visited Ivanka and Jared in their beautiful home in the Kalorama section of Washington. I was met at the door by Ivanka and Jared's four-year-old son Joseph who extended his hand to greet me and introduced himself. I smiled, thinking what an adorable and proper young man. Then he stunned me with a question in perfect diction: "May I get you a drink?" I turned and looked at the Secret Service agent behind me. He nodded to me, as if to say yes. I turned back, looked at Joseph, and said, "Yes, thank you!" To which he inquired, "Would you like a Shirley Temple?" I burst out laughing, and thanked him. Ivanka was dressed in a two-piece white knit outfit, looking casual yet stunning. Together, we walked into a lovely dining room with a table set for lunch. Large windows looked out on a small backyard filled with bikes, toys, and a child's jungle gym. The yard was a feature that helped sway Ivanka and Jared to take the house, she said. Having lived in Manhattan, backyards are a luxury.

Jared walked into the dining room dressed in dark slacks and light-colored casual shirt. The thing that strikes you first about him is how handsome he is in person: tall and trim, with an easy smile and piercing eyes. When you see Jared and Ivanka together, you realize how perfect they are for each other. Theirs is a respectful, loving marriage. It's obvious.

As we sat at the table, their six-year-old daughter Arabella appeared from the living room. Precocious, with her mother's eyes, and a smile like her dad's, she showed us the latest dance moves she'd learned, and recited poetry of Confucius. A born entertainer, Arabella's singing videos have already gone viral. One of them is a song she sang in Mandarin with her brother Joseph at Mar-a-Lago for Chinese president Xi. The children learned Mandarin from a Chinese nanny. The video has had millions of views in China alone.

Ivanka reminded Arabella to introduce herself, which she did with a ladylike bow. Then Joseph, who's a biological stamp of his father, came back in wearing his bicycle helmet, looking ready to hit the trail. Theodore, the baby, is still a little young for banter with adults—Ivanka was pregnant with him during the campaign. Right after he was born, his grandfather went on a winning streak across America, so Ivanka called Theodore their good luck charm!

As a spring sun poured through the windows, we drank mint lemonade and talked about life as working parents. Although they both have been blessed financially and otherwise, Ivanka and Jared worked very hard in their careers, and now in the White House, trive to raise their children in a normal, loving home.

Neither Ivanka nor Jared get the credit they deserve for what they've done in their short time as presidential advisors, and in Jared's case, on the campaign as well. Ivanka worked tirelessly to craft and pass the tax cut legislation, especially championing its working families' provisions which included the creation of the child tax credit, doubling the standard family deduction, lowering individual rates, and preserving the child and dependent care and adoption credits.

She and Jared hosted fifteen dinners at their home for legislators, urging them to vote for the bill and securing critical votes from both the House and the Senate. Whether it's her focus on economic growth and job creation, paid family leave, youth sports, championing apprenticeships and retention in Workforce Development, or global women's economic empowerment, Ivanka's focus on advancing job opportunities for all American workers is laserlike. oday there are more jobs available and unfilled than the number of unemployed. Ivanka champions vocational education for the young and older worker to fill these jobs. The federal government spends little on retraining older workers and, of course, our educational system generally stops at the age of twenty two. Ivanka is currently working on a groundbreaking initiative with CEOs of major American corporations to develop vocational education in order to bring people off the sidelines and into the workforce.

Though she doesn't get the credit she deserves in the main stream media, there's no denying the positive impact she's had on the world stage. Heads of countries around the world have invited Ivanka to speak and shared the stage with her at the W20 conference in Berlin, the Summit of the Americas in Peru, the World Assembly for Women in Japan, and the Global Entrepreneurship Summit in Hyderabad, India. At all these important events, she has been nothing short of sensational, and the perfect representative for America and the Trump White House.

Another case in point is the Winter Olympics. Along with the star turn she took there, she engaged in diplomacy at its highest level. Her private discussions and subsequent dinner at the Blue House with the South Korean President Moon Jae-in and First Lady Kim Jung-sook might very well have laid the foundation for denuclearization talks with Kim Jong-un of North Korea. It was at this dinner that she informed them of the sanctions being issued the following day by the United States against North Korea. She attended the Olympics to celebrate the world's athletes but also to act as a representative of the Trump administration. The people of South Korea were clearly charmed by her, especially how she celebrated the deep alliance between the US and South Korea.

When Ivanka first took the job as an advisor for her dad, LIBERALS were thrilled. They believed that she would talk her father out of the promises he made on the campaign trail, like a wall on the Mexican border or the defunding of Obamacare, and start promoting causes that mattered to them—causes that flew in the face of Donald Trump's agenda.

In other words, they wanted her to make her father into a liar, and blamed her when she didn't. Why is it nobody ever talked about moderating Obama out of his positions?

Leaving aside the fact that manipulating Donald Trump is about as easy as rolling a boulder up the Washington Monument, the whole idea is wrong.

LIBERALS are not paying attention to what Ivanka is doing in the West Wing. Donald Trump was elected our president because of his policies, and Ivanka has no interest in getting her father to change his stripes. What they refuse to acknowledge is that Ivanka is getting her father to add more stripes. She feels privileged and honored to serve her country and there are many areas in which she completely agrees with her father the president.

I managed to get where I am because I'm not afraid to speak out for what I believe in—perhaps too often, I'm told—and Ivanka got to where she is the same way. She's never let anyone tell her what to think or what to do. When people were telling her to study hard at boarding school, she decided to try her hand at modeling instead, just like her mother. When people expected her to join the family business straight out of Wharton, she worked at an outside firm instead. And when they told her she needed to follow the liberal crowd in New York City, she decided to use her head instead. She's advocated policies that made sense to her and joined an administration where she knew her ideas would be heard.

As soon as Ivanka joined her father's campaign, the LIBERAL knives came out. The reporters who used to write positive profiles about her, chose instead to mock her from afar and make cheap jokes at her expense, or reduce everything she does to her clothing. Here's a headline from the New York Times last November: "In India, Ivanka Trump Tried on Some Fashion Diplomacy. Was It a Good Look?" Could you imagine similar coverage of David Axelrod during the Obama years? Maybe a piece about Dick Cheney's shoes?

She's been called a "media darling" and an "adviser-in-training," and that's only in the headlines! It's similar to how reporters can never seem to reference Hope Hicks, one of President Trump's former aides, without reminding everyone that she's a former model. Even in the 1950s, this kind of coverage would smell of sexism and condescension. It's so much worse when it comes from the same outlets that used to praise Ivanka for her ambition and business acumen. What they should write is that she has impeccable credentials that she brings to her job in the West Wing: she ran a huge international real estate company and created her own eponymous clothing company worth hundreds of millions of dollars!

Once Ivanka was a role model for young women who wanted to succeed. Suddenly, now that she's speaking her mind, she's just an inexperienced little girl again, according to the Fake News media.

These are the kind of tactics that no one has ever used on a woman like Chelsea Clinton, who, as far as

I can tell, hasn't had a real job in years. Ivanka used to be quite friendly with her.

The difference between them, as I see it, is that one of these women has a father who ran a successful business empire while the other makes most of his income from donations from foreign despots. One of these women worked hard all through college and became a business executive and entrepreneur, while the other hit the speaking circuit right out of school and made money off her last name. One of these women has a father who makes bad jokes on occasion, while the other has sexually assaulted more women than anyone's ever been able to count, including an intern in the Oval Office.

One of them is viewed by the media as a champion of women. Can you guess which one?

It goes to show you that the LIBERAL Left will let you get away with anything so long as you can buy into their tactics and regurgitate their talking points. But if you believe that, say, illegal immigration is a serious problem, or that abortion is murder? Sorry, they say. That's not what women think anymore. We decided for all of them. What right does the Left have to speak for all women, to exclude women who don't share liberal views—the millions of conservative women who voted for Donald Trump? Ivanka is making sure that their views are being heard.

This kind of mindless groupthink leads to a bad place. You don't need to study history for very long to realize what happens when a group of people starts dictating what citizens are and are not allowed to believe. The struggle that Ivanka Trump is having with the mainstream media is no different than the one faced by millions of women across this country who dare to think for themselves—women who won't be told what they can and cannot believe.

LIBERALS in this country have built a platform of hatred, and anyone who's not onboard is the enemy. If you don't hate like they do, you're not a feminist. You're a racist and a Nazi. Or you're some of the vile names I got called on the streets of Washington, DC, during the women's march. Take your pick. We're sick of being called names and hearing what you're against. Tell us what you're for. Do something productive!

The sad truth is that these rich New York City liberals don't actually believe in anything. They only know what they hate. That's why no one could tell me what the women's march was about. It was only about hatred of one man—a man who, somehow, remains unaffected by it. So, they go after his daughter.

The reason LIBERALS, who once pretended to be Ivanka's friends, don't want to see illegal immigration curbed in this country is they need illegal immigrants to do jobs they won't do: to work on the floors of the factories they own, to help around their penthouse apartments for below minimum wage, to be gardeners for their Scarsdale estates. They don't want to see Donald Trump reform the international trade system because they're already making millions off the current crooked system. They can't stand the thought that it might be Donald Trump—a man who was one of them and decided to strive for something other than the standard rich-guy life in the city—who ends the strife in the Middle East or fully strips North Korea of its nuclear capability. They can't stand it because he doesn't owe them anything, he doesn't need them, and he won without them. He won because the real people of America believe in him.

So instead of doing something, the LIBERALS run back into their bubbles and hide. They cut ties with everyone who thinks differently than they do, and they funnel dirty money into Democrat campaigns, hoping it'll swing their way next time. Or they organize some kind of "women's march."

Next time they have one, I'm going to stay in the studio.

Considering what he's up against, I can't help but marvel at what President Trump has accomplished in barely over a year. He did it despite unprecedented negative news coverage, a spurious investigation based on the left's outlandish Russiagate conspiracy theory, and even resistance from some within his own party. There are times when he seems to be fighting the whole world. But he's fighting for the people who elected him; he's fighting for America. This is the Trump presidency you haven't been told about. And it's going to go on winning, the Swamp be damned.

CHAPTER THIRTEEN

The Trump Boomerang

The anti-Trump hate brigade keeps coming up with new and more ridiculous ways to attack the president, finding ways to not only spin his spectacular accomplishments negative, but to disparage even his most innocuous comments or actions as proof he is evil incarnate. Ironically, whenever they point an accusatory finger at him, as the saying goes, there are three more fingers pointed back at themselves. Like a boomerang, every unhinged hate campaign against the president eventually circles back and hits the hater square in the forehead.

The NFL Boomerang

Donald Trump took on the NFL in his take-no-prisoners fashion, calling out Colin Kaepernick and other players taking a knee during our national anthem by saying "Get that S.O.B. off the field right

now, he's fired, he's fired!" He was accused of everything from creating a divisive controversy to outright
racism. David Remnick of the *New Yorker* called it
"racial demagoguery." Charles Blow of the *New York
Times* opined: "Trump is a racist. Period." It's outrageous that when the President of the United States
stands up for honoring the National Anthem, he's
called a racist!

NFL commissioner Roger Goodell called the president's comments "divisive," adding they demonstrated
"an unfortunate lack of respect for the NFL and all
our players." He added that the president exhibited a
failure to understand the overwhelming force for good
the NFL and its players represent. The assistant executive director of the NFL mouthed off that no one
should have to choose a job that forces them to sur-
render their rights, as if following their employers'
policies to respect our flag and national anthem was
surrendering their rights.

Suddenly, all these guys want to stand up or take
a knee for social justice? When was the last time they
voted, sat on a jury, joined a school board, wrote a letter to Congress, or fought for laws to help the people for whom they supposedly want justice? Instead
of honoring the nation that allowed them to shine
and become financially prosperous, they chose to dis-
respect our flag, inspiring eight-year-olds who hold

them up as heroes to do the same. In high school football games across the country, young players took a knee, thinking they were "cool."

The boomerang was almost immediate. Americans who watched sports to get away from day-to-day stresses, financial woes—and yes, politics—had had enough.

The NFL suffered ratings and attendance losses. Fans canceled their subscriptions and burned their season tickets and team jerseys.[1] Stations that broadcast NFL games all took a hit. Television ratings on games dropped between 13 and 30 percent,[2] costing the NFL hundreds of millions of dollars. As much as they loved football, Americans were angry enough to not watch the game because Goodell, Kaepernick, and company forced them to choose between football and the flag. True Americans chose the flag.

But the Trump boomerang hit more than the franchises and the game. As the NFL kept going down the rabbit hole, with coaches beholden to misguided players and the almighty dollar, Americans made an end run to the Right.

The 2017 World Series was a display of Americanism we hadn't seen in decades. The singing of "God Bless America" by a Coast Guard petty officer preceded the national anthem. At some NASCAR races, the Pledge of Allegiance was recited, including US Olympic team members at one race.[3]

It was a classic boomerang. The NFL took on the president and they were the ones who suffered, not for their phony patriotism as social justice warriors, but for their lack of real patriotism, period.

The Papal Boomerang

During the 2016 campaign, as Donald Trump touted his plan to build a wall between the US southern border and Mexico, Pope Francis decided to chime in from the other side of the world.

Although he did not mention Trump by name, the Pope said societies should build bridges, not walls, to encourage good relations among people—a clear Trump reference. He added, "a Christian can never say 'I'll make you pay for that.' Never! that is not a Christian gesture." Again, that was clearly referring to Trump having said that Mexico would pay for the wall.

Catholics across America panicked and started to wonder if a vote for Trump would be one against the church.

Most politicians would have softened the wall message, or eliminated it, to steer clear of any perceived confrontation with the leader of the Catholic Church. After all, there are certain things that just aren't done.

Not Trump. He responded clearly and firmly, uncharacteristically sticking to his script, "For a religious leader to question a person's faith is disgraceful."

Donald Trump knew any fight with the leader of 1.2 billion Catholics, regardless of whether he won, would not be to his benefit. But he also knew that he couldn't allow the Pope's comments to go unanswered.

The answer was in the form of a tweet. It was a picture of the Vatican, highlighting the wall surrounding the compound adding, "Amazing comments from the Pope—considering Vatican City is 100% surrounded by a massive wall."

Catholics who had held their breath, worried that they might not be able to vote for Trump because of the Pope's message, breathed a sigh of relief. The point was made.

Trump not only didn't lose many votes; he got 50 percent of the Catholic vote to Hillary's 46 percent.

The Trump boomerang struck again.

The Minority Boomerang

The mainstream media and the Left has excoriated anyone of color who says anything remotely positive about Trump. The backlash is always immediate, swift, and severe. In fact, it's so predictable that none dare to bring up anything pro-Trump. They are afraid to even mention that African American and Hispanic employment are at an all-time high.

Kanye West, a cultural leader in the African-American community, has broken this intimidated silence. In a series of social media tweets, West posted a photo of himself wearing a "Make America Great" hat and commenting on his fondness for Trump. This reportedly cost him the loss of nine million followers and resulted in enormous social media criticism.

To his credit, West, a personal friend of the president, pushed back defiantly. He said people didn't have to agree with Trump and that "no 'mob' can't make me not love him," adding, "We are both dragon energy. He is my brother. I love everyone. I don't agree with everything anyone does. That's what makes us individuals. And we have the right to independent thought."

The more the totalitarian Left pushed back against him, the more defiant Kanye became. His pro-Trump message started to permeate through minority communities.

Kanye doubled down. He criticized African-American president Barack Obama. "Obama was in office for eight years and nothing in Chicago changed," he said.

Then, another famous African-American rapper, Chance the Rapper, came to Kanye's defense on social media. "Black people don't have to be Democrats!"

The pro-Trump message's reach expanded exponentially.

In retrospect, even the claim Kanye lost millions of followers was just fake news to intimidate pro-Trump messengers. Twitter later confirmed Kanye remained at about twenty-seven million followers.

The forty-eight-hour frenzy not only boomeranged to Trump's advantage, but instantly destroyed the fear that prevented so many from discussing Trump's "what have you got to lose" message.

The African-American community, suppressed for so long by Democrats who quashed any sign of agreement with a Republican politician, especially one called Donald Trump, had turned around and boomeranged.

The North Korea Boomerang

When President Trump stood in front of the UN General Assembly on September 19, 2017, and called Kim Jong-un "Rocket Man," the Left blew its cork. The *New Yorker* said the president's remark was "perfectly engineered to trigger Kim's paranoia and animosity." The *Washington Post* said Trump had issued, "a reckless threat of war." So-called foreign policy experts from Columbia University and other liberal mental institutions called the president's speech "terrifying" and "delusional."

And when Kim stated a "Nuclear button is on my desk at all times," our president didn't huddle in some corner of the White House with advisers and generals, like milquetoast Obama would have done. He didn't make empty proclamations like Obama's "red line." He didn't send Hillary Clinton or John Kerry to do his dirty work. No, President Trump took matters into his own hands and gave Kim something to think about:

"North Korean Leader Kim Jong-un just stated that the 'Nuclear Button is on his desk at all times.' Will someone from his depleted and food starved regime please inform him that I too have a Nuclear Button, but it is a much bigger & more powerful one than his, and my Button works!"

How did our press respond to a president who has the balls to stand up for America? The *New York Times* called him a "ranting old guy with nukes." The *Washington Post* told us, "This is how nuclear war with North Korea would unfold." The *New Yorker* warned us that, "Trump's taunts will almost certainly compel North Korea to respond in words or actions."

Lo and behold, the old Trump Boomerang came around again. As of this writing, North and South Korea are in talks to formally end the war between them and to accomplish the denuclearization of the North. Kim Jong-un suspended his provocative missile tests and became the first North Korean leader to set foot into South Korea. David Sanger, the *New York Times'* national security correspondent said Trump deserves "enormous credit" for the progress in North Korea. Even Bill Clinton's UN ambassador, Bill Richardson, thinks that the president's handling of North Korea "could pay dividends."

In the press and the halls of Congress there are whispers of a Nobel Prize for President Trump. Wouldn't that be something? And unlike Obama, who received his prize without doing anything and later embroiled America in several disastrous new conflicts, Trump's would be deserved.

The Comey Boomerang

Perhaps the most dramatic example of the boomerang effect is what happened to James "Cardinal" Comey, the sanctimonious former director of the FBI who earned his unflattering nickname by holding himself up as an incorruptible, straight-arrow lawman who defended the rule of law against the forces of evil, regardless of politics.

This six-foot, eight-inch stuffed suit was so determined to ensnare President Trump that he wrote detailed memos purporting to accurately document each conversation he had with the president. But rather than damaging the president, the now-released memos have boomeranged on Comey, exposing him for the LIAR, LEAKER and LIBERAL we always knew he was. Comey repeatedly lied to or misled the president, while leaking a supposedly classified memo to his friend at Columbia, Professor Dan Richman.

Not only did the memos expose Comey, they exposed the president, but not in the way the president's enemies wished they would have. It's clear from the content of these memos the president never attempted to obstruct justice in any way. In fact, they show he was eager for his campaign to be investigated for any evidence of collusion with Russia. The memos also show Comey repeatedly assured the president the FBI wasn't investigating him—technically not a lie—while at the same time leaking the memos in the hopes a special prosecutor would be appointed to do just that.

Rather than incriminate the president, Comey's memos show their author to be a hypocritical, self-serving weasel, and are a key look into the heart of the Deep State conspiracy to bring down the Trump presidency. Like every other hateful attack on this man who truly loves his country, Comey's lying, leaking, and scheming have come back around to hit him instead of their target. And his boomerang may have cuffs attached to it.

If he weren't a personal friend, I'd almost wish the president's deranged opponents would keep coming up with new ways to attack him. Every time they do, Donald Trump and America ends up winning. But regardless of my best wishes, we can expect the hate to continue. I expect Donald Trump to keep on overcoming adversity, the way he did throughout his extraordinary business career.

CHAPTER FOURTEEN

Some Closing Thoughts

In the Museum of the Bible in Washington, DC, there is a special effects exhibit that "soars" you through the city to see biblical texts written on the monuments of our nation's capital. The ride is called "Hidden in Plain Sight," and I've taken it many times. You should, too, when you visit Washington. Although many people seemed to have forgotten, "In God We Trust" is still the official motto of this country.

One of my favorite parts of the ride is when it flies you right into the Jefferson Memorial. Etched into one of the Vermont marble walls are the words: "Indeed I tremble for my country when I reflect that God is just, that His justice cannot sleep forever."

There are people who will tell you there isn't a Deep State. They'll say the idea of entrenched officials trying to overthrow a duly-elected president is just a wacky conspiracy theory invented by a bunch of conservative wingnuts. They'll tell you Cardinal Comey is as good and truthful as he looks—just read his book, they'll say—and that the president had no right to fire him. They'll say the upper echelon of the FBI is not in cahoots against Donald Trump, even though, as of this writing, Andrew McCabe has asked for immunity in exchange for his testimony to the Senate Judiciary Committee. And they'll say President Obama wasn't involved in weaponizing the FBI against the Trump campaign, even though a September 2, 2016 text from Lisa Page to Peter Strzok says, "potus wants to know everything we're doing."

They'll tell you the Clinton Foundation is as honest as the day is long—that the Uranium One sale was a legitimate business deal.

They'll say the *New York Times* and the *Washington Post* print only the gospel truth and that Don Lemon, Anderson Cooper, and Rachel Maddow are reincarnations of Walter Cronkite.

They'll say Christopher Steele's discredited dossier wasn't fake, Hollywood isn't hypocritical, and President Obama was a great president.

They'll tell you the Mueller investigation in not a witch hunt.

They'll tell you all of this—swear to it, in fact—despite a mountain of evidence to the contrary.

They are wrong and misguided. Brainwashed by

an avalanche of disinformation that buries them day in and day out, many of them don't know any better. It's unfortunate. They are incapable of seeing that powerful people put vast amounts of money behind the Fake News, the marches, and the protests.

Those who have orchestrated this conspiracy, the ones who pull all the levers, who seek to steal the presidency, be warned. America is coming for you!

As John Adams once said "Facts are stubborn things; and whatever may be our wishes, our inclinations, or the dictates of our passion, they cannot alter the state of facts and evidence."

I've seen too many leaks of classified information funneled straight to liberal newspapers and cable television networks. I've watched too many political hacks from the RNC who have tried to install their friends and cronies in the Trump White House to keep what's left of their chokehold on our political system. I've seen too many corrupt bureaucrats at the FBI, NSA, and agencies you've hardly heard of plot daily to undercut the agenda of Donald Trump. I've heard too much crap from Hollywood hypocrites and seen too many crooked politicians like the Clintons enrich themselves at the expense of the American people.

I've watched for too long as LIARS, LEAKERS, and LIBERALS try to take what isn't theirs.

It must stop here.

332   LIARS, LEAKERS, AND LIBERALS

As of this writing, the midterm elections are still months away. Fake News tells you the Republican Party is about to be swallowed by a "blue wave." They say the House is a goner, and the slim, one-vote majority in the Senate hangs by a thread.

The Democrats, led by Nancy Pelosi and Chuck Schumer, are rubbing their hands. Undoubtedly, House Democrats and the Deep State are plotting the end game for the Trump presidency. If the Democrats take the Senate, House, or both, Donald Trump's agenda to continue to make America great again is dead on arrival. A Democrat majority in the Senate would also essentially remove the president's ability to appoint Supreme Court justices. As of this writing, rumors swirl that Justice Kennedy is about to retire, and since Justice Ginsberg is eighty-five, she may also be retiring soon. A Democrat-controlled Senate could hold two vacancies on the Supreme Court open indefinitely.

On the local level, the stakes are just as high. As of right now, Republicans control thirty-three governorships and an overwhelming number of state legislatures, seventeen of which are veto-proof supermajorities. But there are thirty-six races for governor this coming election, and half of the state Senate seats, and nearly all the state lower house seats are in play.

There's also the party affiliation of thirty-five state

attorneys general at stake. Party control of the state AG's office is a *big* thing. Before he was accused of abuse that included slapping and choking women, and was forced to resign, New York State's attorney general, Eric Schneiderman did plenty of damage. He took more than a hundred legal (or administrative) actions against the Trump administration and congressional Republicans. That's just *one* state! This is trench warfare. Every state house that turns from red to blue means liberal legislation and a direct hit on conservative values. Every state attorney general we lose means lawsuits aimed at Trump's policies.

As consequential as all that is, the big enchilada has nothing to do with any election. In fact, it's the exact opposite. If the Democrat Party takes the House, you can bet a vote for impeachment happens immediately after swearing-in ceremonies on January 3, 2019.

I want you to picture a country where there are jobs for just about anyone who wants one. Picture an America where business prospers and families grow in safe communities. Picture parents standing on the front steps, waving their kids off to college. Picture a military that is strong and keeps us safe. Imagine a country that gets a fair shake in global trade, and the respect of our allies and, maybe more importantly, from the countries who are not our allies. Picture an America that is great again.

Under Donald Trump's leadership, we're already well on our way to making it a reality. As the president said to me, "2019 will be another great year, Jeanine. We're building the wall and rebuilding the infrastructure of our beautiful country."

Now picture someone trying to take that all away from you. Picture the elitist, globalist economy coming back. Picture the establishment back in control of your life, your liberty and pursuing its happiness at the expense of yours. Picture an unfettered Deep State, bigger and badder than ever, without a president calling them out daily for their abuses of power. Picture the politically correct insanity run amok on college campuses becoming the law of the land.

That, ladies and gentlemen, is what's at stake. The future of our children and their children depend on your actions. They can inherit a nation whose government is dedicated to securing their inalienable rights; or they can be serfs on the globalists' plantation, with a diminishing standard of living, neighborhoods rife with imported crime, and "hate speech" laws to punish them lest they dare to complain.

That's the America Donald Trump's enemies—our enemies—have in mind. They must be stopped.

Justice cannot and will not sleep forever.

Acknowledgments

Writing a book about politics with Donald Trump in the White House is like trying to build a sand castle in a hurricane. No one can keep up with the man! So, I needed some help.

My thanks to Al Pirro for his never-ending insight and assistance, especially in reconstructing our early years with the Trumps. Thanks for jumping on a plane and being there whenever and wherever circumstances required it. Thanks also to his assistant of many years, Deborah Trevorah. She is so unflappable, she amazes me.

To Kate Hartson, editorial director at Center Street who traipsed to DC with me and waited in lines at the White House on freezing cold days, always with a smile, I am grateful. I am even more grateful for her editorial guidance, perseverance and patience. To the whole team at Hachette, especially publisher Rolf Zettersten, vice president of marketing, Patsy Jones, and vice president of sales, Billy Clark, thank you. I am proud to be published by your house.

To Brian McDonald and Tom Mullen, many thanks

for your research and fastidious attention to detail as well as your availability at all hours, given my crazy schedule.

Thanks also to David Vigliano and Steve Carlis for pushing and pushing me to put this experience on paper.

Finally, hugs and kisses to Sir Lancelot for always being there—with me, for me, and by me. Standard poodles are the best.

Endnotes

CHAPTER 2: LYING, LIBERAL FAKE NEWS, AND FICTION

1. Paul Krugman, "What Happened on Election Day: Paul Krugman: The Economic Fallout," *New York Times*, November 9, 2016. https://www.nytimes.com/interactive/projects/cp/opinion/election-night-2016/paul-krugman-the-economic-fallout.

2. Brian Ross, Matthew Mosk, and Josh Margolin, "Flynn Prepared to Testify That Trump Directed Him to Contact Russians About ISIS, Confidant Says," ABC News, December 1, 2017, http://abcnews.go.com/Politics/michael-flynn-charged-making-false-statements-fbi-documents/story?id=50849354.

3. "ABC News Statement on Michael Flynn Report," ABC News, December 2, 2017, http://abcnews.go.com/US/abc-news-statement-michael-flynn-report/story?id=51536475.

4. Brian Flood, "ABC Demotes Brian Ross After Bungled Report on Trump, Russia," Fox News, January 5, 2018, http://www.foxnews.com/entertainment/2018/01/05/abc-demotes-brian-ross-after-bungled-report-on-trump-russia.html.

5. Manu Raju and Jeremy Herb, "Email Pointed Trump Campaign to WikiLeaks Documents," CNN, December 8, 2017, https://edition.cnn.com/2017/12/08/politics/email-effort-give-trump-campaign-wikileaks-documents/index.html.

6. Rosalind S. Helderman and Tom Hamburger, "Email Pointed Trump Campaign to WikiLeaks Documents That Were Already Public," *Washington Post*, December 8, 2017, https://www .washingtonpost.com/politics/email-offering-trump-campaign -wikileaks-documents-referred-to-information-already-public/ 2017/12/08/61dc2356-dc37-11e7-a841-2066faf731ef_story.html? utm_term=.c8941406daa6.

7. Chris Cilliza, "Yes, Mr. President, There Is Total Chaos in Your White House," CNN, March 6, 2018, https://www.cnn.com/ 2018/03/06/politics/trump-chaos-analysis/index.html/

8. Christine Wang, "Rosenstein: No Allegation of American Involvement or Election Impact—In This Particular Indictment," CNBC, February 16, 2018, https://www.cnbc.com/2018/02/16/ deputy-ag-rod-rosenstein-on-grand-jury-indictment-of-russians .html.

9. Mike Allen. "A huge clue about Mueller's endgame." AxiosAM Newsletter, March 19, 2018. https://www.axios.com/robert -mueller-investigation-obstruction-justice-collusion-2128e27f -bbb6-4b82-9e28-c6f1244fb9e3.html.

10. William E. Geist, "ABOUT NEW YORK; Pssst, Here's a Secret: Trump Rebuilds Ice Rink," *New York Times*, November 15, 1986, https://www.nytimes.com/1986/11/15/nyregion/about-new-york -pssst-here-s-a-secret-trump-rebuilds-ice-rink.html.

11. James Rosen, "Mugger's Trumped," *Daily News*, November 20, 1991, http://truthfeed.com/flashback-that-time-trump-heroically -stopped-a-mugger/5909/.

12. Tom Huddleston, Jr., "The *New York Times* Has 132,000 Reasons to Thank Donald Trump," *Fortune*, November 29, 2016, http:// fortune.com/2016/11/29/new-york-times-subscribers-donald-trump.

13. Ken Doctor. "Trump Bump Grows Into Subscription Surge – and Not Just for the New York Times." Thestreet.com. March 3, 2018. https://www.thestreet.com/story/14024114/1/trump-bump-grows -into-subscription-surge.html

14. Margaret Sullivan, "The Disconnect on Anonymous Sources," *New York Times*, October 12, 2013, https://www.nytimes.com/2013/ 10/13/opinion/sunday/the-public-editor-the-disconnect-on -anonymous-sources.html.

15. Claire Atkinson, "Trump's Right: His Media Coverage Is Mostly Negative," NBC News, October 2, 2017, https://www.nbcnews .com/politics/donald-trump/trump-s-right-his-media-coverage -mostly-negative-n806681.

CHAPTER 3: LYING, LIBERAL HOLLYWOOD HYPOCRITES

1. Jennifer Hansler. "Michelle Obama: 'Any woman who voted against Hillary Clinton voted against their own voice.' CNN, September 27, 2017. https://www.cnn.com/2017/09/27/politics/michelle-obama -women-voters/index.html

CHAPTER 4: LYING LIBERAL RINOS

1. Kelly Phillips Erb, "What's Included (and What's Not) in the $1.3 Trillion Omnibus Bill," *Forbes*, March 24, 2018, https://www .forbes.com/sites/kellyphillipserb/2018/03/24/whats-included -and-whats-not-in-the-1-3-trillion-omnibus-bill/#6b2f27f4ff4c.

2. Benjamin Siegel, "McConnell, Ryan Say Congress Will Pay for Trump's $12B Border Wall," ABC News, January 26, 2017, http://abcnews.go.com/Politics/mcconnell-ryan-congress-pay -trumps-12b-border-wall/story? id=45063195.

3. Justin Fishel, John Parkinson, Riley Beggin, Jordyn Phelps, Maryalice Parks, and Cecilia Vega, "Ryan Pulls 'Fundamentally Flawed' GOP Health Care Bill Following Call from Trump," ABC News, March 24, 2017, http://abcnews.go.com/Politics/ryan-pulls-gop-health-care-bill-call-trump/story?id=46346773.

4. Jim Tice, "Army Shrinks to Smallest Level Since Before World War II," *Army Times*, May 7, 2016, https://www.armytimes.com/news/your-army/2016/05/07/army-shrinks-to-smallest-level-since-before-world-war-ii.

5. Christian Davenport, "Congress Boosts Funds for Fighter Jets, Missile Defense in Military Spending Spree," *Washington Post*, March 23, 2018, https://www.washingtonpost.com/business/economy/congress-boosts-money-for-fighter-jets-missile-defense-in-military-spending-spree/2018/03/23/98347796-2e08-11e8-b0b0-f706877db618_story.html?utm_term=.a11523cc4972.

6. Debra Goldschmidt and Ashley Strickland, "Planned Parenthood: Fast Facts and Revealing Numbers," CNN, August 1, 2017, https://www.cnn.com/2015/08/04/health/planned-parenthood-by-the-numbers/index.html.

7. Peter Hasson, "BROKEN PROMISE: Trump, GOP Congress Give Planned Parenthood $500 Million in Taxpayer Funds," *The Daily Caller*, March 23, 2018, http://dailycaller.com/2018/03/23/trump-gop-omnibus-planned-parenthood.

8. Tessa Berenson, "Reminder: The House Voted to Repeal Obamacare More Than 50 Times," *Time*, March 4, 2017, http://time.com/4712725/ahca-house-repeal-votes-obamacare.

9. Bridget Johnson, "McConnell: Trump's 'Drain the Swamp' Term-Limits Vow Going Nowhere in the Senate," PJ Media, November 9, 2016, https://pjmedia.com/news-and-politics/2016/11/09/

mcconnell-trumps-drain-the-swamp-term-limits-vow-going
-nowhere-in-the-senate/1/.

10. Ali Rogin, "Senate Leader McConnell Cautions Trump on Travel
    Ban, Warns Against 'Religious' Tests," ABC News, January 29,
    2017, http://abcnews.go.com/Politics/senate-leader-mcconnell
    -cautions-trump-travel-ban-warns/story?id=45112817.

11. Kyle Blaine and Julia Horowitz, "How the Trump Administration
    Chose the 7 Countries in the Immigration Executive Order," CNN,
    January 30, 2017, https://www.cnn.com/2017/01/29/politics/how
    -the-trump-administration-chose-the-7-countries/index.html.

12. Katie Reilly, "Read Paul Ryan's Speech Calling Donald Trump's
    Victory the 'Most Incredible Political Feat,'" *Time*, November
    9, 2016, http://time.com/4564832/paul-ryan-speech-donald-trump
    -election/.

13. Eric Bradner, "Ryan: 'We Are Not Planning on Erecting a
    Deportation Force,'" CNN, November 13, 2016, https://edition
    .cnn.com/2016/11/13/politics/paul-ryan-donald-trump
    -obamacare-deportation-force/index.html.

14. Feliks Garcia, "How Donald Trump's Victory Has Devastated the
    US Political System, in Two Quotes," *The Independent*, November
    13, 2016, http://www.independent.co.uk/news/world/americas/
    donald-trump-immigration-deportation-paul-ryan-president-elect
    -wall-video-watch-a7415296.html.

15. Max Ehrenfreund, "Paul Ryan Might Not Be Happy About the
    First Item on the Agenda in Trump's Victory Speech," *Washington
    Post*, November 9, 2016. https://www.washingtonpost.com/news/
    wonk/wp/2016/11/09/paul-ryan-might-not-be-happy-about-the
    -first-item-on-the-agenda-in-trumps-victory-speech/?utm_term=
    .beef4012fc55.

16. Lisa Mascaro, "Speaker Ryan 'Does Not Agree' with Trump's Pardon of Arpaio," *Los Angeles Times*, August 27, 2017, http://www .latimes.com/politics/washington/la-na-essential-washington-updates -speaker-ryan-does-not-agree-with-1503856893-htmlstory.html.

17. Kevin Breuninger, "House Speaker Ryan Opposes Trump's Tariffs, Warns of 'Unintended Consequences,'" CNBC, March 8, 2018, https://www.cnbc.com/2018/03/08/house-speaker-ryan-opposes -trumps-tariffs-warns-of-unintended-consequences.html.

18. Howard Blum, "How Ex-Spy Christopher Steele Compiled His Explosive Trump-Russia Dossier," *Vanity Fair*, March 30, 2017, https://www.vanityfair.com/news/2017/03/how-the-explosive -russian-dossier-was-compiled-christopher-steele.

19. Dan Nowicki and Ronald J. Hansen, "John McCain Decries Memo Release: 'We Are Doing Putin's Job for Him,'" *USA Today*, February 2, 2018, https://www.usatoday.com/story/news/ politics/2018/02/02/mccain-nunes-memo-statement/301932002.

20. Julia Manchester, "McCain Associate Invokes Fifth Amendment on Trump Dossier Sources: Report," The Hill, February 22, 2018, http://thehill.com/blogs/blog-briefing-room/news/375205 -mccain-associate-invokes-fifth-amendment-on-trump-dossier.

CHAPTER 5: LIBERAL SANCTUARY CITIES

1. "Remarks by President Trump at Law Enforcement Roundtable on Sanctuary Cities," White House, March 20, 2018, https:// www.whitehouse.gov/briefings-statements/remarks-president -trump-law-enforcement-roundtable-sanctuary-cities.

2. Cleve R. Wootson, Jr. "Widespread panic as Oakland mayor warns sanctuary city of an ICE sweep" *Washington Post*, February 26, 2018, https://www.washingtonpost.com/news/post-nation/

wp/2018/02/25/oaklands-mayor-just-warned-the-sanctuary-city
-about-a-potential-ice-raid/?utm_term=.ada8ec4d852d.

CHAPTER 6: LYING, LEAKING, LIBERAL LEADERSHIP

1. Tal Kopan, "Polygraph Panic: CIA Director Fretted His Vote for Communist," CNN, September 15, 2016, https://www .cnn.com/2016/09/15/politics/john-brennan-cia-communist -vote.

2. Fred Fleitz, "Trump Will Face a Huge Challenge with U.S. Intelligence If He Wins," *National Review*, August 18, 2016, https://www.nationalreview.com/2016/08/ donald-trumps-right-cia-intelligence-politicized-left.

3. Mark Mazzetti and Carl Hulse, "Inquiry by C.I.A. Affirms It Spied on Senate Panel," *New York Times*, July 31, 2014, https:// www.nytimes.com/2014/08/01/world/senate-intelligence -commitee-cia-interrogation-report.html.

4. Awr Hawkins, "Brennan Accused of Involvement in Altered Benghazi Talking Points," Breitbart News, February 27, 2013, http://www.breitbart.com/national-security/2013/02/27/white -house-releases-more-benghazi-information-gop-sees-brennan-s -hand-in-cover-up.

5. Greg Miller, Ellen Nakashima, and Adam Entous, "Obama's Secret Struggle To Punish Russia For Putin's Election Assault," *Washington Post*, June 23, 2017, https://www .washingtonpost.com/graphics/2017/ world/national-security/ obama-putin-election-hacking/?utm_term=.3e8979cc071e.

6. Mark Mazzetti, "Donald Trump and Hillary Clinton to Get Intelligence Briefings," *New York Times*, July 28, 2016, https://

www.nytimes.com/2016/07/29/us/politics/donald-trump-hillary
-clinton-intelligence-briefings.html.

7. *Washington Post* Staff, "Full Transcript: FBI Director James
   Comey Testifies on Russian Interference in 2016 Election,"
   Washington Post, March 20, 2017, https://www.washingtonpost
   .com/news/post-politics/wp/2017/03/20/full-transcript-fbi
   -director-james-comey-testifies-on-russian-interference-in-2016
   -election/?utm_term=.aefc2895a558.

8. Alex Pappas, "Senators Flag 'Unusual' Susan Rice Email on
   Russia Probe from Inauguration Day," Fox News, February 12,
   2018, http://www.foxnews.com/politics/2018/02/12/senators
   -flag-unusual-susan-rice-email-on-russia-probe-from-inauguration
   -day.html.

9. Susan Power, "Bystanders to Genocide," *The Atlantic*, September
   2001, https://www.theatlantic.com/magazine/archive/2001/09/
   bystanders-to-genocide/304571.

10. Dennis Ross, "How Obama Got to 'Yes' on Iran: The Inside Story,"
    Politico, October 8, 2015, https://www.politico.com/magazine/
    story/2015/10/iran-deal-susan-rice-israel-213227.

11. Politico Staff, "The Full Ginsburg," Politico, May 15, 2013, https://
    www.politico.com/gallery/the-full-ginsburg?slide=0.

12. https://www.nytimes.com/2014/06/02/us/politics/bowe-bergdahl
    .html

13. Cheryl K. Chumley. "Susan Rice sought 'detailed spreadsheets'
    on Trump aide calls: Report." *The Washington Times*, April 4,
    2017. https://www.washingtontimes.com/news/2017/apr/4/
    susan-rice-wanted-detailed-spreadsheets-trump-aide/

14. Ellen Nakashima and Greg Miller, "FBI Reviewed Flynn's Calls
    with Russian Ambassador but Found Nothing Illicit," *Washington*

Post, January 23, 2017, https://www.washingtonpost.com/
world/national-security/fbi-reviewed-flynns-calls-with-russian
-ambassador-but-found-nothing-illicit/2017/01/23/aa83879a-e1ae
-11e6-a547-5fb9411d332c_story.html?utm_term=.d0d78e
228ed0.

15. House Permanent Select Committee on Intelligence, FISA
Amendments Reauthorization Act of 2017, S. 139 as amended,
https://intelligence.house.gov/fisa-702.

16. Washington Post Staff, "Full Transcript: Sally Yates and James
Clapper Testify on Russian Election Interference, *Washington Post*,
May 8, 2017, https://www.washingtonpost.com/news/post-politics/
wp/2017/05/08/full-transcript-sally-yates-and-james-clapper-testify
-on-russian-election-interference/?utm_term=.97b2162bdb09.

17. "U.S. Interests at the United Nations," CSPAN, June 16, 2015,
https://www.c-span.org/video/?326583-1/ambassador-samantha
-power-testimony-us-interests-un.

18. Ibid.

19. https://www.judicialwatch.org/press-room/press-releases/judicial
-watch-sues-state-department-samantha-powers-unmasking
-documents.

20. https://www.archives.gov/about/laws/appendix/13489.html

21. Scott Shane, "Court Unbraided NSA On Its Use of Call-Log
Data, *New York Times*, September 10, 2013, http://www.nytimes
.com/2013/09/11/us/court-upbraided-nsa-on-its-use-of-call-log
-data.html?pagewanted=all.

22. Charlie Savage, "NSA Gets More Latitude To Share Intercepted
Communications. *New York Times*, January 12, 2017, https://
www.nytimes.com/2017/01/12/us/politics/nsa-gets-more-latitude
-to-share-intercepted-communications.html

23. United States v. Stephen Jin-Woo Kim, No. 10-225 (CKK)
    https://fas.org/sgp/jud/kim/plea.pdf

24. Annie Gown, "Clinton says 'follow the money' in the Trump-
    Putin relationship," *Washington Post*, March 12, 2018, https://
    www.washingtonpost.com/news/worldviews/wp/2018/03/12/
    hillary-clinton-says-follow-the-money-in-the-trump-putin
    -bromance/?utm_term=.1f3b72647723.

25. Matt Zapotosky and Devlin Barrett, "FBI Has Been Investigating
    Clinton Foundation for Months," *Washington Post*, January 5, 2018,
    https://www.washingtonpost.com/world/national-security/the-fbi
    -is-investigating-the-clinton-foundation/2018/01/05/1aca0d4a
    -f1cf-11e7-97bf-bba379b809ab_story.html?utm_term=.6aeca
    4979ace.

26. William K. Rashbaum, J. David Goodman, and William Neuman
    "Why Mayor de Blasio Is Facing So Many Investigations,"
    New York Times, April 28, 2016, https://www.nytimes.com/
    2016/04/29/nyregion/the-de-blasio-inquiries-a-recap-and-whats
    -next.html.

27. Tom Hamburger, Rosalind S. Helderman, and Any
    Narayanswamy, "The Clintons, a Luxury Jet and Their $100
    Million Donor from Canada," *Washington Post*, May 3, 2015,
    https://www.washingtonpost.com/politics/the-clintons-a-luxury
    -jet-and-their-100-million-donor/2015/05/03/688051d0-ecef
    -11e4-8abc-d6aa3bad79dd_story.html?utm_term=.3e0afb
    9d4acc.

28. Harriet Sinclair. "Fox Host Told Trump to Appoint Special
    Counsel to Investigate Clinton at Private Meeting with President."
    Newsweek, November 14, 2017. http://www.newsweek.com/
    fox-host-told-trump-appoint-special-counsel-clinton-private
    -meeting-711542

CHAPTER 7: LYING, LEAKING, LIBERAL LAW ENFORCEMENT

1. Glenn Harlan Reynolds, "Florida Shooting Yet Another Government Failure to Keep Us Safe: Glenn Reynolds," *USA Today*, February 25, 2018, https://www.usatoday.com/story/opinion/2018/02/25/florida-shooting-yet-another-government-failure-keep-us-safe-glenn-reynolds-column/371372002/.

2. Tammy Bruce, "The FBI and Pulse Nightclub Shooter Omar Mateen," *Washington Times*, March 28, 2018, https://www.washingtontimes.com/news/2018/mar/28/the-fbi-and-omar-mateen-pulse-nightclub-shooter.

3. Dan Barry, Serge F. Kovaleski, and Juliet Macur, "As F.B.I. Took a Year to Pursue the Nassar Case, Dozens Say They Were Molested," *New York Times*, February 3, 2018, https://www.nytimes.com/2018/02/03/sports/nassar-fbi.html?mtrref=www.google.com.

4. Peter Helsel, "McCabe Took Notes of Interactions with Trump, Notes Turned Over to Mueller," NBC News, March 17, 2018, https://www.nbcnews.com/politics/politics-news/mccabe-took-notes-interactions-trump-notes-turned-over-mueller-n857621.

5. Laura Jarrett and Pamela Brown, "Ex-FBI Deputy Director Andrew McCabe Is Fired—and Fires Back," CNN, March 17, 2018, https://www.cnn.com/2018/03/16/politics/andrew-mccabe-fired/index.html.

6. William McGurn. "McCabe, the New 'Deep Throat'." *The Wall Street Journal*, April 16, 2018. https://www.wsj.com/articles/mccabe-the-new-deep-throat-1523915645

7. Matt Zapotosky, "FBI Disciplinary Office Recommends Firing Former Deputy Director Andrew McCabe," *Washington Post*,

March 14, 2018, https://www.washingtonpost.com/world/
national-security/fbi-disciplinary-office-recommends-firing
-former-deputy-director-andrew-mccabe/2018/03/14/c1d0dc1a
-208a-11e8-86f6-54bfff693d2b_story.html?utm_term=.a4293eb
9be1a.

8. John Solomon, "Comey's Private Memos on Trump Conversations
Contained Classified Material," The Hill, July 9, 2017, http://
thehill.com/policy/national-security/341225-comeys-private
-memos-on-trump-conversations-contained-classified.

9. "McCabe, Barbara Jill," FollowTheMoney.org, 2018. https://www
.followthemoney.org/entity-details?eid=31990894&default=cand
idate.

10. Joseph Curl, "REPORT: McCabe Threatened to 'Torch the
FBI' if Forced Out of Bureau Without Pension," The Daily Wire,
January 30, 2018, https://www.dailywire.com/news/26526/
mccabe-threatened-torch- fbi-if-forced-out-bureau-joseph-curl.

11. Brian Fitzgerald, "Hoover Wrecked My FBI Hero Dad, Reveals
CFA Prof," The Bostonian, October 5, 2005, https://www.bu.edu/
today/2005/hoover-wrecked-my-fbi-hero-dad-reveals-cfa-prof.

12. "Melvin Purvis Biography," Biography.com, December 30, 2014,
https://www.biography.com/people/melvin-purvis-9542100.

13. "From TIME's Archives: The Truth About J. Edgar Hoover,"
Time, December 22, 1975, http://content.time.com/time/
magazine/article/0,9171,879566-1,00.html.

14. "ARMZ Takes Hold of Uranium One," World Nuclear News,
June 9, 2010. http://www.world-nuclear-news.org/C-ARMZ
_takes_hold_of_Uranium_One-0906107.html.

15. Peter Koven, "Uranium One Bought by Top Russian Shareholder
ARMZ for $1.3-billion," Financial Post, January 14, 2013, http://

business.financialpost.com/commodities/mining/uranium-one
-bought-by-top-russian-shareholder-armz-for-1-3-billion.

16. Jo Becker and Mike McIntyre, "Cash Flowed to Clinton
Foundation amid Russian Uranium Deal," *New York Times*, April
23, 2015, https://www.nytimes.com/2015/04/24/us/cash-flowed
-to-clinton-foundation-as-russians-pressed-for-control-of-uranium
-company.html.

17. Ibid.

18. John Solomon and Alison Spann, "FBI Uncovered Russian
Bribery Plot Before Obama Administration Approved
Controversial Nuclear Deal with Moscow," The Hill, October 17,
2017, http://thehill.com/policy/national-security/355749-fbi
-uncovered-russian-bribery-plot-before-obama-administration.

19. Ibid.

20. John Solomon, "Senate Seeks to Interview FBI Informant in
Russian Nuclear Bribery Case," The Hill, October 18, 2017,
http://thehill.com/policy/national-security/356155-senate-seeks
-to-interview-fbi-informant-in-russian-nuclear-bribery.

21. John Solomon, "Senate Seeks to Interview FBI Informant in
Russian Nuclear Bribery Case," The Hill, October 18, 2017,
http://thehill.com/policy/national-security/356155-senate-seeks
-to-interview-fbi-informant-in-russian-nuclear-bribery.

22. John Solomon, "Uranium One Informant Makes Clinton
Allegations to Congress," The Hill, February 7, 2018. http://
thehill.com/homenews/administration/372861-uranium-one
-informant-makes-clinton-allegations-in-testimony.

23. Katie Bo Williams, "Dems: Uranium One Informant Provided
'No Evidence' of Clinton 'Quid Pro Quo,'" The Hill, March 8,

2018, http://thehill.com/policy/national-security/377404-dems
-uranium-one-informant-provided-no-evidence-of-wrongdoing-by.

24. Tom Kertscher, "Hillary Clinton's State Department Cut Security
in Libya Before Deadly Terror Attacks, Sen. Ron Johnson Says,"
PolitiFact Wisconsin, May 19, 2014, http://www.politifact.com/
wisconsin/statements/2014/may/19/ron-johnson/hillary-clintons
-state-department-reduced-security.

25. Marc A. Thiessen, "Commentary: Hillary Clinton's dreadful lies,"
Chicago Tribune, September 20, 2016, http://www.chicagotribune
.com/news/opinion/commentary/ct-hillary-clinton-lies-health
-emails-benghazi-20160920-story.html.

26. Tim Hains, "Rand Paul: CIA Annex in Benghazi Shipped Arms
from Libya to Syria; Clinton Lied About It," Real Clear Politics,
August 12, 2016. https://www.realclearpolitics.com/video/2016/
08/12/rand_paul_cia_annex_in_benghazi_shipped_arms_from
_libya_to_syria.html.

27. Kim Ghattas, "Hillary Clinton Has No Regrets About Libya,"
Foreign Policy, April 14, 2016, http://foreignpolicy.com/2016/
04/14/hillary-clinton-has-no-regrets-about-libya.

28. Dakshayani Shankar, "Rod Rosenstein: What to Know About the
Deputy Attorney General Under Sessions," ABC News, June 26,
2017, http://abcnews.go.com/Politics/rod-rosenstein-deputy
-attorney-general-sessions/story?id=48845480.

CHAPTER 8: LYING AND LEAKING TO FIX AN ELECTION

1. Charles R. Kubic, "Hillary's Huge Libya Disaster," *The National
Interest*, June 15, 2016, http://nationalinterest.org/feature/
hillarys-huge-libya-disaster-16600.

2. "Gaddafi Warned Blair His Ousting Would 'Open Door' to Jihadis," *The Guardian*, January 7, 2016. https://www.theguardian.com/world/2016/jan/07/gaddafi-warned-blair-of-threat-from-opening-door-to-al-qaida.

3. Dan Eggen and Paul Kane, "Gonzales Hospital Episode Detailed," *Washington Post*, May 16, 2007, http://www.washingtonpost.com/wp-dyn/content/article/2007/05/15/AR2007051500864.html.

4. Kelly Phillips Erb, "No Criminal Charges Expected in FBI Investigation into IRS Scandal," *Forbes*, January 14, 2014, https://www.forbes.com/sites/kellyphillipserb/2014/01/14/no-criminal-charges-expected-in-fbi-investigation-into-irs-scandal/#4aaf7b4f4ebd.

5. David A. Graham, "The Real Bias at the FBI," *The Atlantic*, February 8, 2018, https://www.theatlantic.com/politics/archive/2018/02the-fbis-principal-loyalty-is-to-the-bureau-itself/552686.

6. Laura Jarrett and Evan Perez, "FBI Agent Dismissed from Mueller Probe Changed Comey's Description of Clinton to 'Extremely Careless,'" CNN, December 4, 2017. https://www.cnn.com/2017/12/04/politics/peter-strzok-james-comey/index.html.

7. *Hearing Before the Committee on the Judiciary House of Representatives, One Hundred Fourteenth Congress, Second Session*, September 28, 2016, https://judiciary.house.gov/wp-content/uploads/2016/09/114-91_22125.pdf.

CHAPTER 9: THE LIBERAL INSURANCE POLICY

1. "FBI Agent Peter Strzok's Texts with Lisa Page Disparage Trump Throughout Campaign," CBS News, December 13, 2017, https://www.cbsnews.com/news/peter-strzok-lisa-page-texts-trump-idiot.

2. Ibid.

3. Del Quentin Wilbur, "In FBI Agent's Account, 'Insurance Policy' Text Referred to Russia Probe," *Wall Street Journal*, December 18, 2017, https://www.wsj.com/articles/in-fbi-agents-account -insurance-policy-text-referred-to-russia-probe-1513624580.

4. Patrick Lawrence, "A New Report Raises Big Questions About Last Year's DNC Hack," *The Nation*, August 9, 2017, https:// www.thenation.com/article/a-new-report-raises-big-questions -about-last-years-dnc-hack/.

5. Ali Watkins, "Obama Team Was Warned in 2014 About Russian Interference," Politico, August 14, 2017, https://www.politico .com/story/2017/08/14/obama-russia-election-interference-241547.

6. Politico Staff, "Full Text: Nunes Memo on FBI Surveillance," Politico, February 2, 2018, https://www.politico.com/story/ 2018/02/02/full-text-nunes-memo-fbi-transcript-385057.

7. "Democratic Rebuttal of G.O.P. Memo," *New York Times*, February 24, 2018, https://www.nytimes.com/interactive/2018/ 02/24/us/politics/house-democrats-memo-rebuttal.html.

8. Erik Sass, "'BuzzFeed' Catches Hell for Publishing Trump Dossier," MediaPost, January 11, 2017, https://www.mediapost .com/publications/article/292720/buzzfeed-catches-hell-for -publishing-trump-dossi.html.

9. Margaret Sullivan, "How BuzzFeed Crossed the Line in Publishing Salacious 'Dossier' on Trump," *Washington Post*, January 11, 2017. https://www.washingtonpost.com/lifestyle/style/how-buzzfeed -crossed-the-line-in-publishing-salacious-dossier-on-trump/ 2017/01/11/957b59f6-d801-11e6-9a36-1d296534b31e_story.html? utm_term=.056d072c5870.

10. "Rule 403," Cornell Law School, https://www.law.cornell.edu/rules/ fre/rule_403.

11. Adam Entous, Devlin Barrett, and Rosalind S. Helderman, "Clinton Campaign, DNC Paid for Research That Led to Russia Dossier," *Washington Post*, October 24, 2017. https://www.washingtonpost.com/world/national-security/clinton-campaign-dnc-paid-for-research-that-led-to-russia-dossier/2017/10/24/226fabf0-b8e4-11e7-a908-a3470754bbb9_story.html?utm_term=.3bfdcad6aba4.

12. Ellen Nakashima, "Justice Dept. Told Court of Source's Political Influence in Request to Wiretap ex-Trump Campaign Aide, Officials Say," *Washington Post*, February 2, 2018, https://www.washingtonpost.com/world/national-security/justice-dept-told-court-of-sources-political-bias-in-request-to-wiretap-ex-trump-campaign-aide-officials-say/2018/02/02/caecfa86-0852-11e8-8777-2a059f168dd2_story.html?utm_term=.ac5a4e30160a.

13. Andrew McCarthy. "Spinning a Crossfire Hurricane: The Times on the FBI's Trump Investigation." *National Review*, May 7, 2018. https://www.nationalreview.com/2018/05/crossfire-hurricane-new-york-times-report-buries-lede/

CHAPTER 10: THE LYING, LEAKING, LIBERAL SWAMP'S SECRET COURT

1. "Senate Select Committee to Study Governmental Operations with Respect to Intelligence Activities," United States Senate. https://www.senate.gov/artandhistory/history/common/investigations/ChurchCommittee.htm.

2. "Foreign Intelligence Surveillance Act Court Orders 1979–2016," Electronic Privacy Information Center. https://epic.org/privacy/surveillance/fisa/stats/default.html.

3. Ellen Nakashima, Spencer S. Hsu, and Matt Zapotosky, "Texts Show Judge Who Recused Himself in Flynn Case Was Friendly with FBI Agent Involved in Probe," *Washington Post*, March 16

2018, https://www.washingtonpost.com/world/national-security/
texts-show-judge-who-recused-himself-in-flynn-case-was-friendly
-with-fbi-agent-involved-in-probe/2018/03/16/3b3736f2-293d
-11e8-b79d-f3d931db7f68_story.html?utm_term=.5e219d0b7325.

CHAPTER 11: THE LYING, LEAKING, LIBERAL WITCH HUNT

1. Jim Sciutto and Marshall Cohen. "Flynn Worries About Son in Special Counsel Probe," CNN, November 9, 2017, https://www.cnn.com/2017/11/08/politics/michaeßl-flynn-son-special-counsel-russia-investigation/index.html

2. Sharon LaFraniere. "Judge Questions Whether Mueller Has Overstepped His Authority on Manafort." *The New York Times*, May 4, 2018. https://www.nytimes.com/2018/05/04/us/mueller-authority-paul-manafort-case-judge.html

3. Paula Reid, Jeff Pegues, and Rebecca Shabad, "Rod Rosenstein Announced Indictments of Russians in U.S. Election Meddling," CBS News, February 16, 2018, https://www.cbsnews.com/news/russian-indictment-2016-elections-rod-rosenstein-announcement-today-2018-02-16.

4. "Mueller Indictment—The "Russian Influence" Is A Commercial Marketing Scheme." Moon Over Alabama, February 17, 2018 http://www.moonofalabama.org/2018/02/mueller-indictement-the-russian-influence-is-a-commercial-marketing-scheme.html.

5. David Stockman. "Mueller's Comic Book Indictment: How to Prosecute a Great Big Nothingburger," David Stockman's Contra Corner, February 20, 2018, http://davidstockmanscontracorner.com/muellers-comic-book-indictment-how-to-prosecute-a-great-big-nothingburger.

6. Tim Hains, Real Clear Politics, February 16, 2018. https://www
    .realclearpolitics.com/video/2018/02/16/watch_live_deputy_ag
    _rod_rosenstein_announcement.html

7. Order No. 3915-2017 "Appointment of Special Counsel to
    Investigate Russian Interference with the 2016 Presidential Election
    and Related Matters," Office of the Deputy Attorney General,
    https://assets.documentcloud.org/documents/3726385/Order-3915
    -2017-Special-Counsel.pdf.

8. Legal Information Institute, Cornell Law School, https://www.law
    .cornell.edu/cfr/text/28/600.4.

9. Mike Allen. "A Huge Clue About Mueller's Endgame," Axios,
    March 19, 2018, https://www.axios.com/robert-mueller-investigation
    -obstruction-justice-collusion-2128e27f-bbb6-4b82-9e28-c6f1244
    fb9e3.html.

10. *United States v. Jicarilla Apache Nation*, 564 U.S. 162, 169 (2011).
    https://supreme.justia.com/cases/federal/us/564/162.

11. The Crime-Fraud Exception to the Attorney-Client Privilege. https://
    www.nolo.com/legal-encyclopedia/the-crime-fraud-exception-the
    -attorney-client-privilege.html.

CHAPTER 13: THE TRUMP BOOMERANG

1. https://www.si.com/nfl/2017/09/26/themmqb-nfl-fans-stopped
    -watching-colin-kaepernick-anthem-protests-donald-trump-nfl
    -ratings.

2. https://www.si.com/extra-mustard/2017/10/27/nfl-2017-ratings
    -national-anthem-protests

3. http://www.richmondraceway.com/Articles/2012/08/Olympians
    .aspx